CHOICE   JAN. '70

History, Geography &
Travel

North America

O'CONNOR, Thomas H. Lords of the Loom; the Cotton Whigs and the Coming of the Civil War. Scribner, 1968. 214p il bibl 68-27783. 7.50

O'Connor's attempts to refute the thesis that an industrial North and an agrarian South were heading for an "irrepressible conflict" in the decades before the Civil War. What Philip Foner's *Business and Slavery* (1941) has done for New York businessmen, he tries to do for their Massachusetts counterparts. The theme is that the Northern and Southern economies were supplementary, not antithetical. The development of the textile economy of Massachusetts is examined for the 60 years preceding the Civil War. In readable style, O'Connor presents a slice of business history showing its relationship to political events. The general reader and the undergraduate should find *Lords of the Loom* profitable reading, but the graduate student and scholar will probably despair at O'Connor's skimpy political survey. He never mentions the opposition of the Taylor Administration to the 1850 Compromise. He ignores the problem of the Cotton Whigs in the party's convention of 1852. Errors such as Toombs and Stephens being listed as Senators in 1850 and Lecompton being drafted in the fall of 1856 might have easily been avoided with a little more care. The lack of any election returns for the period is most frustrating. O'Connor used the

Continued

O'CONNOR

CHOICE   JAN. '70

History, Geography &
Travel

North America

manuscript collections of the Lawrences, Appletons, Robert Winthrop, and other Cotton Whigs as the basis of his work. Why these men were not more successful in their efforts at national reconciliation, especially during the 1850's, he never really analyzes. Probably the polarization of American politics during the decade doomed the efforts of this small group of élitists. Recommended for college and public libraries.

THOMAS H. O'CONNOR

is Chairman of the History Department at Boston College, Chestnut Hill, Massachusetts. He has written and contributed to several textbooks as well as to professional journals. Professor O'Connor lives with his wife and three children in Braintree, Massachusetts.

LORDS OF THE LOOM

*The Cotton Whigs
and the Coming of the Civil War*

THOMAS H. O'CONNOR

❧ *NEW YORK* ❧
CHARLES SCRIBNER'S SONS

To Steven, Jeanne, and Michael

PRINTED IN THE UNITED STATES OF AMERICA
LIBRARY OF CONGRESS CATALOG CARD NUMBER 68-27783

❦ Acknowledgments

IN SOME WAYS, almost every scholarly work that is written must be a testament to the generosity and hospitality of what Professor Dewey W. Grantham, Jr., once aptly described as the "republic of letters" in America. Certainly this book is no exception.

This study of the conservative Boston businessman in the turbulent ante-bellum period began as a research project for the doctoral dissertation in the Department of History at Boston University. Professor Kenneth A. Bernard not only saw the dissertation to its eventual conclusion, but provided stimulating new insights into the whole Civil War era and suggested new dimensions far beyond the original limits of the topic.

At the University of Kansas, the hospitality of Professor George L. Anderson of the History Department and the graciousness of the staff at the University Library greatly facilitated my use of those letters and documents pertinent to the Kansas phase of my research. Especially valuable were the views and suggestions of that state's eminent historian, Professor James C. Malin.

For the opportunity to explore new aspects of the problem and to experiment with new ideas, I would like to express my appreciation for the efforts of Professor Richard W. Griffin of Wesleyan College, Macon, Georgia, editor of the *Textile History Review*.

Since the Lawrence Manuscripts and a significant portion of the writings of prominent New Englanders are housed at the Massa-

v

chusetts Historical Society, I am greatly indebted to Dr. Stephen T. Riley and his excellent staff for the promptness and courtesy with which they assisted me in my work. And to the reference staffs of the Boston Public Library, the Baker Business Library, the John Hay Library, the American Antiquarian Society, and the Boston Athaneum, I am deeply appreciative of the time and the efforts they so generously spent on my behalf.

I would also like to thank Miss Marilyn Brickley, Secretary of the History Department at Boston College, for her painstaking work in typing the manuscript.

Above all, I am profoundly grateful to my wife for the constant encouragement and assistance which made this book possible, and to my children whose affection and forebearance made it all worthwhile.

Thomas H. O'Connor

Boston College
Chestnut Hill, Massachusetts
September, 1968

❧ Contents

✇ Illustrations

INTRODUCTION

IN 1941, Philip Foner, in his *Business and Slavery*, made an appeal for a more detailed study of the Northern businessman and his reaction to the coming of the Civil War. Countering the popular interpretation that the war was the product of two conflicting economic systems, Professor Foner presented his own observations regarding the concerted efforts of the New York financial interests to check any and all movements which tended to precipitate an intersectional struggle. The documented reactions of this particular group of Northern businessmen could not be explained in terms of an oversimplified economic interpretation of the Civil War, and for this reason Professor Foner pointed to the need for more intensive research into the economic sources and materials of the antebellum period.[1] Foner's challenge has failed to arouse very much historical enthusiasm, apparently, for many recent historical treatments of the critical years before the Civil War continue to generalize upon the essential economic antagonisms of the North and the South, and still look upon the Northern industrialist as the catalytic agent which propelled the sections into bloody warfare.

One of the most distinctive presentations of this economic point of view came into the twentieth century with the writings of Charles Beard. The South, according to Beard, was an area of "planters operating in a limited territory with incompetent labor on soil of diminishing fertility," in contrast to the industrial men

1

of the North who "swept forward . . . exulting in the approaching triumph of machine industry, [and who] warned the planters of their ultimate subjection."[2] Not only did Beard consider the Civil War to be an "irrepressible conflict" resulting from the clash of these two conflicting economies, but attributed the immediate cause of the war to Northern "capitalism."[3] So intense was Beard's criticism of the materialistic greed of Northern "capitalism" and its immoderate demands upon the South, that one commentator remarked that "the Southern planters very nearly became the heroes of the narrative, and Beard very nearly became the ally of John C. Calhoun."[4]

This economic interpretation was carried into the twenties by the work of Vernon Parrington, who maintained most of the essential ideas of Beard regarding the origins of the Civil War. Enthusiastic about the "agrarian democracy" of the West, sympathetic at times toward the interests of the South, Parrington had little regard for the ideals of a middle class which was busily engaged in "creating a plutocracy."[5] In the decades before the war, claimed Parrington, the major parties of the United States chose to follow the economic interests of "master groups, heedless of all humanitarian issues"; and once the war was over, the "slave economy could never again thwart the ambitions of the capitalist economy."[6]

Widely circulated during the late twenties and early thirties, the age of the Great Depression, the economic interpretations of Beard and Parrington found easy acceptance at a time when hostility to American capitalism and business methods was unusually strong. Many Southern historians, in particular, seized upon these ideas to lend support to the thesis that war had been thrust upon an unwilling South. Frank L. Owsley, for example, constantly emphasized the conflict between the agrarian South and the industrial North, which resulted in bloodshed when the industrial "plutocracy" of the North tried to force its way of life upon the South.[7] The philosophy of the North was intolerant, crusading and standardizing, wrote Owsley, and as a result, "Juggernaut drove his car across the South."[8]

Although in recent years many of the extreme conclusions of the Beard thesis have been somewhat modified, and concessions have been made in the direction of admitting certain points of similarity between North and South, many historians continue to stress the elements of sectional "divergence" in the years preceding the Civil War.[9] Writers continue to generalize upon New England's "hatred of Southerners and their institutions" and often describe this hatred as so intense that New England would "do everything possible to destroy slavery."[10] The South is still depicted as a "static, agrarian, debtor section," as opposed to a North which was a "dynamic, commercialized, industrializing, creditor section"; and that because of the presence of these conflicting economic tendencies, there existed a "profound and irrepressible clash of material interests" which would inevitably lead to "warfare between the slave industrial system and the free industrial system."[11] Industrial capitalism, "with the banners of righteousness, patriotism and progress over its head," marched out to triumph over the agrarian ideals of the South.[12] "Bourgeois acquisitiveness . . . was in the saddle. Democracy, like the rest of the hindmost, was left for the devil."[13] In short, to what Professor Charles Grier Sellers has aptly called the "myth of the Monolithic South," there has been added another myth—that of the Moloch of the North, a huge, mechanical automaton, breathing flame, and moving inexorably forward to devour the hapless planters of the South.[14]

In reviewing the various economic interpretations regarding the clash of economic interests and the role of the Northern capitalist as the prime mover, one cannot help but compare the sweeping generalities regarding the pre-Civil War businessman, with the actual amount of factual data concerning his influence in the history of the period. In recent years the market has seen many book titles indicating a widespread interest in almost every aspect of the American businessman. Hereditary influences, social backgrounds, intellectual qualifications, and psychodynamic motivations have all been statistically recorded and have provided the background for a plethora of novels, plays, and motion pictures dealing with the dramatic involvements of the American man of business.[15] American historiography, too, has shown a remarkable trend toward reevaluating and reassessing the contributions of the American entrepreneur.[16] It is almost impossible

to recognize the old "robber barons" of Ida Tarbell, Matthew
Josephson, and Henry Demarest Lloyd in Allan Nevins' treatment
of John D. Rockefeller, or in the recently published study on
the Standard Oil Company of New Jersey.[17]

Unfortunately, however, very little of this modern interest in
economic operations has been projected back into the pre-Civil
War period. The American businessman is apparently regarded
by many historians and social scientists as a comparatively new
phenomenon which made its appearance after 1870. As a result,
the antebellum industrialist continues to remain an obscure
figure, half-hidden in the mists and shadows of history.

The field of business history, and the more recent school of
entrepreneurial history, to be sure, have made outstanding contributions to historical knowledge, by furnishing a wealth of
source material on the financial and industrial operations of early
American business enterprises, especially those of New England
origin. The Pepperell Company, the Whitin Machine Works,
and the Saco-Lowell Shops are only a few of the many local ventures whose histories have been recorded by excellent business
historians.[18] Such studies, however, tend to focus attention almost
exclusively upon the financial structure and corporate operations
of the individual companies involved, make little attempt at
historical interpretation, and fail to analyze the interplay of those
powerful social and political forces which were an integral part of
the historical background of the pre-Civil War economy.[19]

Professor Glyndon Van Deusen has suggested that one of the
reasons for the obvious lack of reliable information dealing with
the Northern Whigs, is due, in large measure, to the preoccupation of American historians with the ideas of Jacksonian Democracy, to the virtual exclusion of the other side of the picture.
"So far as I am aware," wrote Professor Van Deusen, "there has
been no systematic attempt to analyze Whig thought and theory
as represented by the writings and speeches of the Whig leaders of
the period."[20] This fatal disregard for important social and economic movements during the antebellum period of American
history has also been underscored by Professor Thomas Cochran.
Although the impact of business enterprise and urban development upon American culture and society between 1840 and 1860

was probably greater than in any period of equal length, "such forces appear only in the form of a few isolated phenomena in the usual treatment of the pre-Civil War period." While the life and thought of such American leaders as Clay, Calhoun, and Webster have been most carefully studied and weighed, writes Cochran, such figures as Nathan Appleton, John Murray Forbes, and other important business figures of the period still await "their first full-length social interpreter."[21]

It is in the hope of contributing additional insights regarding the reactions of the American businessman toward the coming of the Civil War that the author has chosen to study one particular group—the cotton textile manufacturers of Massachusetts, as typified by the Lawrence family among others. In order to appreciate more fully the influence of these men upon the political life and institutions of the United States in the years preceding the Civil War, it will be necessary to analyze not only their industrial capacities and material productivity, but to reassess their influence upon the society in which they lived, and to consider the important demands which that society made upon them.

Throughout much of traditional historical literature, the conservative Northern Whigs in the decades before the Civil War have either been completely overlooked, or else dismissed out of hand with vague generalizations. They are most often represented in caricature form as a group of ossified Brahmins, living complacently amid the past glories and relics of the Revolution, taking little or no interest in the pressing political issues of the day, ignoring the moral and humane aspects of Negro slavery, and concerning themselves exclusively with the profit-and-loss statements of their factories and their mills.

Such a distorted picture is not only at odds with historical evidence, but it also does a serious injustice to a generation of turbulent political history in the United States. In introducing the "colonial mind" to his readers, Vernon L. Parrington had the foresight to caution his readers that "the Puritan and the Yankee were the two halves of the New England whole," and that to overlook or to underestimate the contribution of either element "is grossly to misinterpret the spirit and character of primitive New England."[22]

With Parrington's observation in mind, then, this present study is the story of what happened, later in the history of the Bay State, when the Puritan conscience collided head-on with the Yankee zeal for profit—when the moral desire to uproot the evils of slavery reached the point where it had to be weighed against the economic demands for more slave-grown cotton, and when a decisive answer either way was calculated to endanger the very existence of the Union.

1

THE MERCHANT
AND THE MILLER

BERLIN: NOVEMBER 21, 1806

WITHIN the huge grey walls of the castle at Charlottenburg, the Great Man paced steadily back and forth as he dictated: "Les Îles Britanniques sont declarées en état de blocus. Tout commerce et toute correspondance avec les Îles Britanniques sont interdit . . . ."

The voice droned on as half of Europe lay in ruins. With Italy torn apart and Austria prostrate; with the German states mauled beyond recognition and the Imperial armies even now smashing through the Prussian defences everywhere, the future was no longer in doubt. The Emperor held undisputed possession of every mile of the northern coast of Europe—from Brest to Copenhagen, from Hamburg to Danzig. With such an over-whelming advantage, what could be more natural than that the master should now move to close every European port to ships from Great Britain? It would be only a matter of time before he would force proud Albion to her knees, weak and helpless.

Napoleon Bonaparte smiled as he drew himself erect: "Je veux conquérir la mer par la puissance de la terre!" Snatching up the quill as he bent over the desk, the Emperor signed his famous "Berlin Decree."

LONDON: JANUARY 7, 1807

". . . HIS MAJESTY is thereupon pleased, by and with the advice of Privy Council to order . . . that no vessel shall be permitted to trade from one port to another, both of which ports shall belong to or be in the possession of France or her allies . . . ." So read Britain's austere reply to the Napoleonic blockade—the Order in Council. Highly indignant, particularly outraged that France should have the effrontery to threaten England at a time when the French fleet itself was ignominiously bottled up by His Majesty's navy, the British not only declared Napoleon's coasts under a state of blockade, but for all practical purposes required that neutral shipping be forced to trade through British ports.

Spencer Perceval, then Chancellor of the Exchequer, summarized the British attitude quite succinctly when he stated in clipped tones: "Our Orders say to the enemy, 'If you will not have *our* trade, as far as we can help it you shall have *none!*' "

WASHINGTON, D.C.: DECEMBER 7, 1807

THE TALL, lanky gentleman eased himself awkwardly back into his chair and read over the words, slowly and carefully: "I deem it my duty to recommend the subject to the consideration of Congress, who will doubtless perceive all the advantages which may be expected from an inhibition of the departure of our vessels from the ports of the United States . . . ."

An Embargo. Yes, mused President Thomas Jefferson, that was the only possible solution. The massive millstones of French assault and British retaliation had begun to grind exceeding fine, and already American ships were being caught up in the thrashing foam. In vain attempts to make their way through the continental barriers nearly five hundred American vessels had been seized by both belligerents during the year 1807. The insulting procedure of the British "impressment" technique had long outraged the dignity and the honor of the nation when, in the summer of 1807, a final challenge had been flung in the face of the United States. In June, the American frigate *Chesapeake* was blasted to a limping hulk by His Majesty's ship *Leopard* just outside Norfolk harbor, after the American vessel refused a demand that she be searched for British deserters. A roar of protest arose throughout the nation: the Governor of Virginia was forced to call out the militia to prevent mob violence, and public sentiment everywhere demanded that the President take immediate action.

To yield to the humiliating demands of the European belligerents was, of course, out of the question. But the nation was without the barest of military and naval requirements which any show of force would require, for shortly after his election to office President Jefferson had reduced the standing army to a mere skeleton and had laid up all the frigates in the Potomac while urging the construction of a "gunboat navy" for coastal defense. As a matter of practical expediency, therefore, if not for theoretical principle, Jefferson determined to retaliate against the foreign powers in kind—with his own version of economic warfare. Realizing that both England and France were relying heavily upon the United States for foodstuffs and other scarce commodities, the President concluded that to withhold these products would force both parties to cancel their Decrees and their Orders and assume a more reasonable and respectful attitude toward America's neutral rights.

Despite heavy Federalist opposition, Jefferson succeeded in forcing through Congress a sweeping Embargo which virtually prohibited the export of any goods from the United States, by sea or by land. To those who protested the severity of this decision, the Virginian nodded sympathetically, but added in a tone of quiet assurance that it was better to "discontinue all intercourse with these nations till they shall return again to some sense of moral right."

But what a blow the Embargo was to the State of Massachusetts which controlled about one-third of the total tonnage of the entire nation, and whose total merchant and fishing fleet by 1810 had already reached 500,000 tons! From 1803 to 1805, the United States was the largest carrier of goods from European ports, up to one million tons—of which almost half belonged to Massachusetts alone. So expansive was this worldwide sweep of commercial activity that it has been estimated that during these years Massachusetts ships brought home some $15,000,000 in freight money alone, as the value of American exports increased from $2,500,000 to $20,000,000 annually during the period from 1790 to 1807. Virtually every phase of the Bay State economy depended upon a vigorous maritime commerce, and even the agricultural interior relied upon the seaports as the chief markets for such farm produce as lumber, potash, butter, and grain.[1]

It was this expansive mercantile empire, with its comfortable fortunes, cultivated society, and political dominance, which Jefferson and his Embargo threatened to destroy. By forbidding any American vessel to leave an American harbor and by restricting fishing and coastal shipping to the immediate coastal areas, the tightening fingers of regulation slowly began to throttle New England's economic lifelines. Before long, a million tons of shipping lay idle. Shipowners, seamen, captains, and merchants faced unemployment and ruin. Farmers found themselves deprived of both their American and European markets. Soup kitchens made their appearance in the seaport towns of the Northeast as men exhausted their family savings or went across the border into Canada in search of work.[2]

This was no paper panic. In a single year, 1807–1808, national imports fell off almost two-thirds, and fishing tonnage was sliced in half. Shipbuilding practically came to a halt, and the trade of Salem, Newburyport, and Plymouth was so seriously damaged that these seaport towns would never again recover their former position or prosperity. In a special edition, the Boston *Gazette* mournfully predicted that the loss of trade in Massachusetts alone would amount to $38,200,000—or more than one-fourth of the nation's total amount. President Jefferson was flooded with memorials and petitions from Massachusetts communities and towns which denounced the policy of the administration and predicted dire consequences if that policy were not immediately rescinded.[3]

It all finally proved too much for President Jefferson, who was now being pelted with memorials and petitions not only from New England (he had expected the Federalists to oppose everything he did because of political motives), but from his beloved Virginia as well. Apparently he had never suspected that the agricultural states, deprived of their foreign and domestic markets, would eventually be as hard hit as the commercial states of the North. Reluctantly he was forced to retreat, step by step, before the angry onslaught until, shortly before his administration came to a close in 1809, he signed the repeal of the hated Embargo, conscious that his noble experiment had failed.

With the lifting of the Embargo, it was "business as usual" as far as the Yankee merchants and skippers were concerned. They headed for the open waters, anticipating whatever commercial opportunities the spring of 1809 would bring. While it is true that a Non-Intercourse Act, which forbade trade with both England and France, had been passed in place of the Embargo, the new regulations were either blithely ignored or skillfully evaded as the quest resumed to recoup lost fortunes. A surprisingly bright source of prosperity was located in far-off Russia which was finding most of the European ports locked up tight, thanks to the efforts of Bonaparte. Like bees swarming after honey, the Yankee schooners headed for the northern seas in an effort to exploit the profits of the arctic regions. Within a year American tonnage registered in foreign trade had jumped again until it reached the unprecedented figure of 981,000 tons—with no apparent reason why it should not go higher. President Madison's administration in 1810 was to see the highest peak of American tonnage in the nation's history, a figure which would not be equalled until the merchant fleet was expanded during World War II.[4]

With trade lanes repaired and with commerce prospering once again, canny New England merchants were anxious that no more Federal laws, regulations, or restrictions should cripple their economy again. Consequently they made every effort to conceal or to minimize any incidents of spoliation and impressment. One special committee from Nantucket took pains to point out that, from the thousand seamen which the community sent out, only *one* had been impressed. James Lloyd, a member of Congress, went on to assure his listeners that *no* impressments had taken place on any of his ships, and that he had never received so much as a single complaint from any of his constituents. Throughout Massachusetts "peace meetings" were organized in an obvious effort to demonstrate to the Government, and to the rest of the nation, that circumstances were peaceful and quiet and no longer required Federal attention or interference—above all, no more Embargoes![5]

Despite these protests of peace and the almost frantic assurances of security from the Northeast, however, other pressures were at work pushing the nation toward war with Great Britain. In place of the obviously ineffective Non-Intercourse Act, Congress had passed Macon's Bill which stipulated that if either belligerent would repeal its Decrees the United States would, in turn, resume nonintercourse against the other. Bonaparte immediately seized the opportunity. On August 5, 1810, he declared his Berlin and Milan Decrees to be annulled (while quietly signing the Decree of Trianon which kept his confiscatory policies in effect) and then called upon President Madison to keep his part of the bargain.

With dogged naïveté Madison walked into the trap, and at the close of 1810 announced that nonintercourse would be reestablished against Great Britain. While Napoleon was enjoying the spectacle, Anglo-American relations deteriorated with amazing swiftness, until many persons on both sides of the Atlantic came to the opinion that war was the only solution to the international problems which confronted the two nations. On June 1, 1812, President Madison sent his war message to Congress, and in less than three weeks the vigorous War Hawks had swept up sufficient support from the South and the West to force a declaration of war through Congress over the protesting votes of a majority of the representatives from New England.

The Northeast reacted to the news of war with Great Britain with anything but an outburst of patriotic fervor. Flags in such cities as Boston, Providence, and Hartford drooped mournfully at half-mast. Angry mass meetings were held throughout the Bay State, and a new flood of memorials came pouring into the nation's capital protesting this calamitous turn of events. In Boston, John Lowell sardonically labeled it "Mr. Madison's War,"

while an incensed mob burned the unpopular President in effigy
—with a figure of Bonaparte perched upon his shoulder. "We
view the declaration of war as we view the cataract at Niagara,"
snarled the *Connecticut Courant*, "as one of the wonders of the
world."[6]

At first, New England was both surprised and relieved to find
that a complete commercial disaster did not develop right away.
For a while business proceded smoothly as Britain winked at
commercial violations and maritime irregularities. New England
took full advantage of the unusual situation, building up a back-
log of economic security against the day when rigid maritime
restrictions would be strictly enforced. During the first six months
of the war, every Atlantic port was trading with England itself,
under special license from the British blockading squadron. Massachusetts skippers took out Portuguese papers in order to evade
the British men of war they might encounter on the high seas,
speculators avoided the open Atlantic waters by lugging their
heavily laden whaleboats across the neck of Cape Cod and lowering them again into Buzzard's Bay, and during the winter enterprising merchants used sleighs to bring their products across the
New Brunswick frontiers into Canada so that the British Army
might feast on American beef and flour. New England's burst
of commercial activity was reflected in the economic statistics of
the Commonwealth. Bank deposits moved steadily upwards from
$2,671,000 in 1810 to $8,875,000 in 1814, while the amount of
specie during that same period correspondingly increased from
$1,561,000 to $6,393,000.[7]

In time of war, however, it was too much to expect that such
conditions could last. Slowly but surely the gates of the British
blockade began to swing inward—then closed with an ominous
clang. At the close of 1813, only five American vessels had cleared
for foreign ports from Boston Harbor, choked with some 250
vessels of all sorts swinging idly on their rusty anchor chains,
with their topmasts housed and their masts covered, like useless
furniture in a deserted house. During the summer and fall of
1814, British squadrons moved in to patrol the New England
coastline, and then captured any vessel that dared to venture
out. Two enemy frigates actually set up headquarters at Province-

town and policed the area from Cape Cod to Cape Ann. So effective was this British surveillance that in order to get its produce to markets in the South, maritime Massachusetts had to resort to the ignominious expedient of horse and wagon traffic![8]

The effect upon the Bay State's economy was swift and disastrous. Deprived of its main source of income, Massachusetts now had to depend upon whatever it had managed to save during the course of the past few years in order to purchase necessary raw materials and foodstuffs. Yankee traders were forced to look around for new sources of enterprise in which to invest their capital now that commerce was no longer profitable. Specie which had amounted to over five million dollars in 1814 dropped to less than two million—a loss of $3,500,000 in only six months! National taxes, rising to unprecedented heights because of the increase of the national debt, cut so deeply into depleted local funds that the State government was nearly bankrupt. As far as Massachusetts was concerned, the economic and military picture was a dismal one. Its ships were rotting at the wharves, its specie was being rapidly depleted, its coastline was under attack, and its interior was threatened with possible invasion at any moment.[9]

The salvation of New England during these trying times proved to be not in wooden hulls, countinghouses, or captain's cabins— but in factories. That portion of New England capital which was fluid was hastily diverted into manufacturing, rather than into mercantile enterprises which were no longer paying dividends. While John Lowell was excoriating "Mr. Madison's War," and calling for a New England Confederation, his brother, Francis C. Lowell, was picking up information over in England about power looms—information which he would shortly incorporate in his mills at Waltham.[10]

As an alternative to commercial oblivion, manufacturing was a practical solution, since it would not only provide an outlet for a remarkable amount of surplus Yankee capital (capital which "good" Federalists refused to lend to the Government), but would also provide an income for New England which would in part compensate for its growing maritime losses. The stretch of embargoes, sinkings, nonintercourse, and now the restrictions of the war itself had forced the interior sections of the United States to go without manufactured goods for so long that they were crying for commodities at any price. Woolens for the white folks, homespun for the children, cottons for the slaves, pots and pans, hammers and files, boxes and wagons—all these things and hundreds of others were being eagerly sought by consumers in all parts of the country. Yankee enterprise was only too happy to respond. If there was a demand, New England would supply it. This was especially true with regard to the production of cotton textiles with which New England had been cautiously experimenting in recent years.

Early experiences with the mechanical production of cotton textiles had proved rather disappointing, since the crude machinery performed poorly—if it performed at all. Fortunately, however, a number of English workmen managed to slip away to the United States where they proceeded to reconstruct models of the textile machinery which was so jealously guarded by the laws of the island kingdom. Once begun, despite foreign competition and domestic setbacks, the production of cotton goods started to expand slowly, with New England taking the lead in this form of domestic manufacturing. In Beverly, a group of citizens, including a number of the Cabots, had incorporated the Beverly Cotton Manufactory in 1787, received State aid, and were honored with a personal visit by George Washington who enthusiastically noted the new types of machinery in use there. Down in Providence, Rhode Island, Moses Brown persuaded a recently arrived Englishman by the name of Samuel Slater to work with him, and before long the skilled artisan who had worked with the Arkwright machinery and system of production in England had successfully duplicated the complicated techniques from memory, enabling power-driven machinery to be applied to the spinning of cotton yarn.[11]

In the twenty years that followed the ratification of the Constitution, some dozen cotton mills were erected in the United States, providing eight thousand spindles for the new industry. By 1810, however, after two winters of Jefferson's Embargo, the figure had jumped to eighty-seven mills and eighty thousand spindles, three-quarters of which were located within thirty miles of Providence. With the outbreak of the war itself and the

gradual strangulation of American shipping, cotton textile manufacturing became the most important of the many new industrial
fields into which enterprising speculators poured their time, their
money, and their talents. With surplus capital now being diverted
from maritime investments, and with the additional incentive
of ready-made domestic markets literally begging for products,
Yankee ingenuity went to work. A New York newspaper was soon
pointing with pride to the fact that President Madison himself
was wearing a coat which was manufactured in Springfield, Massachusetts. "Wheels roll, spindles whirl, shuttles fly," rhapsodized
the *Connecticut Herald.* "We shall export to other states many
more productions of industry than ever were exported in any
one former season." At a time when the rest of the nation was
insolvent, New England was drawing upon untapped resources of
the national economy, and its spindles had already surpassed the
hundred thousand mark when the War of 1812 suddenly came to
an end.[12]

It was February, 1815, when the news of the Treaty of Ghent
finally arrived in America. Peace at last! Bells began to clang
the joyous news from Bay State meetinghouses which up to now
had stubbornly refused to acclaim a single American victory during the war. Peace! The news was shouted by stamping seamen
through billows of frozen breath as they hacked away at the
glistening hulks of ice which shrouded their ships like white
phantoms in the frozen harbor. New England rejoiced, shook off
the lethargy of enforced wartime idleness, and began eager preparations to return to its former maritime predominance. As the
ice-choked harbors began to melt and swell with the spring thaws,
ports hummed with the sounds familiar to the ears of seafaring
communities. New England determined to flood the world with
Yankee bottoms and take advantage of the trade of a world elated
with the prospects of peace. And behind the clatter of the wharves
could be heard the whirring of spindles. There seemed to be no
reason why New England's newly found prosperity in manufacturing should not keep pace with the expansion of Yankee shipping in the postwar world. With the Northern mills producing
more textiles than ever before, the news of peace presented the
textile manufacturers with the glittering picture of a world market
which would supplement its already expanding domestic sales.[13]

But this bubble soon burst. Instead of maritime prosperity and industrial expansion, the Treaty of Ghent brought an economic disaster to the shores of the Northeast which sent the local enterprises reeling back in shocked amazement. Instead of opening wide their gates to receive the Yankee vessels, the European nations now concentrated on cultivating their own carrying-trade, jealously guarding it against the onslaughts of Yankee opportunists. With sullen contempt Great Britain refused to open her ports to American shipping and doomed New England's bright maritime hopes to bitter disappointment.

If Yankee shipping was badly shaken, New England cotton mills were virtually obliterated by this unexpected reaction. Anticipating an eager world market for its textile products, New England suddenly found itself virtually buried under an avalanche of British manufactured goods. Long denied access to world markets during the Napoleonic wars, Great Britain now proceeded to dump its stockpiles of manufactured goods onto American markets in such prodigious amounts and at such ridiculously low prices that New England industrialists gaped in alarm.[14]

Now it was the turn of the Northeast to cry panic—and who could blame a Southern State or a Middle State for regarding the situation as a case of just retribution? Facing ruthless foreign competition, Yankee shipowners and merchants struggled for their lives. Flooded with English goods whose cut-rate prices resulted in double the normal consumption, the infant New England textile industry was badly hit. Credit was strained to the breaking point, money was hoarded, banks throughout the Commonwealth were either closing their doors in alarm or else curtailing their loans with complete disregard of need. Thousands of native New Englanders were packing up and moving out to the Mohawk Valley and western New York. In a memorial to Congress, dated October 20, 1815, the cotton manufacturers of Rhode Island complained that they could no longer work profitably their 140 factories and their 130,000 spindles, and they pleaded that some form of Government assistance be provided so that they might escape certain bankruptcy. Such fears were reechoed throughout the newly created milltowns of Massachusetts where the loss of great amounts of capital was not a matter of theoretical speculation but of immediate and evident certainty. Most of the factories which had been hastily equipped and loosely managed were being forced to close down operations completely. Industry in the Northeast had all but stopped now; and it appeared that Hamilton's cherished "infant American industry" had been still-born.[15]

As the situation worsened, more and more of the manufacturers began to petition Congress for assistance—and they found surprisingly influential and vocal allies throughout the nation seconding their cries for protection and assistance. *Niles Register* chose to ignore its former critical attitude toward New England's behavior during the late war and, in an obvious attempt to get other sections of the country to adopt a more sympathetic attitude toward the distress of New England, pointed out to its readers that the manufacturer bore a relationship to the government like that of "an infant to its mother." It offered the reassurance that if cared for and nourished in their early years, these manufacturers would later grow in strength and repay the other sections of the nation "all that is done for them."[16]

The Sage of Monticello, too, had moved far enough away from his traditional position as the defender of an exclusively agrarian form of economic life to add his voice to the growing appeal for protection of those who could supply the manufactured goods needed for the nation. Anyone who is opposed to domestic manufacturing, Jefferson wrote to Benjamin Austin of Boston, "must be for reducing us, either to a dependence on that foreign nation, or to be clothed in skins, and live like wild beasts in dens and caverns. I am not one of these," the former President emphasized; "experience has taught me that manufactures are now as necessary to our independence as to our comfort . . . ." With such unqualified sentiments issuing from his mentor, James Madison had no reason to falter, and soon, in clear and forthright language, he took the occasion of his Annual Message of December, 1815, to call upon the Congress to erect a tariff barrier so that American manufacturing enterprises would be "not only safe against occasional competitions from abroad, but a source of domestic wealth and even of external commerce."[17]

Certainly President Madison's words fell upon most fertile grounds, for there were few Congresses more favorably disposed to a program of national protection than the Fourteenth Congress which began its deliberations on December 4, 1815. Control of Republican policy was, for the most part, in the hands of the generation of 1812, those War Hawks who had helped to bring about the war and who felt responsible for seeing that the nation should reap all the fruits to which victory had entitled her. These men represented a national party which upheld the majesty of the Union and championed a bold and progressive program designed to benefit the nation as a whole. It was a Southerner, for example, William Lowndes of South Carolina, Chairman of the Ways and Means Committee, who introduced the new tariff bill into Congress. It was another Southerner, John C. Calhoun, also of South Carolina, who added his brilliant oratory to the support of the measure, pointing out the importance of domestic manufacturing to the continued security and welfare of the nation and insisting that the combination of agriculture, commerce, and manufacturing were *all* necessary and that each "cannot exist without the other." Henry Clay of Kentucky, then Speaker of the House, brought in the voice of the West on the side of the distraught manufacturers as he, too, vigorously championed the cause of national protection, pointing out the dangers that faced a nation which lacked complete self-sufficiency during time of war.[18]

Undoubtedly the cotton manufacturers of the Northeast, witnessing this display of legislative sympathy, must have had every reason in the world to feel encouraged about the prospects of obtaining some form of ironclad tariff protection. A program was quickly mapped out providing a duty of 33⅓ percent with no time limit and a "minimum" clause designed to shut out cheap Indian cotton goods altogether. On this latter point Francis C. Lowell himself had come down to Washington to urge the passage of a proviso which would set the values of cotton from India, regardless of their actual cost (which at this time would be about nine cents a yard), equivalent to twenty-five cents a yard the minute they entered an American port. Certainly, with the Congressmen from the South and the West so obviously in favor of American goods for American markets, who could possibly object to such a protective policy?[19]

And yet, despite all the assurances of support for a protective tariff which had issued from the Fourteenth Congress, the final record clearly indicates that when the Tariff of 1816 was actually passed—the advocates of *low* duties had carried the day! The iron-makers who had agitated for higher rates found themselves cut down to 40 percent. The sugar-growers who had complained that a four cents duty was not enough, found themselves reduced to two and a half cents a pound. The wool manufacturers saw their duty first reduced 50 percent—and then rejected entirely. But it was the cotton manufacturers who suffered the most startling setback. Their goal of a duty of $33\frac{1}{3}$ percent with no time limit had been reduced to 25 percent for only three years, at which time it would revert to 20 percent. While they had been guaranteed a "minimum" clause to stop the influx of cheap Indian cloth, this promise turned out to be a masterful hoax, for the "minimum" would not go into effect for at least a year—during the very time when the manufacturers needed protection most. And when it did function, it would not provide any more protection than had been in force before the Tariff Act was passed.[20]

Viewed in hindsight, the Tariff of 1816 was obviously not what the members of Congress originally intended—although most of the Congressmen were still under the impression that they had passed a relatively stiff piece of protective legislation. The explanation for this surprising turnabout lies in the complex and often intangible aspects of political action. For one thing, there were still enough hardcore Federalists from New England left in Congress who were ready to oppose any program which the hated Republicans might try to pass, regardless of its merits. Then too, economic jealousy and sectional rivalry played a significant part in preventing the passage of anything like a coordinated tariff policy: Northerners opposed the sugar duties, Southerners protested against the textile tariffs, and both North and South combined to squelch the hopes of the Middle States for the protection of iron. Such partisan reaction against the economic interests of the other sections had obviously gone far toward disrupting any uniform national tariff policy.

But if there was one specific group represented at Washington during the spring of 1815 that set out to undercut the program of protective tariffs and high duties, it was the shipping interest of the Bay State which at this very same time was clamoring for free trade. The postwar years were frightening ones for sea captains and merchants who were straining every nerve and muscle to stay alive in the face of an openly hostile world market. The last thing they wanted was a national policy of restriction and control which they felt would lash a heavy anchor around a maritime economy that they hoped was just getting under way again after a disastrous war. Timothy Pickering, former Secretary of State and now Congressman from the important seaport town of Salem, Massachusetts, was on his feet constantly during the debates over cotton tariffs, and had been particularly indignant over the proposals to shut off the imports of cotton from India. Congressman Pickering had no intention of letting Essex County lose the profits of the lucrative India trade! Warmly seconded by his colleague from Massachusetts, Artemas Ward, and by the young Daniel Webster who was then representing the State of New Hampshire, Pickering pleaded the cause of justice for American shipowners and warned that manufacturing must not be nourished at the expense of the great mercantile communities. The Representative from Salem then offered what appeared on the surface to be only a slight modification of the "minimum" clause, proposing that all Indian goods be admitted on a duty of 25 percent of their cost in India, with the additional charge of 20 percent— and further asked that these rates go into effect at least a year later.[21]

Influential as the newly emerging manufacturing interests had become as a consequence of the late war, the traditional shipping interests of the nation still continued to hold tremendous power and prestige. If the country felt a sense of responsibility to those who furnished their material wants, it held in even greater esteem those Americans who had furnished the brave seamen, the bold privateers, and the gallant fleets which had written such a glorious chapter in the annals of the War of 1812. In an effort to assure the nation that America's merchant marine was not being the subject of economic discrimination, the legislators adopted Pickering's amendment by a large majority—without apparently realizing that they had returned the duty on cotton to exactly the same amount already in force, under which the country was being flooded with cheap foreign goods. As of 1816, at least, it would seem that the advocates of free trade had beaten down the proponents of protectionism, taking the first round of what was to evolve into a classic battle between the merchants and the millers of the Commonwealth of Massachusetts.[22]

For the next two and a half years, the cotton manufacturers were faced with an impossible situation, as they found themselves being battered between a domestic situation of high commodity prices and an international condition of low purchasing power. In America, from 1816 to 1819, the prices of most breadstuffs, provisions, and other staple products were phenomenally high, while cotton prices soared to heights of over thirty cents a pound. A series of bad harvests in Europe caused a greater demand than ever for all staple food products, and British manufacturers tried to keep pace with the rising costs of cotton. All this meant, of course, that production costs for the struggling American manufacturer were equivalently high as he was forced to divide any profits he might make between high-standard wages and high-priced cotton. Nor could he make up the difference by raising his own selling prices, because the heavy foreign exports, especially those from England, had already caused such a serious oversupply of finished goods in the United States that the prices of all manufactured commodities were dragging along at an all-time low.[23]

Suddenly the bottom fell out of the market. Late in 1818 the glittering bubble burst and the inflated economy floated to earth. The British manufacturer, no longer willing or able to keep abreast of the fantastic American cotton prices, gave up in disgust and began to buy the less expensive East India cotton, importing over two hundred thousand bales during 1818. This decision shattered the great cotton spiral, and when Americans heard the shocking news that Liverpool prices had already dropped to twenty-four cents, domestic prices began to plunge downward at such a rapid rate that soon cotton was averaging only fourteen cents at New Orleans. Caught in the avalanche, all other commodity prices were dragged down in the thundering spectacle. Bloated land prices, which had sent the value of likely cotton lands in the Southwest as high as a hundred dollars an acre, now collapsed in a welter of worthless paper, causing the most disastrous financial repercussions in an economy whose condition was already unreal and unsound. Steadily improving harvests in Europe and the effects of the recently enacted British corn laws simultaneously cut into the prices of the agricultural products of the American South and West.[24]

In the midst of the shambles of this economic debacle, it was the manufacturer who emerged not only unscathed, but actually in better shape than ever before. The prices of manufactured goods had already been depressed to the point where no further decline was possible. When, therefore, the prices of cotton, foodstuffs, raw materials, wages, and rents suffered a serious decline, the general result was most advantageous to the textile manufacturer. Now, for the first time, he could begin to produce at a profit, even at pre-panic prices—prices which had seemed so low before, but which now seemed almost high by comparison. Then too, public sentiment in the United States was beginning to clamor for a home market. Shocked by the sudden fall in the prices of staple commodities and by the virtual disappearance of foreign buyers, and especially angered at what they considered to be the unnecessary and arrogant economic restrictions of the British, Americans now adopted a much more sympathetic attitude toward the idea of protection for young American industry. It was painfully clear that Europe could no longer be relied upon to purchase their products or furnish their wants.[25]

The struggle was on once again—the second round in the battle of the wharf and the waterfall—as the manufacturers took full advantage of the sudden change in economic fortunes to try and bend the mercantilists over to the cause of protection. Events in the nation's capital looked promising. A new House of Representatives, notoriously in favor of protection, had just assembled in December, 1819, elected the popular Henry Clay once again as Speaker, and created separate committees—one for Commerce and one for Manufacturing—in place of the single committee which had previously handled both topics. Speaker Clay took special pains to see that only friends of protection were appointed to the Manufactures Committee, so that it came as no great surprise when that body introduced a bill, early in the session, calling for a complete revision of the tariff with a general increase in the scale of duties, including a boost for cottons and woolens from 25 percent up to 33 percent.

The next two weeks were spent in bitter debate over the relative merits of protection and free trade. Speakers such as Henry Baldwin of Pennsylvania waxed enthusiastic over the wealth and prosperity which an industrial America would realize, while other speakers, like John Tyler of Virginia and William Lowndes of South Carolina heatedly condemned the discriminatory practices of a tariff bill that would add to the profits of one class of citizens while penalizing the economy of another. In the House, at this time, however, it was clearly a victory for the protectionist forces, as a strong block of votes from the Middle and Western States proved sufficient to push aside the opposition of a solid South and a divided New England by a margin of eight votes. With their hopes higher than ever, the protectionists saw their bill immediately sent up to the Senate, where it was promptly killed on the strength of a single vote—significantly enough, the vote of Harrison Gray Otis, Senator from Massachusetts, who considered that the tariff bill would jeopardize the commercial and mercantile interests of the Bay State. It would seem, at first glance, that the textile manufacturers had lost round two.[26]

The only difference, now, was that the cotton manufacturers did not seem quite as disappointed as they had been in 1816. As a matter of fact, there was very little disturbance at all. This was because the cotton mills of New England, having managed to survive the ordeal of the postwar doldrums, had finally begun to operate at a profit, and were no longer passively awaiting whatever assistance the Congress might provide. The financial crisis of 1818–1819 had worked to the cotton manufacturer's advantage, and he exploited the fallen price market to the utmost as a means of handicapping his foreign competition. This was not merely the result of a fortuitous set of economic circumstances, for the leading manufacturers had been hard at work during those lean years, rearranging managements and establishing new forms of mechanical apparatus. Especially important in this regard was the general introduction of the power loom as a substitute for the handloom in the process of weaving the spun yarn into cloth. Originally introduced into his Waltham mills by Francis Lowell, where for the first time the entire process of converting cotton into cloth took place under one roof, the power loom was gradually adopted by many other factories in Rhode Island, New Hampshire, and Massachusetts after 1817.[27]

With lower manufacturing costs made possible by the economic depression and with greater production resulting from the introduction of power machinery, cotton manufacturing was soon able to recover from its depressed position in such short time that in 1821 *Niles Register* could nod approvingly and applaud the fact that "the manufacture of cotton now yields a moderate profit to those who conduct the business with the requisite skill and economy."[28] Profits led to prosperity and prosperity led to self-confidence, as cotton manufacturing experienced an unprecedented growth and development during the early twenties. New factories were being built every day and milltowns were mushrooming as Boston saw two distinctive industrial areas come into being to its north and to its south.

In the southern part of the region, the cotton industry, which had first seen the light of day in the Providence-Pawtucket area, spread up along the Blackstone River moving northeast into Massachusetts, where it exploited the phenomenal water powers of the Fall River. It was here that two brothers, Richard and Jefferson Borden, gradually took over nearly all the water power and mill sites and after 1820 stimulated the industrial growth of the town of Fall River. Richard Borden supervised and directed the Fall River Iron Works, which turned out nails and other iron products, and saw to it that the profits were used to construct the textile factories which were under the management of his brother Jefferson. Throughout the 1820's and 1830's the number of milltowns multiplied, strung out along the various small rivers like carbon copies with their rows of workers' houses, the small water power, the factory, and the ever-present "big house on the hill" where the owner lived. These characteristics of multiplicity and decentralization which typified the physical aspects of the southern manufacturing area were carried through into the financial operations as well. Ownership was usually in the hands of in-

dividuals or partnerships, with certain prominent families exert-
ing considerable influence over several localities or many
enterprises in which entire families were employed. Capital funds
continued to be fairly limited, seldom extending beyond the
original financing and reinvested small profits.[29]

To the north of Boston, however, industrial operations were
developing in a much more highly organized and centralized
manner. The original factory at Waltham, with which Francis C.
Lowell, Nathan Appleton, and Patrick Tracy Jackson had been
associated, had proven so successful that the investors decided to
expand their facilities, and as early as 1820 were looking about
for a suitable location. The splendid water power of the Paw-
tucket Falls on the Merrimac River came to their attention, and
the sight of the thirty-foot drop of the river convinced them that
such a location would be ideally suited for the type of manufacturing they had in mind. Moving quickly and quietly, the
enterprisers bought up the titles to most of the water power and
real estate in the locality from "The Proprietors of the Locks and
Canals on Merrimac River," and on December 1, 1821, they
formed themselves into the "Merrimac Manufacturing Company"
with a capital stock of six hundred shares. Patrick T. Jackson
and Nathan Appleton were the principal stockholders with 180
shares apiece; Kirk Boott, Treasurer of the company and Manager
of the new enterprise, held 90 shares; while Paul Moody, the expert technician, possessed 60 shares; and the rest was assigned to
a handful of prominent friends. The wheels of the new plant
began to roll on September 1, 1823, turning out not only increased amounts of the regular cloth and sheeting which the
facilities of the Waltham plant could not provide, but also manufacturing fancy fabrics and printed calicoes on a scale never seen
before in the United States.[30]

So successful were the operations of the new plant, and so
rapidly did the new industrial locality build up—due in great
part to the organizing genius of Francis C. Lowell and his ideas
regarding a paternal mill community—that by 1824 the district
was able to be incorporated into a town which was named, ap-
propriately enough, "Lowell." As the new town prospered and
the Merrimac Manufacturing Company paid out encouraging

dividends (one hundred dollars a share in 1825), other companies began to spring up. The Merrimac Company was selling land and water rights to the Hamilton Manufacturing Company as early as 1825, and that company started operations with a capital of $600,000. By 1828 the Appleton Company and the Lowell Company had been incorporated, and in 1830 the Suffolk and the Tremont Companies had selected sites along the Merrimac and were starting production.[31]

The dominant characteristics of these northern manufacturing enterprises, even during the initial decade of their industrial development, were the high degree of capital organization and the corporate structure of their administrations. The original capital of the Lowell mills, for example, had already passed the million dollar mark, as increasing numbers of observant Boston capitalists began to see the possibilities in widening the scope of their investments. With increased liability and the further complexity of managerial responsibility, however, neither partnerships nor joint-stock arrangements were considered sufficiently adequate or safe, and so the corporation form, authorized by state charter, came into greater use. With this financial system, not only were the liabilities of the shareholders themselves limited, but, more important to the enterprisers, much larger amounts of capital stock could be obtained through the sale of corporate securities.

From a small, localized and struggling operation of the early 1800's, New England cotton manufacturing had mushroomed by the 1830's into a multimillion dollar industry which utilized all the advantages of mechanical power, corporate methods, and capital finance. This combination of technical operation and managerial planning led one commentator to observe that in the "northern mills," "manufacturing was specialized completely and no longer retained even subordinate relations with household industry or general merchandising." One of Hamilton's "infants" had come of age.

2

THE COTTON
ARISTOCRACY

BOSTON had always been noted for
its own kind of aristocracy. Officers of the Crown, young English
bloods, prosperous colonial merchants, conservative Federalist
squires—all these and many others had been a part of the long
genteel heritage that started with European traditions and continued on into the post-revolutionary years. There were, it is
true, other towns of the Commonwealth where fortunes were
evident and where first families were prominent, but Boston
overshadowed them all.

And yet, even Boston had never seen anything like the new
aristocracy of wealth which now began to characterize the fashionable society of Beacon Hill and to set the economic patterns of
State Street. During the early years of the nineteenth century,
old established mercantile classes which had grown rich on the
profits of Europe and the Orient began to merge with the manufacturers of cotton cloth in an association which was to produce
an economic and social elite whose influence would be felt
throughout the Commonwealth.

By 1824 there had occurred a significant transfer of shipping
capital into cotton manufacturing, as exasperated shipowners to
the north and south of Boston saw their mercantile profits falling
behind in the years that followed the War of 1812.[1] Almy and

Brown of Providence, the Lowells, the Cabots, the Appletons, and, most recently, the Lawrences, had already completed the merger of the shop and the factory. Using their stores as local outlets for their own manufactured goods, they found that they could also employ the profits from their commercial enterprises to tide over the factory operations when times were slow.[2] Their success was quickly noted, and before long growing numbers of shipowners, in search of greater profits with which to compensate for their loss in trade, threw in their lot with the Lowells, the Appletons, and the Lawrences in developing the profitable cotton industries. New England manufacturing was given an even greater impetus, now that new wealth was released for additional investment, and as a demand increased for those manufactured goods which had been previously imported from England. This is not to suggest, of course, that shipowners and mill owners immediately put aside their differences of opinion on matters of economic policy. Shippers still stumped for free trade, and manufacturers continued to clamor for the principles of protection. Although these points of contention continued to exist, the bitterness and intensity of feeling which had characterized them prior to 1824 gradually began to diminish.[3] The shipowners, for their part, modified their opposition to the nation's tariff policy when they saw that their foreign trade did not necessarily suffer. The mill owners, on the other hand, no longer fearing foreign competition now that lower production costs and more efficient power machinery had given them a more secure position in the domestic market, placed much less emphasis on the importance of high protective duties. They continued to favor a *general* national protective policy, as a matter of principle, but assumed an almost indifferent attitude on the subject of specific rates and duties. Nathan Appleton, for example, insisted that by 1825 profits in the cotton industry were so high that it would have been highly profitable "even without protection at all," and that after the introduction of the power loom a protective tariff was "of little or no importance."[4]

The changing attitude of both interests can be seen most clearly in the tariff question. Urged by the manufacturers of iron, lead, wool, hemp, and cotton-bagging who wanted a high rate of tariff quite desperately, new tariff proposals were presented in 1824 which actually offered little benefit to the cotton manufacturers of the Northeast. New England industrialists, therefore, joined with the shipping interests and with the Southerners in opposing the act which was eventually carried through on the votes of the Middle and Western States. "The merchants and manufacturers of Massachusetts and New Hampshire repel this bill," sneered John Randolph sarcastically, "while men in hunting shirts . . . want protection for home manufactures." Again in 1828, when the tariff question was revived by the iron and woolen interests, the cotton men were little in evidence to lobby and fight for the passage of the measure as they had done so vigorously back in 1816. When Abbott Lawrence came down to represent the state of Massachusetts at the Harrisburg Convention, he indicated what could be expected of the cotton group. Waving aside the demands of many of his colleagues that the cotton men demand a specific forty-cent minimum, Lawrence was content to write a general recommendation that Congress should merely impose "adequate duties."[5]

While the manufacturers were modifying their stand with regard to the protective tariff, the concessions of the commercial interests of Massachusetts were reflected in the support which Daniel Webster, once the political spokesman for free trade, was now giving to the new protective tariff. He calmly indicated that the merchants and shippers were now willing to yield to the inevitable and adjust their financial policies to what had obviously become an accepted part of the national economic program. Replying to Senator Hayne's charge of inconsistency during their heated exchange over nullification in 1830, Webster snapped back: "Between the ground I stood on in 1824 and that I took in 1828, there was not only no precipice, but no declivity." "It was," emphasized the spokesman of the New England commercial interests, "a change of position to meet new circumstances."[6]

And so, with their formerly divergent interests gradually moving in the direction of a more harmonious relationship, the merchants, the shippers, and the manufacturers of Boston began to build a financial empire. They still did not see eye-to-eye, but at least by 1828 they were beginning to look in the same direction.

Additional capital and eager investors produced a rash of new mills and factories all over New England; and this steady concentration on manufacturing resulted in a rapid growth of industrial cities and towns. Established enterprises were expanding profitably, new factories were developing new markets and customers, and the manufacturing interests of Massachusetts found that by 1840 they had built up a total capital investment of some twelve million dollars—with every indication that the figure would go much higher.[7]

Not satisfied to rest on their economic laurels, however, the cotton men were constantly exploring every opportunity for additional investment. When a Daniel Saunders of Andover told them about a new source of power on the Merrimac River the Lawrences, the Lowells, the Lymans, together with Nathan Appleton and Patrick T. Jackson were soon busy buying up the land, laying out the sites and drawing up the papers for a new company. The "Essex Company," as it was called, was incorporated in 1845 with a stock of a million dollars, and the new town was named "Lawrence," after the company's first president and outstanding stockholder, Abbott Lawrence.[8] Branching out from here, Lawrence became president and principal stockholder of the Atlantic Cotton Mills which was started in 1846; and when the Pacific Mills was incorporated in 1853, with an original capitalization of two million dollars, its president was also—Abbott Lawrence. Although other individuals were permitted to buy stock in the various manufacturing enterprises of Massachusetts as they were established during these middle years, it is noticeable that few were taken into active partnership. Control of the expanding industry always remained in the hands of the Lawrences, the Lowells, the Appletons and their immediate associates in Boston, so that before long, a small group of some twelve or fifteen Boston capitalists were exercising effective control over most of the great corporations of the state.[9]

As the interests of the merchant and the manufacturer grew closer, the profits from both the production and the sales of cotton cloth began to mount. Quite naturally the interested parties began to look for cheaper and more efficient means of transportation between the sales and exchange center of Boston and such inland points of market and production as Lowell, Lawrence, Providence, Fall River, Worcester and Springfield. It is not surprising, therefore, to find the manufacturers interesting themselves in the prospects of railroad transportation during its formative years. In order to develop railroad connections between Boston warehouses and the cotton factories, the leading textile manufacturers, in 1830, voted $100,000 as a bonus to the Boston and Lowell Railroad. Abbott Lawrence was active in promoting various trunk lines and was a liberal subscriber to such projected developments as the Boston and Providence Line as well as the more daring undertaking of the great "Western Railroad" which was scheduled to extend from Worcester, Massachusetts, to Albany, New York.[10]

The techniques of combining foreign trade with domestic manufacturing and overland transportation, however, only added to the complexities of the financial problems. The conversion of foreign currency, the expense and inconvenience of redeeming notes from the various local banks, and the general instability of the State's decentralized currency situation, served to convince the economic leaders of the Commonwealth that they must take a hand. The Suffolk Bank, therefore, was established in 1818 under the leadership of the original group of Waltham manufacturers, including the Lowells, the Lawrences, and the Appletons, closely followed by members of Boston's oldest merchant families, with John A. Lowell and William Lawrence serving on the Board of Directors. As a closely knit group which was already well on the way to controlling the prominent features of the Massachusetts economy, the Suffolk Bank provided a financial stability that was beneficial to both its investors and to the State. At the same time, by rigidly controlling the extension of credit and the payment of specie, the Suffolk was able to suppress speculative local banking and check expansion of undesirable and less organized forms of economic enterprise.[11]

With interlocking financial interests now fusing the profits of manufacturing, transporting, selling and financing cotton textiles, the new "aristocracy" of the Commonwealth commanded both economic allegiance and social acceptance. Like a great golden magnet Boston not only displayed its own glittering society, but exerted a powerful attraction upon the various local elites scattered throughout the State, gradually drawing them into its own orbit where they would be absorbed and integrated with "Boston's own." Nathan Appleton had come down from New Hampshire as a merchant to become a leader in the textile industry. The Lawrence brothers had moved in from Middlesex County to set up in the importing business before they engaged in manufacturing. Every day new families were moving down from Salem, Newburyport, Worcester and New Bedford to blend their social and economic fortunes with those of the Boston groups. The Lowells, already associated with such prominent mercantile families as the Cabots, the Higginsons and the Russells, had now linked with the Jacksons through the marriage of Francis C. Lowell to Patrick Tracy Jackson's sister, Hannah. John Amory Lowell's son, Augustus, was married to Abbott Lawrence's daughter, Katherine; and in 1842 Abbott's nephew, Amos Lawrence, married Sarah Elizabeth Appleton, the niece of Nathan Appleton. Thus the cycle was complete. Not only were the Lowells, the Lawrences, and the Appletons partners in industry and colleagues in business, but now they had further integrated their interests through the powerful agency of kinship and marriage.[12]

Moving into Boston society, the new manufacturers were gradually accepted in the higher social echelons along with the older mercantile families. By the 1830's the industrialists were beginning to take up residence in the fashionable red brick houses in Louisburg Square and Mount Vernon Street, receiving their guests in the dignified and comfortable houses with colonnade porches and small balconies which were such a characteristic part of the homes along Beacon Hill. In 1836 Abbott Lawrence moved into the old Amory house at number eight Park Street, situated, conveniently enough, next door to the residence of his daughter's father-in-law, John Amory Lowell.[13]

On Sundays, the Lawrence brothers would join with such prominent figures as Nathan Hale, the noted editor; Harrison Gray Otis, the Magnificent Federalist; and various members of the Perkins family, on their way to Unitarian services. Carefully they would make their way past "Brimstone Corner" at the junction of Park and Tremont Streets, where one of the latest ministers from orthodox Yale College would be upholding the traditions of the Bible and the Trinity. Finally arriving at the Brattle Square Church of Boston, the Unitarians could settle back in their pews and absorb what they deemed a more reasonable and intellectual approach to the Christian spirit—a theology which Ralph Waldo Emerson once caustically described as "the best diagonal line that can be drawn between Jesus Christ and Abbott Lawrence."[14]

The rest of the week was spent in a fairly constant routine of work, conversation, coffee, and commuting. Early in the brisk mornings the businessmen, walking down from their homes on Beacon Hill, would nod pleasantly to those who were just arriving from their suburban dwellings in Brookline, Milton, and Newton. First they would go to their respective offices to spend most of the morning preparing their correspondence, surveying the latest financial statements, and issuing whatever instructions were necessary for the operations of the day. About noon, the gentlemen of business and trade would gather up their hats, sticks, and gloves, in order to make their way to the "Change" to discuss some of the more informal—yet extremely important—aspects of economic enterprise with their relatives and associates. This midday walk usually took them to the old State House on the corner of State Street and Washington Street, where the center of attraction was the famous "Topliff News Room" on the first floor overlooking State Street—a combination club and reading room for Boston's leading merchants, bankers, and businessmen. Everything pertaining to their interests was available—newspapers and periodicals from all over the world, listings on the entrances and clearances of vessels from every port, and information bulletins from foreign correspondents. Samuel Topliff had even arranged a system of signals from Long Island to his own home on Fort Hill to inform him of arriving vessels. He would then send out a swift rowboat to get the foreign news as soon as possible for the benefit of his commercial clientele.

Here, during the noon hours, the business elite would discuss matters of mutual interest until it was time for them to return home. Back up the Hill, or out into the country they would go for dinner, which would be served at two or three o'clock, fol-

lowed by recreation or exercise; while back in Boston, the office
staffs carried on the details of the business. In the warmer weather
riding and hunting were favorite pastimes, and in the winter
sleighing and skating made for delightful afternoons.[15]

The move from economic prominence to political dominance
required only one giant step. This was accomplished when Nathan
Appleton, manufacturer and protectionist, defeated Henry Lee,
merchant and free trader, in the congressional elections of 1830.
From this point on, protection was triumphant over free trade,
and the industrialists proceeded to consolidate their political
gains. Coalescing behind a strong National Republican Party, the
conservative elements of the Bay State found their interests being
sponsored at home and in the nation's capital by an impressive
array of talent. With the State administration headed by such
men as the popular Levi Lincoln, and later the handsome, polished Edward Everett (reputed to be the wealthiest man in Massachusetts as a result of his marriage to Peter C. Brooks's daughter),
Massachusetts was bound to follow the "right" path in all things.
"Honest John" Davis could be relied upon to represent the protectionist point of view in the United States Senate; and his colleague, Daniel Webster, was already solidly allied with and
financially dependent upon Nathan Appleton and Abbott Lawrence who had sold him shares in their textile corporations and
who later led subscriptions of $100,000 each in order to maintain
the influential orator in public office. And in the House of
Representatives, the indomitable John Quincy Adams, more terrifying than ever in his old age, majestically held the line—
supporting principle over mere expediency.[16]

With such a team of political experts leading the way, it is
small wonder that the business interests of Massachusetts could
feel certain that before long the political atmosphere would reflect that same stability and order which already characterized
the economics and society of the State. Many, certainly, would
agree with the words of Amos Lawrence to his son, as he rhapsodized: "Our local affairs are very delightful in this state and city.
We have no violent political animosities; and the prosperity of the
people is very great."[17]

Political affairs, however, were to prove anything but "delightful" as the disturbing ideas of Jacksonian Democracy began to make their unsettling effects felt not only at the national level, but at the state level as well. In local politics, new parties were already popping up almost everywhere. A rich druggist by the name of David Henshaw (who had never been accepted into Boston's social elite) had formed a Jackson Party in Massachusetts made up of rural and urban democrats, and including a number of so-called "silk-stocking democrats" who represented those die-hard maritime families who still refused to make peace with the johnny-come-lately manufacturers. Although the National Republicans were able to prevent the Jackson men from gaining any measure of effective control in the Bay State as the new Democratic Party came into being, the political problem became more difficult when federal patronage passed into the hands of the local Democrats after Old Hickory's election in 1828.[18]

In 1828, too, a third party came into existence, the Anti-Masons who had already elected three state senators and a score of house members by 1830. A diverse group, made up of former Federalists, dissatisfied Republicans, and unrewarded Democrats, the Anti-Masons became extremely popular, representing all things to all men. Dedicated to the destruction of all kinds of special privileges and powers (such as the Masons were charged with having), they gained considerable headway in New England and the Middle Atlantic States. Particularly disturbing was the tendency of this new group to absorb elements of existing parties by combining appeals for protection and internal improvements with demands for reform and "general welfare" legislation. It was obvious that this new party was confidently looking forward to the elections of 1833 as a true test of its political strength.[19]

As if the political picture in the Bay State were not sufficiently confusing, a *fourth* political party put in its appearance that year —the Workingmen's Party. Although this organization did include such "workingmen" as mechanics, ship caulkers, and urban laborers, it drew its chief supporters primarily from the ranks of the hired hands and farm workers of the outlying rural districts, who were putting their hostility to the "idle city rich" into political form. Representing something of an early version of the Populists of the late nineteenth century, the members of the

Workingmen's Party considered themselves to be the "real" producers in the democratic tradition and they proposed to use political means to oust the mere "accumulators" of wealth whom they accused of manipulating not only economic enterprises but public affairs as well.[20]

The business interests of the city were particularly annoyed at the implications of this new party, and Amos Lawrence took particular exceptions to its name. "We are literally all working men," he wrote indignantly to his son, "and the attempt to get up a 'Working Men's Party' is a libel upon the whole population, as it implies that there are among us large numbers who are not working-men!"[21] Nevertheless, the Workingmen's Party, too, was looking forward to the elections of 1833 with much enthusiasm and confidence as it organized with surprising swiftness in the inland towns of the western counties and in the seaport towns of the East.[22]

The elections of 1833, then, produced not only four political parties, but a flurry of excitement and campaign oratory the like of which had not been seen in Massachusetts for many years. And the results were as exciting as the preliminaries. There was a deadlock: John Davis, the Anti-Mason candidate, received the largest number of votes, but failed to get a majority. He was followed by John Quincy Adams, Republican, with Marcus Morton, the perennial Jackson candidate, in third place. It was Adams, now, who held the balance of power, and he made up his mind with typically calm deliberation, as everyone watched and waited. After prior consultation, Adams publicly withdrew from the race in favor of Davis, the Anti-Mason candidate. No Jackson man was going to get the benefit of *his* vote![23]

The election of Davis through the support of Adams not only produced a virtual merger of the Anti-Masons and the Republicans (the combined groups now called themselves "Whigs" in opposition to "King Andrew" Jackson), but caused the Anti-Mason Party to lose its distinguishing characteristics and cease to be a possible threat to the established community of the Bay State. The year 1833 also marked the decline of the Workingmen's Party as a separate political movement, as the losses sustained in the elections convinced many of the leading members that success lay in combining with the national party of Andrew Jackson. Before long, then, a large number were filing into the ranks of the Democratic Party, leaving the "Whigs" holding the field.[24]

The only other dark cloud on the political horizon during the thirties, was the bothersome issue of the National Bank. When Jackson published his famous Veto Message back in the summer of 1832, refusing to countenance the re-chartering of the Second Bank of the United States, Boston businessmen had reacted in genuine alarm. Not that the closing of the Second Bank caused undue panic or excitement in itself. Boston business interests had long ago taken the precaution of creating their own private banking system which, by this time, controlled as much capital as the Second Bank and was actually a financial rival of the national banking system. Many Bostonians, as a matter of fact, took a rather dim view of the way in which the Director, Nicholas Biddle, managed the Second Bank; and even before the Veto Message Nathan Appleton, Abbott Lawrence, and several other prominent Bay State businessmen had urged Biddle to modify the charter of his bank—but to no avail. And later, when the "bank fight" was on, many Boston business leaders were convinced that Biddle was deliberately manipulating finances as a counterattack against Andrew Jackson.[25] In 1834 Nathan Appleton headed a committee of Boston financiers who joined with a similar New York group demanding that Biddle cease his capricious policy which they claimed was playing havoc with financial credits.[26]

No, it was not the attack upon the Second Bank or the implications for Mr. Biddle's future that alarmed the conservative elements of the city—it was the fear that Jackson's Veto Message was only the initial step in an outright attack on property and position, a prelude to class warfare. "This is the most wholly radical and basely Jesuitical document that ever emanated from any administration, in any country," protested the conservative *Daily Atlas*. "It falsely and wickedly alleges that the rich and powerful throughout the country are waging a war of oppression against the poor and the weak. . . . "[27] Undoubtedly, many Bostonians experienced the same apprehension as the Whig who sarcastically remarked that if Jackson had his way all banks would be eventually suppressed, all paper currency destroyed, and the nation returned to the "barter of the patriarchal age." It was more on a basis of principle, then, rather than enthusiasm for the Second Bank or regard for Nicholas Biddle, that led Boston business leaders to support the Second Bank against Jackson's determination to destroy it.

The repercussions of the bank fight, however, proved even more disastrous than New England had anticipated. With Jackson withdrawing government deposits, and with Biddle contracting and expanding credit almost at will, the financial situation throughout the country became alarmingly unstable. As the government money, now deposited in "pet" banks, was put into land speculations and internal improvement schemes, scarcity of funds caused a new crop of banks to appear. Larger issues of paper money came pouring out, prices spiraled upward, and credit was stretched to the breaking point. The business community watched in horror.[28] Then came the crash.

Hardly had the portly Martin Van Buren seated himself in the presidential chair in 1837 when the financial crash precipitated the worst depression the nation had ever seen. Banks everywhere suspended payments, the most important mills in Lowell were practically closed, nearly half the spindles of Massachusetts ceased operations, and scarcely a manufacturer in the boot and shoe industry escaped bankruptcy. Almost unable to believe his eyes, Amos Lawrence called it "the most violent pecuniary revulsion that has been anticipated for more than a year," and said it was "more severe than our worst fears."[29] But Massachusetts business held on tight, trimmed its financial sails, and rode out the frightening storm. Special scrip was issued by the government of Massachusetts during the crisis and the State commanded higher prices in loans overseas than any other state in the Union. Over a million dollars in State Bonds were issued and the proceeds appropriated to railroad construction all through the Commonwealth. Gradually Massachusetts banks began to resume specie payment on a limited basis as the amount of specie on deposit in the vaults started to increase. In his message to the State legislature in 1839, Governor Edward Everett could report an increase of $900,000 in specie on deposit in Massachusetts bank vaults, making a total of $2,394,624.[30]

Unexpectedly, however, it was the Jackson Party and its associates which suffered some of the worst effects of the financial panic in Massachusetts. The officers of the local "pet" bank, the Commonwealth Bank, had, like so many others, engaged in land speculations involving bank funds. By the fall of 1837, the first director died, personally bankrupt, the second director was found to be $80,000 in debt to the bank, and the bank itself was falling to pieces. With dramatic irony, the Whigs themselves were able to supply the *coup de grâce*. When the Commonwealth applied to the Suffolk Bank for financial assistance—the Suffolk refused. The Commonwealth was forced to close January 11, 1838, and brought down with it such affiliated corporations as the Commonwealth Insurance Company and the Warren Association, whose funds had been invested in the bank.[31]

Delighted at the way in which economic developments were matching their most dire predictions, the local Whigs swarmed all over the Jacksonians. In Washington, Daniel Webster was thundering for a special investigation by the Secretary of the Treasury and demanding a report to Congress. Back home, the Massachusetts Whigs continued to torment the Democrats with the responsibility for causing bank failures and business depression, and they directed their sharpest attacks against David Henshaw, local Democratic manager, who had been a leading figure in the defunct bank and the bankrupt corporations. Hit from every side, the Jackson men did not have a chance in the Bay State, and in the elections of 1837 Edward Everett beat Marcus Morton by nearly five to three. After this, although the Democrats might snatch an occasional gubernatorial election now and then, the Whigs remained in firm control of state politics for the next decade.[32]

Boston businessmen settled back to review their position by the close of the 1830's—and found it good. In spite of the jealous pretensions of former Federalists, the competitive ambitions of Anti-Masons, the levelling tactics of Workingmen, and the absurd theories of Jacksonian Democracy, the men of wealth and influence seemed to be seated more firmly in power than ever before. "The result of the election in Massachusetts is a matter of devout and grateful feelings to every good citizen," wrote Amos Lawrence; and there were many "good" citizens who would agree with him.[33] Everything, once again, seemed to be normal, orderly and quiet.

Quiet, that is, if one chose to ignore the fanatical outbursts of that madman up at Merchants' Hall, William Lloyd Garrison, and his ridiculous position regarding slavery!

3

YANKEE MILLS
AND DIXIE COTTON

HIS HONOR, Harrison Gray Otis, Mayor of the City of Boston, did not understand it at all. On his desk were explosive letters from the Governor of Virginia and the Governor of Georgia, demanding that he take action against some "incendiary" newspaper, published in Boston, that was being circulated among the plantations, inciting the black people to riot and revolt. Nat Turner's abortive uprising in August, 1831, had recently struck terror into the heart of the entire South, and many Southern leaders blamed the *Liberator* for inciting the Negro rebellion. Although there was no evidence that either Turner or his associates had ever seen the paper, the South demanded an end to such outrageous publications. Senator Hayne of South Carolina had just sent a blistering letter insisting upon action against the editor of the offending newspaper, and the *National Intelligencer* even now was publicly inquiring of "the worthy mayor of the City of Boston" whether any law could be found to prevent publication of such "diabolical papers."[1]

Mayor Otis was at a complete loss. Although the *Liberator* had been making its appearance for almost a year now, he had never heard of it—nor had any of his friends or acquaintances. Obviously, however, this was a matter that must be looked into; and the Mayor ordered an investigation of the offending publication.

In due time His Honor was informed that the newspaper called the *Liberator* was edited by a man named Garrison, whose office was nothing but an "obscure hole," whose only "visible auxiliary" was a Negro boy, and whose supporters were only a few "insignificant persons of all colors."

Harrison Gray Otis breathed a sigh of relief—it was obviously only a tempest in a teapot—and sat down to assure his friends in the South that this unfortunate incident was of no consequence. This new "fanaticism," he wrote, had no influence whatsoever among persons of consequence in the Bay State. "Nor was it likely," he emphasized, "to make proselytes among the respectable classes of our people."

"In this, however," wrote a bewildered Harrison Gray Otis, some years later, in a masterpiece of understatement, "I was mistaken."[2]

Just *how* mistaken he had been, even Otis himself would never know. This "obscure" little paper and its "fanatic" editor were destined to revolutionize completely the antislavery movement in the United States, and tear apart what has been called the "great conspiracy of silence."

There had been antislavery agitation long before America had ever heard of William Lloyd Garrison; but for the most part the approach had been rational, the technique gentlemanly, and the demands moderate and gradual. One of the most popular of all early emancipation programs was the plan for "colonization," which proposed to solve the slavery problem by purchasing Negroes and settling them in Africa.

But plans and programs regarding slavery did not seem to matter very much during the 1830's, when issues like the bank, Nullification, the tariff, party battles, and Western lands were occupying the center of the national stage. Who could blame Mayor Otis for underestimating the efforts of William Lloyd Garrison? The editor himself complained that he found "contempt more bitter, opposition more active, detraction more relentless, prejudice more stubborn, and apathy more frozen" in New England "than among slave owners themselves." The early issues of his papers caused hardly a ripple upon the smooth surface of Boston. "Suspicion and apathy," moaned Garrison, were the reactions to his paper, and the rent became harder to meet each month.[3]

Even when apathy gave way to curiosity, and Boston did begin to take notice of Garrison and his little coterie, the results were anything but encouraging. Looked upon generally as agitators and cranks, Abolitionists were not socially acceptable in any respectable circle. "They did not go to work like Christian gentlemen," observed the Congregationalist minister, Reverend Horace Bushnell; while William Ellery Channing, representing Unitarian principles, agreed that they only stirred up "bitter passions and fierce fanaticism." Financial opinion reflected in the powerful *Niles Register*, claimed that Garrison was "doing all possible injury to the cause of emancipation," and the Washington *National Intelligencer* accused him of "poisoning the waters of life to the whole community."[4]

Garrison seemed to thrive on opposition, however. Imperturbable, self-assured and fanatic, Garrison struck back, blow for blow, gradually gathering a small band of followers about him. "Professional reformers" were, of course, one element which gravitated toward Garrison's cause. Advocates of such varied causes as abolition, temperance, peace, women's rights, and labor unions rallied around the banner of the *Liberator*—but this was to be expected. What was *not* expected, however, was the surprising number of converts who were beginning to appear, representing some of the oldest and the "best" families of the Bay State. The Abolitionists counted as members the young Unitarian minister from Connecticut, Samuel May, Harvard '17, who could trace his ancestry back to the Sewalls, and the Quincys; Samuel Sewall, a promising young Boston lawyer and a direct descendant of old Judge Samuel Sewall himself; Ellis Gray Loring, a lawyer who counted many of Boston's leading families among his clientele and traced his family back to 1634; and Amasa Walker, whose forebears came to New England in 1630, a competent businessman who would soon be lecturing at Harvard, Amherst, and Oberlin, in the field of political economy.[5]

Encouraged even by this meager indication of support, Garrison enthusiastically proposed the formation of some sort of organization in order to formulate policy and gain new adherents. By the opening of the year 1832, the New England Antislavery Society had been formed, as the Abolitionist continued to crusade for immediate emancipation, lashing out furiously at any and all who might continue to suggest a program of moderation or of compromise. Garrison condemned what he sneeringly called "that popular but pernicious doctrine of gradual abolition," and went out of his way to single out for attack the policy of "colonization" which had the support of many prominent Bostonians. Charging that the American Colonization Society had been deliberately organized by Southern slaveholders, Garrison claimed that the organization was "solemnly pledged not to interfere with a system unfathomly deep in pollution," nourished on "fear and selfishness," and encrusted with "corroding evil." This judgment struck a deliberate blow at such conservative Bostonians as Amos Lawrence who had shown great interest in the experiment at Liberia and regarded the colonization movement as destined to make "a greater change in the condition of the blacks than any other event since the Christian era."[6]

Over almost insurmountable obstacles, the Abolition movement in Massachusetts slowly advanced as its membership daily increased with ministers, teachers, lawyers, and merchants—men of standing and property in the community—who came to join themselves with Garrison's program. Up to this time, conservative Boston could laugh at Garrison, sneer at his little newspaper, and ostracize those who saw fit to follow the movement. But by the mid-1830's, there were developments which prevented the Abolitionists from being scoffed out of existence. Stronger measures were necessary.

Boston businesmen in general, and the cotton manufacturers in particular, were outraged by what they considered an irrelevant issue, dragged in by the heels, that might very well upset the peace and prosperity of the Commonwealth. Already there were ominous rumblings from outraged planters in the South who threatened serious economic reprisals unless Northerners put an end to Abolitionist agitation. "The people of the North must go to hanging these fanatical wretches if they would not lose the benefit of Southern trade," threatened the *Richmond Whig*, while the prominent Southern economist and editor, James D. B. De

Bow, began to conjure up the awful picture of grass growing in the streets of Northern cities.[7] When it was learned that there had been an outburst of pro-Abolitionist sentiment among the workers in the Lowell mills, the Southern press flew into a rage. Lamenting the fact that such ideas had been allowed to gain such headway among the working classes, Southerners threatened to impose a boycott that would cause the textile city of Lowell to "wither or be forced to expel the Abolitionists." Colonel William Sparks, a prominent Louisiana planter, hastened to warn his friend, Amos Lawrence, of the latest sentiments below the Mason-Dixon line: "There is much excitement in the whole South upon the subject of Abolition," he wrote in obvious agitation, "and I fear the late Lowell affair will cause some resolutions which will be acted on, aimed at her manufactures." Then, as if to add to the urgency of his appeal, the planter closed with a thinly veiled warning: "There will be strong measures taken in this state during the winter, some which I can not now mention but which will be alarming to the people of the North."[8]

Boston manufacturing in alliance with the shipping interests sought some way out of this frightening situation. The businessmen of Massachusetts were now bound to the fortunes of the Cotton Kingdom—and the South knew it. The manufacturing, the financing, and the transportation of cotton had become so important in the industrial and financial life of the whole New England area that it was considered nothing short of economic suicide to tamper with the mutually advantageous arrangement.

Within ten years after the appearance of Eli Whitney's famed cotton gin the cotton crop of the South had quadrupled. With the vast cultivation of the inexpensive and hardy "upland" or short-staple cotton (superseding the more expensive "sea-island" or long-staple cotton), production grew at phenomenal rates. Huge areas of the South were gradually given over entirely to sprawling white fields which grew larger and larger each year in order to keep pace with the hungry demands of British machines and American factories.[9]

As the world's first great industrial power, Great Britain used by far the larger part of the South's valuable output during the early part of the nineteenth century.[10] Gradually, however, the fluffy product was finding its way into the expanding mills and factories of the Northern states. With cotton spindles increasing from one million to over two million between 1830–1840, American factories used over one hundred million pounds of Southern cotton in the same period. After 1830 the industrial North had become wedded, not only to the South's production of cotton, but to the institution of slave labor which made such valuable production possible. Northern factories depended upon a steady flow of cotton upon which to base their profits. Northern bankers who grew rich by extending liberal (but risky) credit to Southern planters against next year's crop, insisted on good relations and a stable economy. Northern shipping looked forward eagerly to increasing cotton production as one of America's chief items of export. In 1821 cotton was already America's leading export, constituting over 35 percent of the total; by 1850 Southern cotton would account for nearly 60 percent of total exports—a major factor in the consideration of Northern shipping interests. Yankee shipping looked to the busy looms of Lawrence and Lowell for one of its valuable export commodities; and at the same time the shipping interests depended upon the increasing production of raw cotton in the South to provide the most important cargo of the Massachusetts carrying trade.[11]

The growth of the cotton manufacturing industry in Massachusetts had brought the influential business and commercial classes of New England into close relationship with the powerful cotton-raising, slave-owning groups of the South. The result was that economic interests of the otherwise disparate sections drew both parties into an unusually tolerant, friendly, and cordial relationship. The New England mills were accustomed to follow the practice either of sending Northern purchasing agents southward to purchase cotton at such centers as Memphis, Mobile, New Orleans, or Galveston, or else of contacting Southern factory representatives who selected the grades of cotton specified by the mill owners back North.[12] In addition to the official employees and purchasers sent into the South, the Northern manufacturers also employed close friends and relatives to ascertain the economic situation, and to improve the personal relationships that were being steadily developed. One of the best examples of this combina-

tion of market research and public relations can be seen in the
extended tour that was conducted by young Amos Adams Lawrence through the South and West, as a commission agent for
various Boston firms—most notably that of "A & A Lawrence."
Determined that at least one of his sons should take over the
business and preserve the "good name" of the company, Amos
Lawrence, Sr., arranged with his brother Abbott to supply the
young man with letters of reference and send him through the
country to learn the work from the ground up.

Nothing but hospitality and goodwill greeted the young New
Englander as he traveled down to Charleston, South Carolina,
and then returned via Pittsburgh. Commenting on the "solid
wealth" of the latter city, Lawrence carefully sent back to his
father a list of the best commercial prospects wherever he went,
and expressed the hope that an "inexhaustible source of wealth"
could be diverted to "our city." The young traveller left Pittsburgh
for Wheeling, Virginia, and he proceeded to Cincinnati and
Louisville before descending to Florence, Alabama, making new
contacts and adding to his list of future prospects. From Florence
he went to Memphis, and then he took the boat down the Mississippi to Natchez, only taking time out to stop at crowded little
taverns and admire the "pretty ladies" who were travelling the
same route.[13]

On his arrival at New Orleans, Lawrence was given a warm reception by the prominent cotton planters and merchants of the
city who were close friends of his father and uncle. "I like your
New Englanders," boomed the prosperous Mr. Pritchard expan-
sively, as one of the old cotton planters laughed and suggested to
the novice that if "you manufacturers and we planters" find a way
to bypass those New Yorkers, "it will be a great benefit to us
both!"[14]

A visit to Mobile was followed by a trip to Macon, Georgia,
early in 1837, where the young man took time to visit the cotton
mills along the falls of the Chatahoochie, near Milledgeville.
"Everybody called upon us," he wrote, "because we brought letters from A & A L & Co. who have a great reputation here."
Indicating the value of the personal relations which the New
Englanders had been careful to cultivate, Lawrence told his
father: "Every man here who knows anything about Boston says

he feels under great obligations to Mr. Abbott Lawrence (or to you sometimes) that he was very civil to them in Boston, and that they *attended a party* at his house." Then he added: "I never saw the good results of politeness so plainly before. . . ."[15]

The multiplicity of these professional and personal contacts between the enterprisers in the North and their counterparts in the South led to extremely amiable relations. Southern planters vacationed at Boston hotels as they might at summer resorts, and they were frequently and warmly received into the best private homes in the city.[16] Wealthy Southerners also sought out cool places in the North where they could retreat from the oppressive heat of the plantation country, their favorite resorts being at Newport, Rhode Island, and Saratoga, New York, where they mixed with Northern manufacturers and commercial men under the most friendly circumstances. Here, as one English traveler observed, the "reciprocities of civilities" and a "better acquaintance with each other" gradually led to the loss of "their sectional and colonial prejudices."[17]

The sons of Southern planters attended school at Harvard, Yale, and Princeton. With dashing manners and generous allowances they courted the ladies of New England, attended dinners and parties in Beacon Street homes, and reported regularly to such gentlemen as Amos Lawrence and Josiah Quincy on their marks and deportment—which would be promptly reported to their fathers in the South. Before 1800, thirty-nine Carolinians had graduated from Princeton, and "scores of South Carolinians were found in the leading Northern colleges after that date." Oliver Wendell Holmes, Harvard '29, recalled the polished and dapper Carolinians in Cambridge who, with their swallowtail coats and their calfskin boots, were objects of great admiration.[18] Wealthy Easterners and prominent Southern families became even more closely associated through marriage. Amos Lawrence of Boston, for example, took as his second wife Nancy Means Ellis, a cousin of Robert Means, a prominent planter of Beaufort, South Carolina. Correspondence between Lawrence and Means continued to hold the two families together, and Means often urged Lawrence to quit his "frightful winter climate" and spend the cold seasons in the "more genial South."[19]

A complementary economic system between the North and the

South, a tolerant regard for the rights and the privileges of the other, and a warm social relationship which augmented the close economic ties—these were the valuable contributions to national unity and harmony that conservative Bostonians felt were now being jeopardized by what they considered the immoderate demands and dangerous threats of the Abolitionists. The North, they felt, must reassure its Southern friends that the disturbing elements were only a small lunatic fringe which was not at all representative of Northern views; and at the same time, take positive steps to curtail the activities and the influence of the offending elements themselves. Mayor Harrison Gray Otis, himself a heavy investor in cotton manufacturing, wrote to his friend, Nathan Appleton, then Representative from Boston in Congress, pleading for a program of Federal colonization. The project of dividing an annual appropriation among the various Plantation States, which would then be used, *"in its own mode,"* for colonization, would, argued Otis, cut the ground away from the present violent demands for abolition. Writing to Daniel Webster in the Senate, the Mayor repeated his proposals, adding ominously "there will be no peace or security for us untill [sic] you buy up the Virginia negroes & send them off. . . ."[20]

In emphasizing the fact that any solution of the slavery problem was to be accomplished only in accordance with the mode of each Southern state, Otis was touching upon one of the most significant points of the conservative argument against abolition. Slavery, they felt, was an integral part of the American historical process, given specific sanction by the terms of the Constitution of the United States itself. While the average Boston businessman might personally deplore the institution of slavery itself, he was firmly convinced that any change in the situation could be made only by and with the consent of the respective states. Although Webster, in his famous "Reply to Hayne," might publicly castigate slavery as a moral and political evil, he was forced to admit that the Federal Government could have nothing to do with an institution which "has always been regarded as a matter of domestic policy left with the States themselves."[21] Amos Lawrence made it clear to Robert Rhett of South Carolina that he would never interfere in the question "unless requested by my brethren of the Slave-holding States"; and his son, Amos A. Lawrence, expressed the opinion that as a Whig he was honor-bound to preserve the original compact of the Union by which slavery was recognized.[22] When Harrison Gray Otis wrote to Benjamin Faneuil Hunt, an eminent lawyer of Charleston, he assured him that he "never doubted that the states of this union are inhibited by the federal compact from interfering with the plantation states in the management of their own slaves. The letter and the spirit of the constitution are opposed to it. . . ."[23] The majority of conservatives in Massachusetts would seem to agree with Jared Sparks, the historian, who considered slavery a great calamity but a problem which was impossible of solution. "Slavery exists," he wrote, "by the Constitution and the laws."[24] As far as Boston businessmen were concerned, that ended the matter.

As far as the Abolitionists were concerned, however, the mere fact that the Constitution of the United States countenanced the institution of slavery settled nothing. It only meant that the Constitution was wrong, and must either be changed—or abandoned. As early as 1842 William Lloyd Garrison was preaching disunion, calling for "the repeal of the union between the North and the South," and establishing the basis for a growing attack upon the whole American political system. "The ballot box," charged Garrison in his *Liberator,* "is not an anti-slavery, but a pro-slavery argument, so long as it is surrounded by the U.S. Constitution"—a Constitution, moreover, which he classified as "a covenant with death and an agreement with hell." Wendell Phillips agreed that one of the "primary objects" of Abolitionists was "to dissolve the American Union."[25]

Any compact with slavery was evil, the Abolitionists argued, and such a Union must necessarily be dissolved in accordance with the principles of the "higher law." Dissolution of the Union of the States, then, would be the only solution in America, especially since it would not only end the complicity of the Northern states in maintaining the immoral institution of slavery, but would also eliminate once and for all the dangers of the extension of slavery into the territories of the North.[26]

A shudder of horror ran through the conservative North at this

latest evidence of political blasphemy. To preach abolition was
one thing—there was no accounting for personal idiosyncracies—
but to denounce the sacred Constitution and advocate the dissolution of the Union were quite different. There was too much at
stake to let a disorganized group of maniacs and anarchists continue to go their way unchallenged and unopposed! The time had
come for action, if the friendship of the South were to be retained.
Even while excited petitioners were flooding Congress with their
memorials, a huge meeting of some fifteen hundred citizens was
called for Faneuil Hall on August 21, 1835. Presided over by
Mayor Theodore Lyman, Jr., and Abbott Lawrence, the assembly
was attended by leading members of Boston society. Invita-
tions had been sent to prominent slaveholders to come and witness the good intentions of Boston's men of business; and as the
hall began to fill up, Mr. Benjamin Robbins Curtis could note
with satisfaction the "numerous Southern gentlemen [who] came
from all parts of the country to be present at the meeting."[27] With
nods of approval the Bostonians and their guests listened to the
words of the venerable Harrison Gray Otis, now seventy, as he
warned that slaveholders would regard any attempt at abolition
as "war in disguise upon their lives, their property, their rights
and institutions, an outrage upon their pride and honor, and the
faith of contracts." By the close of his eloquent oration, the
elderly statesman had his audience on their feet cheering his
appeal that "the thirteen stripes may not be merged in two dismal
strains of black and red!"[28]

Even the most sanguine of the visitors from the South should
have been satisfied by the Boston meeting.[29] Denunciations of
Garrison and his colleagues had come so fast and furiously that
Garrison's friends, fearing for his life, pleaded with him to leave
the city. Reluctantly he consented, and for about a month he and
his wife stayed away from Boston. In October, however, Garrison
made known his return, and the *Liberator* announced that the
regular meeting of the Boston Female Anti-slavery Society would
be held at three o'clock on October 21, 1835. Garrison apparently
felt that the recent Faneuil Hall meeting had cleared the air and
provided him with an opportunity to resume operations. Having
vented their spleen against the Abolitionists, the conservative

elements of the Bay State would undoubtedly be satisfied with their public assurance to the South that the worst was over and that everything would be well. The only thing left for the frustrated "fiery spirits" of the South to do, then, would be to try to suppress the Abolition movement through legal enactments, or else resort to "mobocratic violence"—and this Garrison dismissed as a practical impossibility.[30]

Despite Garrison's feelings of confidence trouble was already brewing. The rumor had spread through the city that George Thompson, a prominent British emancipationist (that "infamous foreign scoundrel" one placard called him), would address the women's society. A menacing crowd was already at the doors of 46 Washington Street when Garrison arrived at his office, which adjoined the small lecture hall, but the preparation inside went on as scheduled. Promptly at three o'clock, however, the mob burst in, broke up the ladies' meeting, and began a search for Garrison who had just escaped through a rear window. The shouting mob finally caught up with the Abolitionist leader, pummeled him severely, threw a rope around him, and dragged him triumphantly through the streets.[31] Ragged and torn, he was rescued from the mob and spirited off to the local jail for his own protection—after being booked as a "rioter." The next day Mayor Lyman dismissed the charges, released Garrison, and advised him to leave town. Garrison decided to follow the Mayor's advice and journeyed to Providence with his wife for a much needed rest.[32]

Of the nature of the mob which had attacked him, Garrison had no doubt. "It was planned and executed," he insisted, "not by the rabble, or the workingmen, but by 'gentlemen of property and standing from all parts of the city'."[33] Wendell Phillips, who had been a nonpartisan witness to the event, later gave a classic description of the assault being conducted by the "gentlemen" of the city—in "broadcloth and in broad daylight."[34] The conservative character of the rioters was confirmed by a visitor from Baltimore, Mr. T. L. Nichols, who chanced to see the historic outburst as he walked through the city. "Merchants and bankers of Boston, assembled on Change in State-Street," he related, "and believing him [Thompson] to be at the office of Garrison's *Liberator*, they gathered tumultuously, and came around from State-Street into

Washington Street, determined to put a stop to the eloquence of the English Abolitionist."[35] Although the evidence is largely circumstantial, there is little doubt that Boston's leading merchants and businessmen had decided to demonstrate their goodwill to their Southern brethren by deeds as well as by words.

Garrison's almost fatal encounter was only one of a number of bloody episodes that occurred during the mid-thirties, which indicate the violent and almost hysterical nature of the anti-abolition sentiment in the North. Under continual pressure from the Southern states which demanded the suppression of the movement, Northern opposition resorted to desperate measures as a means of stamping out the dangerous agitation. In New York, mobs sacked the home of Lewis Tappan, wrecked churches, and destroyed homes in the Negro section of the city. Although Mayor Lawrence called out the militia, it took three days for the riots to be put down. In Cincinnati repeated attacks were directed against the *Philanthropist*, published by James G. Birney, a converted Alabama slaveholder who led the Ohio Anti-slavery Society. The final blow came with the news that Elijah Lovejoy, a prominent Presbyterian minister who edited the Alton *Observer*, had been shot and killed by an Illinois mob while trying to prevent his presses from being wrecked—for the fourth time.[36]

If there were many who expected that the years of "terror" would intimidate the Abolitionists into inactivity and serve as a strong deterrent to further membership—they were doomed to disappointment. The violence of 1835–1836 not only failed to halt the Abolition movement—it acted as a positive incentive by providing more sympathy and more converts than the movement had ever been able to gain through its own exertions. The acts of unrestrained mob violence had aroused many complacent Bostonians out of their lethargy; and the murder of Lovejoy had been particularly influential in arousing public indignation. Men of wealth, background, and position joined themselves to Garrison's cause as Dr. William Ellery Channing headed a petition signed by one hundred prominent citizens, requesting the use of Faneuil Hall for a protest meeting. Wendell Phillips, Harvard '31, a young lawyer who belonged to one of the city's leading families, had never been particularly interested in abolition until the afternoon he saw Garrison being dragged through the streets of Boston at the end of a rope. While still not converted, he became more interested in the cause, and when he fell in love with an ardent Abolitionist, Miss Ann Terry Greene, the following spring, he publicly joined the Massachusetts Antislavery Society. The news of Lovejoy's murder completed the transition. Burning with outrage, Phillips ascended the platform at Faneuil Hall to deliver a thundering oration on behalf of liberty and freedom that not only brought the audience to its feet, wildly cheering, but marked him from that moment on as the foremost orator of antislavery in the United States.[37]

The list grew alarmingly. Edmund Quincy, son of Harvard's great President, Josiah Quincy, joined the movement; and the prominent Dr. Henry Ingersoll Bowditch who had witnessed the Boston mob scene "from that moment became an abolitionist" and subscribed to Garrison's *Liberator*. Even the influential merchant, John Murray Forbes, confessed that although he had been indifferent to the problem of slavery, Lovejoy's death and Phillips's speech "changed my whole feeling with regard to it," although he still would not join Abolitionist societies because of what he regarded as the "bigotry and pigheadedness" of their leaders.[38] James Russell Lowell was soon adding his writing abilities to the antislavery movement, and by the 1840's Ralph Waldo Emerson had become a warm adherent of the cause. Together with John Greenleaf Whittier, who had been one of Garrison's first disciples, the "literary Abolitionists" were destined to become an influential factor in the drive for emancipation.[39]

The movement continued to mushroom. By 1838 there were over two hundred antislavery societies in the state of Massachusetts alone, with enough funds to send out propagandists and supply literature to all parts of the country. Membership was increasing every day, and the *Liberator's* circulation continued to go up. "We are becoming Abolitionist at the North fast," exulted Charles Sumner, as the fortunes of the antislavery crusade began to rise.[40]

To make matters worse, the slavery question was becoming an important political issue. Up to now, Massachusetts had witnessed its own version of the Victorian Compromise as both Whigs and Democrats uniformly sidestepped the problem of slavery and refused to have anything to do with Garrison and his unpopular program. Garrison himself resisted all attempts to involve his Abolition movement in politics, emphasizing his ideal of "non-resistance" as the method best calculated to effect a solution.[41]

But the question of slavery could hardly be denied access to the turbulent political arena. Western abolitionists under the leadership of such political activists as James G. Birney and Theodore Weld had already committed themselves to political action. The New York group, headed by William Jay and the Tappan brothers, were finding Garrison's "no-government" leanings a little too impractical for their taste. Even in Massachusetts, Garrison's leadership was being challenged by such men as Henry B. Stanton and John Greenleaf Whittier who considered political action to be of greater value to the cause of abolition than their leader was willing to admit. Although Garrison was able to stay on top in Massachusetts, and even retained control of the national organization after a bruising contest at the 1840 convention in New York City, his brand of "passive abolitionism" began to fall behind as an isolated pocket of resistance.[42] More and more, Abolitionists came to believe that the future success of their crusade lay in the power that political pressure could give it; and they swung in behind the newly formed Liberty Party which had nominated Birney for the Presidency as early as 1840. Weld and Joshua Leavitt were now maintaining an Abolitionist lobby in Washington; and with the appearance of antislavery legislators in the National Capital the center of abolitionism was gradually shifting from Boston to Washington. Joining their protests with those of John Quincy Adams, the Congressmen from Vermont, William Slade and John Mattocks, proved themselves vigorous opponents of slavery, and the Ohio Congressmen, Joshua Reed Giddings and Sherlock J. Andrews, supported the contentions of the Senator from their State, Thomas Morris, in condemning slavery as the greatest national sin.[43]

To those who still controlled the conservative policy of the Whig Party in Massachusetts the situation had not yet become critical, and they could see no imminent threat to Whig fortunes in the Bay State. Abbott Lawrence, Nathan Appleton, and Daniel Webster continued to direct State affairs, while sending quiet assurances to their friends in the South that the agitation would soon blow itself out.[44] Nevertheless, there were definite danger signals which indicated the possibility of trouble. The new Abolitionist-sponsored Liberty Party was slowly picking up votes in the State—not many, of course, compared with the major parties, but enough to give the antislavery element an uncomfortable advantage in the event of a close election. Despite the efforts of the Whigs to minimize the problem, the slavery question was drawing greater popular interest than ever before in State and local elections. What about the morality of slavery? What about the extension of slavery? What about slavery in Texas? What about the slave trade in the District of Columbia? These and many other pertinent questions were being asked of candidates for public office, shocking the party leaders into recognizing the fact that slavery had become a serious campaign issue.[45]

Then too, all was not harmonious within the ranks of the Whig Party itself. Rising young political leaders like Charles Francis Adams, John G. Palfrey, and Horace Mann were chafing at the bit, demonstrating an ambition to capture influence in the party and direct it into different channels. Nothing serious had occurred yet—but the new pro-Abolitionist activity needed watching.

Most disturbing was the alarming rate at which the slavery issue was being brought into national prominence. If the South had been outraged and dishonored by the activities of one lone man and his puny newspaper, what would happen if the same sort of irrepressible vituperation were brought into the very halls of Congress itself? If the long white thread that stretched from the plantation to the mill had been endangered by the ravings of a single insignificant reformer, what would happen when the Capital resounded to the voices of dozens of national legislators?

And Boston's merchants and mill owners worried with good cause.[46] By the 1840's, slavery had become a serious national issue, directly involved in the significant crisis of territorial expansion. It was in trying to find a moderate and workable solution to these explosive developments that the Northern manufacturers began their search for a way in which they could balance their economic security with their moral principles.

4

COTTON
VERSUS CONSCIENCE

THE BOSTON manufacturer did not like slavery—as a matter of fact, he personally abhorred it as a grievous affliction—but he had repeatedly gone on record to assure the Cotton Kingdom that he would not lift a finger to interfere with its "peculiar institution" where it already existed under the formal sanction and protection of the Constitution of the United States. This attitude was appreciated by many prominent Southerners at the time. Writing from Louisiana, for example, William H. Sharp told Amos Lawrence that he deplored actions by his fellow Southerners which would force a "reluctant union" between the Abolitionists of the North and that "great mass of wealth, talent, and virtue of the North who though disapproving in the abstract of slavery, still felt that they had nothing to do with it and who were as anxious to put down the agitation as we of the South. . . ."[1] Most Boston Whigs were quite clear in their decision not to tamper with the institution of slavery in the Southern states, and they felt that they had given their Southern brethren tangible assurances that they would continue to hold that position.

The extension of Negro slavery *outside* of these constitutional limits, on the other hand, was an entirely different matter; and most industrialists felt no compunction in taking issue with

territorial expansion whenever and wherever it seemed to fore-
shadow the simultaneous expansion of slavery. "While . . . I feel
it to be my duty distinctly to say that I would leave to the masters
of slaves every guaranty of the Constitution and the Union . . . ,"
said Rufus Choate to a meeting of the Young Men's Whig Club of
Boston, "I still controvert the power, I deny the morality, I
tremble for the consequences, of annexing an acre of new territory, for the mere purpose of diffusing this great evil, this great
curse, over a wider surface of American earth!"[2]

When Amos Lawrence wrote to a friend in South Carolina, it
was quite consistent with the conservative policies of Northern
businessmen that he assured his correspondent that the "peculiar
institution" would never be interfered with by "sober, honest
men." Equally significant, however, was the fact that Lawrence
made it a point to add his conviction that the same institution
would "never be allowed to be carried where it is not now under
the Federal Government."[3] Since this question of territorial
expansion was regarded as completely outside the original constitutional provisions which had insured the security of slavery
in the states, men like the Lawrences were quite comfortable in
their convictions that the South could have no possible grounds
for thinking that its constitutional rights and prerogatives were
being assailed.

The most serious threat to this Whig position on slavery came
during the late 1830's with the movement for Western expansion
in general, and the issue of Texas in particular. Once the American settlers in Texas had declared their independence from
Mexico, sentiment in favor of immediate annexation began to
grow increasingly strong on the part of the northern Republic.
Soon there were many who were not only talking about adding
Texas to the Union, but speculating upon the possibilities of the
vast western lands beyond.[4]

There were many other Americans, however, who flatly opposed
the admission of Texas, convinced that such a step would not only
upset the balance of political power, but would also permit the
institution of slavery to spread beyond its prescribed constitutional limits. As one might suspect, violent Abolitionists like
William Lloyd Garrison immediately set themselves against an-

nexation, and even went so far as to demand secession if Texas were admitted to the Union.[5] The more moderate antislavery groups also took up the cry, and thrilled to the words of the Reverend William Ellery Channing who thundered in protest: "The Free States declare that the very act of admitting Texas will be constructed as a dissolution of the Union!"[6]

But by now apprehension had struck deep into even the most conservative elements of the Boston community. Abbott Lawrence, the leading cotton manufacturer and capitalist in New England, warned that the movement for annexing Texas created the most significant crisis for the Union since the Constitution had been written. The ramifications of the Texas question, he felt, were enormous. With the admission to the Union of a slave-holding territory whose size was sufficient to create six future states, the threat to the political future of the free states was undeniable. "Where will be the patronage and Executive power of the Government?" he asked. "Will it not be gone, forever departed, from the Free States?" Such a thing must not happen, Lawrence insisted. The North must "resist every attempt at the acquisition of territory to be inhabited by slaves!"[7]

Abbott's brother, Amos Lawrence, expressed similar views and stated that he regarded all other questions of the day as "insignificant in comparison with this." Writing to Jonathan Chapman, former Mayor of Boston, and member of the Whig Committee, Amos Lawrence emphasized his belief that the annexation of Texas and the subsequent extension of slavery would be the first step toward national destruction. "Let us work," he urged, "in a Christian spirit as we would for our individual salvation, to prevent this sad calamity befalling us."[8] From New Orleans, Lawrence's friend, Judge Henry Adams Bullard, agreed most heartily. A transplanted Yankee, Bullard had first gone south to fight for the liberation of Mexico, and then stayed on to practice law in New Orleans, where his fluency in languages and his cultured manner made him a popular figure. Now Judge of the Supreme Court of Louisiana, Bullard corresponded with Lawrence frequently and provided him with firsthand evidence of the Southern point of view. "The greatest *humbug* in this life of *humbugs* is that Texas business," he growled. "Only think of a scattered population which never exceeded 25,000 men, women, children, vagrants, runaways, cutthroats and all, absolutely without resources, asking the United States first to recognize their independence as a nation and then to admit them into the Union." The fact that most of the new citizens would be leaving American creditors "with the bag to hold," only made the prospect more dismal than ever.[9]

Private opinions such as these were given open political expression in Daniel Webster's widely discussed address at Niblo's Saloon in Washington when he condemned the extension of an institution which he denounced as "a great moral, social and political evil." Asserting his own personal opposition to any such expansion, Webster was convinced that "the people of the United States will not consent to bring into the Union a new, vastly extensive, slaveholding country. . . . In my opinion," he added, "they ought not to consent to it."[10] In the House, Robert C. Winthrop, close friend of the Lawrences and the Appletons, added his protests against the annexation of Texas. It would, he charged, "break up the balance of our system, violate the Compromises of the Constitution, and endanger the permanence of the Union." Voicing the opinion of Boston's men of business, Winthrop announced that he was "uncompromisingly opposed to the extension of domestic slavery, or to the addition of another inch of slave-holding territory to this nation."[11]

In the face of such strong feelings on expansion most politicians hesitated to commit themselves in public on the issue. While Martin Van Buren endeavored to sidestep the explosive issue during most of his term as President, Whig Party leaders were hard at work on a plan to unseat the Democrats from national power in the coming elections of 1840. Deciding to bypass their nominal leaders, Henry Clay and Daniel Webster, the Whigs chose, instead, William Henry Harrison, the aged military hero who had won his reputation in 1811 because of a victory over the Indians at Tippecanoe Creek.[12] After a raucous campaign in which log cabins and cider jugs played a conspicuous part, the old general swept into office by an even greater electoral majority than had been expected. Jubilant Whigs everywhere were delighted that "the wicked Administration of the last twelve years" had at last been overthrown, and were thankful for "the deliverance that has at last appeared."[13]

Confident that the "old fellow" would quietly collapse into the Presidential chair and "sit still" while conservative Whigs like Henry Clay and Daniel Webster guided the nation's destiny, most party leaders assumed that with the election of Harrison the question of Texas was a dead issue.[14] "We believe Mr. Webster and yourself are to be of the Council," wrote Abbott Lawrence to Senator John J. Crittenden of Kentucky, "and we feel that the success of General Harrison's Administration depends upon those who are to be his Ministers; and the appointments made *through them* of the Federal officers throughout the Country."[15] Certainly things were starting out beautifully. Henry Clay was getting his legislative program ready for Congress, while his friends and colleagues took over their new Cabinet posts. Daniel Webster had just received his appointment as Secretary of State; and Abbott Lawrence was named as one of the commissioners to discuss the Maine boundary dispute with Great Britain. It looked as though the growing impulse for unlimited national expansion was definitely a thing of the past.

But the elderly President Harrison died soon after taking office, and he was succeeded by the Vice-President, John Tyler of Virginia. A confirmed Democrat who hated the tariff and the Bank, but who loved the idea of western expansion, Tyler had been nominated for the second position on the Whig ticket merely as a matter of political expediency; and his unexpected succession threw the Whigs into despair. When Clay tried to create a new national bank in the spring of 1841, Tyler vetoed the bill. When a revised version of the proposal was enacted, he vetoed that as well. When the Whigs passed a new tariff measure, he vetoed it, relenting only when serious modifications were made in the rates. Denouncing Tyler's defection from their party principles in no uncertain terms, ("a traitor, a base traitor!" one Southern planter called him), the Whig hierarchy began to look around almost immediately for a candidate to groom for the next election.[16] One of the hardest workers in this program was Abbott Lawrence of Massachusetts, who added his voice and his influence to the campaign against Tyler, convinced that the coming election was "the most important since the adoption of the Constitution."[17]

Presiding at the State Whig Convention in the fall of 1842, Lawrence came out publicly in support of the candidacy of Henry Clay—much to the disgust of the devoted followers of Daniel Webster.[18] Although he admitted the great local appeal of Webster and praised his contributions to the nation, Lawrence nevertheless considered Clay the head of the Whig Party, and he judged also that the Kentuckian had more "national influence" than the Senator from Massachusetts.[19] As a member of the National Whig Convention, and as an elector from Massachusetts in 1844, Lawrence continued to voice his support of Clay, and he called upon the voters of the Bay State to do likewise. "How any man . . . in New England can cast his vote for Mr. Polk, with his ultra view of national policy, is more than I can comprehend," said the noted manufacturer. "Upon the subject of Texas and the Tariff, Mr. Polk entertains the views of the State of South Carolina. . . . Mr. Polk has come out boldly in favor of the extension of slavery." Opposing Polk, free trade, and South Carolina "abstractionisms," Lawrence led the fight for Clay. "Let us go," he cried, "for Clay and Freylinghuysen—and the American System—and the Union as it is!"[20]

The election of 1844 proved to be close and exciting, with the question of Texas always a critical campaign issue. Trying to keep a foot in both electoral camps, Henry Clay, the unanimous choice of the Whigs, straddled the question of annexation.[21] The Democrats, on the other hand, supported an articulate, pro-Texas Southerner in the person of James K. Polk of Tennessee who campaigned on an open enunciation of the doctrine of Manifest Destiny. It was a neck and neck race down to the finish line, with Polk nosing out Clay by fewer than 50,000 popular votes, as many antislavery votes were switched to the Liberty Party at the last minute in reaction to Clay's vacillating tactics. Although it was a hairline finish—with the electoral votes, 170 to 105, indicating the precarious political balance—the results demonstrated decisive support for expansion.

When President Tyler, before his term of office ended, recommended the annexation of Texas by a joint resolution of both Houses, Congress did not hesitate to take up the question, and a series of violent debates commenced. It was obvious that the Bay State congressmen feared the outcome of the voting. In the

Senate, Rufus Choate argued vehemently against the resolution as both unconstitutional and inexpedient, while Robert C. Winthrop continued the fight against annexation in the House.[22] By letter, Amos Lawrence pleaded with the Massachusetts congressmen to hold the line—"if Texas can be kept off, there will be hope for our government"—and he kept in constant touch with the proceedings.[23] Winthrop provided the latest information in the capital, the Boston newspapers printed all the rumors and gossip they could get their hands on, and Faneuil Hall was filled to capacity with delegates from the various towns who came to attend the highly publicized "Anti-Texas" convention.[24] All their hopes were vain, for both Houses finally passed the resolution; and on March 1, 1845, just three days before he left office, President Tyler had the pleasure of signing the document which admitted Texas to the Union.[25]

With the admission of Texas an accomplished fact, Northern Whigs began to issue dire warnings that this was merely the opening gun in an all-out assault upon the Western lands. War with Mexico would be the inevitable result of such a policy, they prophesied, and they declared that they would have no part of the consequences. "If any battles and wars shall grow out of this affair," warned the Lowell *Courier*, "Massachusetts will let those do the fighting who brought the war upon us. . . . The Bay State will send no militia to the South to fight the battles of slavery or to suppress Negro insurrections."[26] "Texas is not yet annexed!" protested the Boston *Advertiser*; and the Boston *Atlas* circulated a public pledge committing the citizens of Massachusetts not to "countenance or aid the United States Government in any war which may be occasioned by the annexation of Texas."[27] The Massachusetts legislature, with a Whig Senate and a Whig-controlled House, passed resolutions stating that an act of Congress admitting Texas to the Union had "no binding force whatever on the people of Massachusetts."[28]

Especially outspoken in their condemnation of annexation were the younger members of the Whig Party—men like Henry Wilson, Charles Francis Adams, Charles Allen, and Charles Sumner—who were already dissatisfied with their obscure position and nebulous influence in political circles and who had begun to rattle the bars of party conformity by challenging the leadership of the older members and by demanding that the Whig Party come out boldly and take a definite stand against Negro slavery.[29] Already they had produced a dynamic young leader in the person of Charles Sumner who had become famous (or infamous—"the young man has cut his throat!" sputtered former Mayor Eliot) as a result of his Fourth of July speech at Faneuil Hall in 1845 in which he shocked the prominent gathering by denouncing national glory and territorial expansion in general, and the United States armed forces in particular.[30]

The growing breach between the younger and the older elements in the Massachusetts Whig Party was visibly widened with the news of what happened to Judge Hoar in South Carolina. Concerned about the fact that Negroes were being forcibly removed from Massachusetts vessels in Charleston harbor and detained in jail, the Massachusetts legislature in 1844 sent Samuel Hoar, a prominent citizen and eminent lawyer, to seek some kind of legal solution to the problem. Judge Hoar was completely unprepared for the explosive reactions which greeted his arrival in the city. The South Carolina legislature passed resolutions directing the Governor to expel him from the State, a hostile mob threatened to burn down the hotel at which he was staying, and a committee of prominent citizens warned him that if he did not leave the city voluntarily they would carry him aboard his ship bodily![31]

All Massachusetts was soon buzzing over the insulting treatment accorded its official representative, and the young antislavery Whigs stepped up their demands that the old leadership adopt a more severe attitude toward the slaveholding South. Ralph Waldo Emerson loudly proclaimed that no self-respecting Boston merchant could any longer entertain a Southern planter as a respected guest at his dinner table; and Ebenezer Rockwood Hoar, Judge Hoar's son who was serving as a Whig congressman from Concord, protested that the Massachusetts legislature should show greater interest in reflecting the "conscience" as well as the "cotton" of Massachusetts.[32]

From that moment, the terms "Cotton" and "Conscience" were used to characterize the growing split within the ranks of the

Whig Party over the extent to which the slavery issue should be allowed to play a significant role in the party's plans and programs.

Seeing the possibility of their traditionally conservative party being taken over by young firebrands and hotheads, leading Cotton Whigs like Abbott Lawrence, Nathan Appleton, Robert C. Winthrop, and Rufus Choate became more apprehensive than ever when some of their extremely conservative members broke away from the Whig Party during 1844–1845 and formed themselves into what they called the American Republican Party.[33] This Nativist faction succeeded in electing a mayor of Boston in 1845 ("At this moment, our City Government is imbecile— being the miserable offspring of Native Americanism," complained Charles Sumner), and was now threatening to cut further into Whig votes by supporting a separate candidate for the governorship and campaigning on a platform calling for the restriction of Irish immigration.[34]

The situation had become so serious that even the sacrosanct name of Daniel Webster failed to produce the degree of reverence and respect it had done in former days. When Rufus Choate retired from the Senate early in 1845 and offered his seat to his friend Webster, party managers had all they could do to scrape together the subscription of $100,000 (the third time such a collection had been taken up), which would allow the great man to leave his personal financial obligations and return to public life.[35] This episode was just one more outward manifestation of the fact that the "Cotton Whigs" were beginning to lose their hold upon a state which up to now hardly even questioned their superior position. The appearance of a new party, the growing dissatisfaction of the younger elements within their own party, and the obvious loss of much local political support now prompted the Cotton Whigs to mend their political fences and to redouble their efforts to maintain themselves in power.

As one means of readjusting their precarious political situation, the Cotton Whigs endeavored to establish closer and more personal economic ties with the South. A more friendly political understanding with the planting community might conceivably produce unexpected dividends. Watching the interplay of economic interests with cynical amusement, Ralph Waldo Emerson sneered: "Cotton thread holds the union together; unites John C. Calhoun and Abbott Lawrence. Patriotism for holidays and summer evenings, with music and rockets, but cotton thread is the Union."[36] Emerson was nearer to the truth than he perhaps suspected, for even as he was writing these lines, Abbott Lawrence was negotiating with John C. Calhoun regarding the possibility of a personal loan of $30,000. A group of New Englanders would advance the sum, Lawrence suggested, in return for an annual payment of 100,000 pounds of Calhoun's best cotton. Although Calhoun eventually declined the offer—feeling that he might not be able to meet the payments and fearing that the too generous advance might be misinterpreted in some quarters—his reply indicates no irreparable conflict over economic issues. "I am no opponent to manufactures or manufacturers," he wrote in closing, "but quite the reverse. I rejoice in their prosperity."[37]

The Cotton Whigs pressed on. Was there anything else they could do to relieve sectional tensions? Calhoun had mentioned the tariff question, and had expressed his view that duties on manufactured items should be lowered.[38] Possibly something could be done here. In a letter marked "Private and Confidential," Abbott Lawrence confided to Calhoun that although New England manufacturers considered a high tariff an economic necessity, a suitable working arrangement could be worked out. "We are quite ready," assured Lawrence, "at a proper time to meet the question in a spirit of compromise, and settle it upon such a basis as will insure repose for ten years."[39] Adding his influence to this argument, Edward Everett, former Minister to Great Britain and now President of Harvard, wrote to Calhoun urging him to make "some equitable compromise between the tariff and anti-tariff parties. If it is possible to be effected," he added, "it can only be done by you."[40] A short time later, Lawrence cautioned his friend and fellow manufacturer, Congressman Nathan Appleton, not to push the South too far on the tariff issue. "We can afford to yield something to the prejudices of the people," wrote Lawrence, "and I am ready for a new bill with discriminations and specific duties at lower rates than those of '42."[41]

Not even recent Southern proposals to industrialize the region in order to produce its own cotton cloth could dampen the efforts of the Northern industrialists in trying to arrive at an amiable and harmonious working arrangement. Here was another potential clash of interests which Northern Whigs were convinced could be peacefully settled to the mutual advantage and satisfaction of both parties.

For some time there had been a small but vocal group below the Mason-Dixon Line who were trying to impress upon the leaders of the South the necessity of developing a "home" economy. One of the best examples of these early Southern industrialists, William Gregg of South Carolina, was vehement in his protest against the ideas of his political contemporaries who were urging nullification as a weapon of protest. Instead of embittering "our indolent people" against the North, wrote Gregg, these extremists would do well to encourage "the same zeal" in "promoting domestic industry and the encouragement of the mechanical arts."[42] From Georgia came similar sentiments on the part of Congressman J. H. Lumpkin who called upon the South to rise above its traditional prejudices against manufacturing and develop an industrial economy which would, in turn, stimulate an even greater agricultural production in the South.[43]

James D. B. De Bow added his voice to the movement for Southern manufactures going so far as to advocate the employment of Negroes in Southern factories.[44] While on a visit to Boston, Mr. R. L. Allen, a planter from South Carolina, repeated these views to Amos Lawrence. If the South continued to oppose domestic manufacturing, and hold on to their "foolenes [sic] and nonsense . . . the whole state in fifty years will not be worth as much as the parchments on which to draw title deeds . . . ." Even their "frugal file leader in folly," said Allen in a bitter reference to Calhoun, "will require aid for his support unless he allows his Negroes to make their own cloth."[45]

Far from being angered, indignant, or fearful at the prospects of Southern industrial competition, businessmen of the North actually offered their Southern counterparts advice and assistance. Charles T. James of Rhode Island, former superintendent of the Slater Mills and considered one of the greatest factory engineers in the country, gave public support to the demands of Southern industrialists. Writing in 1849, James pointed out the great waste in sending cotton "abroad" to be manufactured, when it "might well be done at home."[46]

It fell to the son of old Amos Lawrence, young Amos Adams, to provide a more complete and formalized answer to these Southern demands for factories in the South. A more typical example of the Yankee entrepreneur and industrialist could hardly be found than this young man, now in his mid-thirties, who had established himself in his own business after graduating from Harvard College in 1835. As a senior, poised eagerly on the threshold of his future, he candidly admitted: "to be rich would be my delight." Although he realized with perfect frankness that with the successful "machine" which his father and uncle had painstakingly created, "my advantages for becoming rich are great," the mere accumulation of wealth for its own sake was far from being his life's ambition. He was determined not to become one of those "plodding, narrow-minded" merchants who were cooped up in the noisy city, with their minds chained to the counting room. No, he was going to be a man of the world, a literary man "in some measure," and a farmer too, with a happy, rustic cottage somewhere in the suburbs.

In an exposition of ideas which were to reemerge a generation later in the writings of his own son, William Lawrence, the future Episcopal Bishop of Massachusetts and noted proponent of the "Gospel of Wealth," young Amos Adams Lawrence considered that a man should be "willing and glad to be rich." "A good man will willingly endure the labor of taking care of his property for the sake of others whom he can so much benefit by it," he wrote, anticipating the idea of the "stewardship of wealth" by half a century.[47] Now, only ten years after his graduation, the ambitious young man was President of the Cocheco Mills, Treasurer of the Salmon Falls Mills, and held directorates in such important corporations as the Suffolk Bank, the American Insurance Office, the Boston Water Power Corporation, and the Middlesex Canal.[48]

Replying to James through the columns of *Hunt's Merchants' Magazine*, Lawrence took issue with the engineer by indicating his belief that immediate prospects for Southern textile mills seemed dim because of the absence of sufficient capital and a "radical defect" in steam power. Nevertheless, the New Englander assured his friends in the South that with sufficient skill, industry, perseverance, and capital, "success will follow at the South as well as at the North."[49] Young Lawrence, however, was particularly disturbed by what he considered the general Southern notion that the Northern textile manufacturer did little work, suffered few risks, and made fabulous profits over night. "General James," he wrote to a friend, "is doing considerable harm by writing to the southern market, stating the great profits which we make by manufacturing at the North," and he expressed his fears that this would lead to a rash of hastily constructed factories throughout the South which would only add to the "over-growth of factories which already presses us down."[50]

In a similar vein, young Lawrence wrote to the Southern industrialist, William Gregg, commenting favorably upon several articles which Gregg had written for *Hunt's*, advocating industry in the South. Praising the calmness and objectivity with which the Southerner viewed the relative advantages of the North and the South for manufacturing cotton, Lawrence went out of his way to demonstrate the risks and dangers of industrialization. Business is not good in the North, he warned: cotton is high, labor is high, prices are low, and goods have stockpiled alarmingly. "At the present time," he complained, "we are in a sad condition."[51] Gregg's personal reply to Lawrence was equally candid. Although Gregg felt that Lawrence did not fully appreciate the "Southern character and the capacity of the poor of our country to compete with the Yankees in manufacturing," he acknowledged that the New Englander's treatment of the economic problem was substantially correct. Despite the difficulties in the path of Southern industrialism, Gregg maintained, the South would achieve its goal. This did not mean, he hastily assured Lawrence, that economic conflict would necessarily result. On the contrary, Gregg continued, "I don't think that you Eastern manufacturers need have any fears of serious competition from the South, for such investments are slowly made in all countries where manufactures are introduced . . . ."[52]

Gregg's opinion, that neither section had anything to fear from the other, had its echo in the North. In a personal letter to Robert

Barnwell Rhett, of South Carolina, old Amos Lawrence insisted that New England would never stand in the way of the South's industrial progress. In response to Rhett's boast that in ten years South Carolina would be spinning its own cotton crop, Lawrence offered nothing but encouragement, and indicated that there was plenty of room for everybody. "We of Massachusetts," he wrote, "will gladly surrender to you the manufacture of coarse fabrics and turn our industry to making fine articles."[53]

So well known in fact, had the conciliatory and encouraging attitude of prominent New England manufacturers become in the South, that in 1846 a number of the leading citizens of Richmond, Virginia, most of them members of the State Legislature, requested Abbott Lawrence to come down and establish a manufacturing town at the Great Falls of the Potomac, just as he had founded the city of Lawrence at the great falls of the Merrimac. "We look to New England's noble, intelligent and enterprising sons and daughters," they wrote, "to rear those industrial and truly national monuments of labor in the 'Sunny South,' which now add so much to the energy, sagacity and wealth of our Eastern brethren . . . ."[54] Although Abbott Lawrence found it impossible to accept the offer, due to the heavy responsibilities of his enterprises in New England, the flattering invitation itself indicates the fact that neither the industrial interests of the North nor those of the South considered that their respective economic interests precluded intersectional aid or mutual assistance.

The leaders of Boston capital obviously could see no conflicting economic problem—personal, sectional, or national—which could not be compromised to the satisfaction of all concerned. This was not merely a temporary policy of convenience and expediency, but a matter of permanent economic survival. Northern industrialists did not look upon the economy of the North as competing with, or essentially antagonistic to, the economy of the South—rather, they regarded both economies as complementary. The South produced the raw materials, the North manufactured them—and one section was an economic nonentity without the other. With these convictions firmly in mind, in the decades to follow the "Cotton Whigs" worked to subordinate sectional economics to the greater interests of national political unity. Only by means

of compromise, concession, mutual understanding, and forbearance, could the unity of the nation be maintained and the north-
ward flow of cotton go on uninterrupted.

Meanwhile, however, the rapid progress of national events was
running counter to the feverish attempts of the Cotton Whigs to
develop sectional harmony and national peace. Ever since the annexation of Texas, the coming of war with Mexico was only a
matter to time. On May 11, 1846, President Polk sent his famous
message to Congress, stating that American blood had been shed
"on American soil" and asking that all means for "prosecuting the
war with vigor" be placed at the disposal of the Executive. The
answer was prompt enough: The next day war was declared, as
Congress provided an appropriation of $10,000,000, and author-
ized an army of 50,000 volunteers. The war with Mexico was on![55]

The Mexican War was far from popular with large segments of
the American populace—both in the South as well as in the
North—although the reasons varied greatly.

In the South, prominent Democrats as well as Whig Party
leaders took a dim view of the consequences of a long war which
would be prosecuted by the Federal Government. Increased national costs which would arise from an enlarged military establishment, together with the inevitable increase in the numbers of
federal officeholders, would certainly lead to demands for higher
taxes and heavier tariffs; and any expansion of the military powers
and nationalizing tendencies of the central government in Washington would surely pose a serious threat to states' rights. Alexander H. Stephens and Robert Toombs of Georgia both denounced the war in open terms, the Charleston *Mercury*
consistently opposed hostilities, and John C. Calhoun, the great
pro-slavery spokesman, was unsparing in his criticism of both the
justice and the wisdom of a war which would not only impose
new responsibilities upon the nation but might well lead to
sectional strife and bitterness.[56]

From New England, too, came the uproar and clamor of outspoken opposition to the policies of the Polk administration.
Convinced beyond argument that this war with Mexico was the
direct outgrowth of slavocracy's insatiable greed for empire, an
amazing array of politicians, Abolitionists, pacifists, reformers,

and anti-expansionists set up a fearful din. But traditional anti-slavery elements in the Bay State now found themselves joined by such young Conscience Whigs as Henry Wilson, James G. Palfrey, Charles Francis Adams, Horace Mann, and Charles Sumner who added new vigor and a greater degree of organization to the protests against expansion. In May, 1846, these men took over a daily newspaper, the Boston *Whig*, as a means of getting into print those "conscience" views which were not reflected in the conservative *Advertiser* or the *Atlas*. Through this new medium they were better able to communicate more effectively the violent opinions of those who ascribed every aspect of the Mexican War to the machinations of a diabolical slaveholding plot.[57]

Reluctant to go to these extremes because of their sensitive associations with the South ("Further actions would only embarrass our Southern Whig friends in Congress," Abbott Lawrence confided to Crittenden of Kentucky), yet sincerely opposed to further territorial expansion, the Cotton Whigs cautiously tried to base their opposition to the war with Mexico on what they hoped were the less explosive and more rational grounds of constitutional principles.[58] Daniel Webster accused President Polk of having usurped the constitutional powers of Congress: "What is the value of this Constitutional provision," he asked, "if the President of his own authority may make such military movements as must bring on war?"[59] In the Senate, John Davis, a Cotton Whig from Massachusetts, conscientiously provided one of the two negative Senatorial votes against the war.[60] In Boston, Governor Briggs steadfastly refused to commission officers of a company of volunteers unless they promised not to march beyond the boundaries of the state.[61] Amos Lawrence sneered at Massachusetts volunteers as "the most miserable, dirty and worn-out wretches that can be scraped up this side of the infernal regions," and even refused to give a young friend, on his way to the war, enough money to buy a pistol. "I could not wish them success in Mexico," the elderly man wrote gravely, "but gave him some books, a Bible, and good counsel."[62] Congressman Robert C. Winthrop eloquently summed up the conservative position: "So far as we have power—constitutional or moral power—to control political events, we are resolved that there shall be no further extension of the territory of this Union subject to the institution of slavery."[63] This did not mean, he was quick to emphasize, that he was being "false to the North or to the South," but that, on the contrary, he was trying to combine "that sense of the evils of slavery which is common to the Free States" with "that respect for the Constitution and the Union which would infringe on no right of the Slave States."[64]

The young radicals and eager Abolitionists of Massachusetts, however, showed little patience with the passive resistance and the vague constitutional gestures of the Cotton Whigs which they contemptuously regarded as nothing more than an obvious subterfuge for maintaining their precious economic relations with the South. Through the columns of the Boston *Whig* the Conscience Whigs bitterly criticized such conservatives as the Lawrences and the Lowells who "truckled to expedience in every thing, for the sake of . . . slaveholding gold," and they denounced the war as a by-product of the alliance between the Cotton Whigs and the slave-expansionists of the South. The Massachusetts legislature went so far as to state that the war had been "unconstitutionally commenced by the order of the President to General Taylor . . . ," and it accused the United States of acting like an aggressor and a conqueror. It was a Christian and patriotic duty, stated the Legislature, "for all good citizens to join in efforts to arrest this war."[65]

Sectional opposition to the war with Mexico appeared to be confined to isolated pockets of resistance, however, as these grave tones of disapproval from the Northeast were virtually drowned out in the wild enthusiasm which came rolling in from the Western plains. Spurred on by visions of conquest, gold, and glory, thousands of Western volunteers eagerly joined the colors. The Mississippi Valley and Texas together supplied almost fifty thousand volunteers—as compared with the thirteen thousand who came marching out from the seaboard states.[66]

Once the war was actually begun, and American troops were meeting the enemy on the field of battle, even hostile public opposition took on a decidedly different complexion. There was, after all, no point in continuing to hurl hypothetical arguments at a *fait accompli*; and so most of the opposition shrugged hopelessly and admitted no other alternative but to prosecute the war to a victorious conclusion.[67] Care would have to be taken, however, to see that this undesirable conflict did not produce equally undesirable consequences. Beaten in its attempts to prevent the war itself, the opposition adopted a "watchdog" attitude pledged to eliminate the evil results of unwarranted aggression. Regarded as especially disastrous would be the acquisition and annexation of the vast stretches of Mexican lands in the far West. In the House, Winthrop denounced the idea that "it is worthy of us to take advantage of this war to wrest it [territory] from Mexico by force of arms and to protract the war until she will consent to cede it to us by a treaty of peace."[68]

Southern slaveholders again formed a rather incongruous alliance with Northern Whigs in opposing this possibility—although for completely different reasons. The South feared that free states would be formed out of conquered territory, and thus the precarious balance of power would be upset; the North feared that slave states would result from expansion and that the slavocracy would be extended into the Western lands. Emotion proved more powerful than logic, then, as Northern Whigs and Southern Democrats stood shoulder to shoulder, agreeing only that intersectional accord should vanquish Manifest Destiny.[69] "We believe that this war ought never to have been begun," declared Robert C. Winthrop in the House, summarizing the convictions of his Boston colleagues, "and we do not wish to have it made the pretext for plundering Mexico of one foot of her lands."[70]

But they argued in vain. The voices of restraint and moderation were practically unheard amid the mounting demands that the victorious United States should stop at nothing less than the acquisition of *all* of Mexico. Public opinion was chanting the theme of Manifest Destiny, urging that the pending treaty be scrapped, and demanding that the lands of Mexico be seized without further notice or negotiation.[71] President Polk, however, anxious to head off an "all-Mexico" campaign, accepted the Treaty of Guadalupe Hidalgo and sent it immediately to the Senate for ratification. In March, 1848, with a stroke of the pen, the United States relieved Mexico of about two-fifths of her lands.[72]

The Cotton Whigs were appalled at the enormity of the crime, and terrified at the consequences—especially if the victory over Mexico were to be the signal for the opening of all the Western lands to the institution of slavery. "I do not believe as individual men, that one fourth of our people would sanction in their neighbor's conduct towards their fellow men, such as they vociferously approve in the Government towards poor Mexico," wrote William Sharp to Amos Lawrence from his plantation in Louisiana. "Nothing good can come of this. You and I may not live to see it, but our children will," he prophesied. "Retribution will come in some shape at some day."[73] Yes, indeed, agreed Lawrence, "God's curse will assuredly rest upon the iniquity of our nation. We have acquired military renown in this war," the old man sighed, "at the cost of our national character for justice and truth. The whole course of our Government from the admission of Texas to the present time has been such as to make me feel that our *foundation* (the virtue and intelligence of the people) is not a sure one for us to rest upon!"[74]

Although the Whigs were relieved that the movement for the acquisition and absorption of all Mexico had been checked, they were still concerned at the prospects of the unconditional expansion of slavery. There was only one way in which the evil consequences of the war might be mitigated satisfactorily—and at the same time assure the continued friendship and cooperation of the South: That was for the "right" Whigs—the Cotton Whigs —to gain political control in the approaching election of 1848. With the right kind of a President and a sufficient number of the right kind of votes in Congress, the possibility of uncontrolled slavery in the Western territories might at least be postponed— if not prevented. With a zest and enthusiasm proportionate to what they conceived to be the seriousness of the occasion, the "Cotton Whigs" began elaborate preparations for the campaign of '48. Slavery must be kept out of the territories—but not at the cost of secession, disunion, and war.

5

GENTLEMEN'S AGREEMENT

THE NOISE of the war with Mexico had hardly subsided, and the excitement over the Treaty had barely abated, when the nation began to prepare for the coming Presidential election. James K. Polk, exhausted by the experiences of his hectic single term, declined to run for reelection in 1848; and so the Democrats chose Lewis Cass of Michigan, a well-known and outspoken advocate of territorial expansion, to carry out the ambitious demands of Manifest Destiny.

The Cotton Whigs made their preparations carefully, conscious of the disastrous effects which would inevitably follow a defeat at the polls. If the Democrats should win, the subsequent discussions in Congress regarding the future of the Western lands would undoubtedly be controlled by a pro-slavery element which might throw all Western lands open to unrestricted slavery. If, on the other hand, radical young Conscience Whigs were able to get a slate of liberal candidates into office, slavery in the territories would certainly be opposed—but by a group so openly hostile and so obnoxiously outspoken, that the friendship and cooperation of the Southern states would be lost forever. No, the only possible alternative was for the Cotton Whigs to exercise strict control over the state and national political conventions, to see that men of property and standing were elected to public office, and eventually to work out a national policy regarding Western lands that would place definite restrictions upon slavery in the terri-

77

tories. At the same time, they hoped to assure the South that neither its social customs nor its economic well-being would in any way be impaired.[1]

With this thought in mind, Whig Party leaders at the national convention which opened at Philadelphia in June, 1848, passed over such regular candidates as Henry Clay, Daniel Webster, Winfield Scott, and John McLean, and nominated, instead, the new military hero of the day, General Zachary Taylor, the colorful hero of Buena Vista.[2] The "Conscience Whigs" were furious at this obvious bid for popularity and votes. Taylor, they charged, was a "favorite candidate of the slaveholders," and was selected solely because he was the "only Southern man who could be elected."[3] The fiery Charles Allen was on his feet to denounce "the perpetual surrender" by Northern Whigs to their "Southern confederates" of the "high offices and powers of the Government." "You have even presumed," he continued, turning in the direction of Abbott Lawrence, who was rumored to be the favored nominee for Vice-President, "that the state which led the first revolution for liberty will now desert that cause for the miserable boon of the Vice-Presidency." "Sir," he roared out, "Massachusetts will spurn the bribe!"[4] Seconding his colleague, Henry Wilson labelled Taylor's nomination as "another and a signal triumph of the Slave Power," and publicly vowed—"so help me God"—to do "all I can to defeat the election of that candidate." In the midst of uproar and wild disorder, the two "Conscience Whigs," Allen and Wilson, strode out of the convention hall.[5]

The Cotton Whigs went serenely ahead, however, disregarding the outbursts of their younger members, and then proceeded to the work of selecting their Vice-Presidential candidate. One of the most prominent candidates was Abbott Lawrence and usually reliable sources had long ago agreed that there would be a Taylor-Lawrence ticket, with Robert C. Winthrop mentioned as the new Secretary of State.[6] Certainly there was much to be said for the nomination of Lawrence. He had served in the House of Representatives, had held a position on the Maine Boundary Commission, and had been an active Whig Party worker for many years. He was more than acceptable to most Southern Whigs. Judge Henry Adams Bullard of New Orleans assured his old friend, Amos

Lawrence, that the delegates from Louisiana would certainly back Taylor and his brother Abbott. "A stronger ticket could not be formed for the South," he declared.[7] Similar word came from H. M. Judge of South Carolina, who told Amos Lawrence that "it would please us all very much" to see Abbott elected. "He would not only be ornamental," he added, "but useful in Washington in these times of trouble."[8]

Abbott Lawrence was to find, however, that he had more enemies in his own home state than in the entire South. His active support of Henry Clay back in 1842 and 1844 had angered the die-hard Webster men, and his support of General Taylor at the 1848 convention had turned the Clay men against him.[9] At this point Free-Soil men and "Conscience Whigs" provided another solid bank of opposition to the manufacturer's nomination, growling that cotton should not be put at both ends of the ticket —a bitter reference to Taylor's background as a Louisiana slave-holder.[10] It was a hard core of these pro-Webster, antislavery Whigs who steadfastly refused to yield a crucial bloc of six votes to Abbott Lawrence, with the result that Millard Fillmore of New York had to be brought forward to receive the nomination as Whig candidate for the Vice-Presidency. This was sweet revenge, and with obvious satisfaction, Henry Wilson took pride in the fact that he and his Free-Soil colleagues were primarily responsible for Lawrence's defeat. "Unquestionably the declarations and actions of Mr. Allen and Mr. Wilson led to this result," Wilson wrote, "and gave to New York the honor which was intended for their own Commonwealth."[11] Burning with rage, Robert C. Winthrop denounced the "Conscience men" who had turned against their own party and their own state. "First they tried to defeat me as Speaker," he told Nathan Appleton. "Second, they tried (and succeeded) to defeat Mr. Lawrence as Vice President."[12] Lawrence, however, accepted the defeat with good grace —he had not looked upon the office very highly, anyway—and went on to fight what he considered the greater battle, the maintenance of moderation and cooperation between the sections. "I intend . . . to abandon all business of a private character and give myself up entirely to the great and more important business of the country in the election of General Taylor," Lawrence told

Senator Crittenden of Kentucky. "I have already made engagements to address the people, and as far as *writing, speaking* and *paying,* my friends *will not find* me wanting."[13] "I am willing to spend and be spent," he wrote to Nathan Appleton, to promote "the great cause of conservatism."[14] He worked hard for the success of the Taylor-Fillmore ticket unaware that destiny had just passed him by; for, since President Taylor died soon after taking office, Mr. Abbott Lawrence might have become the twelfth President of the United States but for the margin of those six votes.

The election of 1848 was marked by the appearance of a third national party, the Free-Soil Party, which was formed by a combination of those who already disapproved of the Democratic platform of pro-slavery expansion, and those who had now come to regard the regular Whig Party as too vacillating and compromising any longer to command their political allegiance.[15] Abolitionists, members of the Liberty Party, antislavery Democrats, the dissatisfied "Conscience Whigs" of Massachusetts, and the radical "Barnburners" of New York, all banded together under the slogan: "Free Soil, free speech, free labor and free men."[16] Moving forward with all the fervor of an evangelistic crusade, the Free-Soilers selected the former New York Democrat, Martin Van Buren, as their new Presidential candidate, and chose Charles Francis Adams, a prominent Bay State "Conscience Whig" as their Vice-Presidential candidate.[17]

Although the new Free-Soil Party failed to carry a single state, it succeeded in taking so many New York votes away from the Democratic candidate, Lewis Cass, that the Whigs were able to capture that State. In 1848, as New York went, so went the nation, and the Whigs victoriously put General Zachary Taylor in the White House.[18] But this was destined to be one of the classic Pyrrhic victories of American political history. With its subterfuge candidate, "Old Rough and Ready," who knew nothing about politics and less about the slavery issue, the old-time Whigs may have succeeded momentarily in disrupting the Democratic machine, but they had also succeeded in providing the basis for their own destruction. For, regarding Taylor's nomination as the final outrage, the "Conscience Whigs" could restrain themselves no longer, and bolted the Whig Party for good. Violently condemning the "conspiracy" between the "cotton-planters and flesh mongers of Louisiana and Mississippi" and the "cotton spinners and traffickers of New England," Charles Sumner branded Taylor's election as the result of the union of "the Lords of the Lash and the Lords of the Loom."[19]

Without fully realizing the long-range implications of what had happened, the Whig Party had lost the dynamic young "Conscience Whigs" forever, and without young blood in its veins it would only be a matter of time before political *rigor mortis* set in. Even though some of the more conservative Conscience men like Charles Francis Adams, Richard Henry Dana, John G. Palfrey, and Stephen Phillips might have preferred to develop a *rapprochement* with their former friends in the Whig Party after the heat of the battle was over, the rigid attitude of the old-line Cotton Whig leaders practically ruled out such a possibility. Determined neither to placate their alienated members nor to offer them the hand of friendship, conservatives made it clear that the party was not big enough to hold both of them now that they had disowned the principles of Whiggery and taken up the banner of Free-Soil. In referring to the "Conscience Whigs, alias the Abolition party," Abbott Lawrence told Robert C. Winthrop that he hoped they could drive these dissident elements out of the Whig Party for good. "We gain nothing by allowing any portion of these people to attend our primary, or other public, political meetings."[20]

Satisfied that they had purified their ranks of those who would water down traditional Whig policies, the old-line Whigs were content to accept their political victory at face value and they used the precious time to get their own trustworthy members into key positions as quickly as possible. Although Senator John J. Crittenden of Kentucky had been offered any Cabinet post in return for his staunch support of Taylor, he preferred to accept his election as Governor of Kentucky.[21] Nevertheless, Crittenden carefully scrutinized every new Cabinet appointment, to be sure that only moderate, pro-Taylor Whigs were admitted to the magic circle. John M. Clayton of Delaware, William M. Meredith of Pennsylvania, Reverdy Johnson of Maryland, William B. Preston of Virginia, and G. W. Crawford of Georgia were Cabinet appointees whose views were consistent with the conservative Whig tradition.[22]

For his part in Taylor's victory, Abbott Lawrence of Massachusetts was first considered for the post of Secretary of the Treasury, and then offered the position of Secretary of the Navy.[23] When Lawrence declined the offer, apparently because it involved too much routine administrative work, the new administration saw fit to honor the prominent manufacturer with the post of Minister to the Court of St. James, an appointment that Lawrence proudly accepted as a suitable tribute to the name of his family and his own brilliant career.[24]

With the new administration in the hands of well-known moderates and conservatives, it was difficult to guess what the outcome of the crisis would be, and when the Thirty-First Congress assembled in December of 1849, the electricity of the situation could be felt everywhere as men hunched forward in their seats, waiting, expectant. It took 63 ballots just to elect a Speaker of the House, and tempers had reached the boiling point by the time the explosive issues created by the Mexican War came up for discussion.

Northern sentiment was clearly determined to keep slavery out of the newly won territories, was opposed to slave trade in the nation's capital, and was openly hostile to the idea of returning fugitive slaves. Southerners, on the other hand, were equally determined that slavery should be permitted in the territories, that slave trade in the District of Columbia was perfectly permissible, and that the Northern attitude toward fugitive slaves was morally and constitutionally indefensible. Flare-ups were frequent and fistfights were not uncommon, as taunts, jeers, charges, and countercharges reverberated through the chambers. "Upon the whole," wrote Robert C. Winthrop to Nathan Appleton in a masterpiece of understatement, "a seat in Congress is a most undesirable possession."[25]

It was against a background of debate and furious recrimination that the elderly Henry Clay rose slowly in his place in the Senate to provide a solution which might salvage some semblance of national unity and restore a measure of sectional harmony.

Clay's famous plan was a compromise, pure and simple, designed to appeal to as much of the moderate sentiment of all parties as possible. "Taken altogether, in combination," he explained, "they propose an amicable arrangement of all questions in controversy between the free and slave states, growing out of the subject of slavery."[26] Peace and conciliation were the basic ingredients of the famous Compromise of 1850—but the question was, would any leading political figure second the proposals of Clay?

On March 7, 1850, Senator Daniel Webster of Massachusetts, defender of the Union, statesman of national renown, and spokesman of the interests of tradition, property and respectability, rose to speak. In the last great speech of his life, the aging Senator gave an eloquent defense of the proposals of Clay, and added his own plea for compromise and peace. Urging a national policy of tolerance and mutual concession, Webster condemned the inflexible attitudes of radical Abolitionists as well as radical secessionists as being equally dangerous to the future of the Union.[27]

Antislavery elements in Massachusetts rose to attack Webster in violent and outraged indignation. Condemned in newspapers, magazines, speeches, and sermons, the "god-like" Daniel was excoriated as a self-seeking traitor and an opportunistic rascal. Theodore Parker called him another Benedict Arnold, Horace Mann likened him to a fallen Lucifer, and James Russell Lowell more prosaically characterized him as a statesman "whose soul had been absorbed in tariff, banks and the Constitution, instead of devoting himself to the freedom of the future." He believes that "government exists for the protection of property," sneered Ralph Waldo Emerson; while Whittier sadly lamented "the light withdrawn which once he wore!"[28] Even some of Webster's staunch supporters admitted that they could follow the great man no longer when it came to supporting a fugitive slave law. Old Amos Lawrence angrily compared him to Lord Bacon and growled: "I do most sincerely believe him among the wickedest men I ever knew . . ."; and John Murray Forbes broke with the Whig Party forever because of what he considered to be the dishonorable defection of its best-known leader.[29] The Boston *Atlas*, usually a reliable index of conservative opinion, admitted that Webster's speech caused widespread "dissatisfaction" throughout the North; but the editor hastily took occasion to assure his readers that these were not the sentiments of the Whigs of New England.[30]

To the business community of the entire Northeast, to a majority of the men of wealth and property and standing, Senator Daniel Webster was the man of the hour. In their correspondence with friends and associates in the South, these people had become terrified at the repeated references to secession, and talked about little else but the serious economic disasters that would follow any permanent division between the two sections. In New York City, Philip Hone expressed horror at reading about the "daily harangues" in Congress that threatened the dissolution of the Union; and in Boston, Rufus Choate prophesied that "the future historian will pause with astonishment and terror" when he later came to record the crisis of 1850.[31]

Given the serious national situation, and realizing how close the South had come to secession, the merchants and businessmen of the North were prepared to clutch at almost any plan which offered even the slightest measure of national peace. The Compromise of 1850 was by no means the best solution, most businessmen agreed, but it was far better than disunion and war.[32] As the conservative *Daily Advertiser* expressed it: "The Boston public *fully* support Mr. Webster—not with an enthusiastic rush of blind admiration, but with a calm belief that he has placed a vexed question in a position in which it can be and must be fairly settled. . . ."[33] Webster's Seventh of March Speech, commented the *Advertiser*, was "a monument of his power of analyzing public affairs, and of his devotion to the interests of the Union, and the defense of the Constitution that is the heart and life of that Union."[34] As for the "dissatisfaction" reported by the *Atlas*, the *Advertiser* assured its readers that it had conducted its own "extended inquiry" and found that the "general disposition" was to receive Webster's speech with favor. Moreover this feeling "has gained ground and is gaining ground as the speech is read and re-read."[35] In order to impress upon its readers the beneficial effects that the speech was having upon the nation, the *Advertiser* cited the *Journal of Commerce* which reported that "Mr. Webster's views are acceptable to the South, who are [sic] willing to carry them out by legislation."[36] The following day, the *Journal* expanded further upon the importance of Webster's statesmanship. "Mr. Webster's views have opened to us a new and cheering prospect," said the influential organ. "He has inspired confidence in the future which was not felt before . . . . The position of Northern conservatives is gloriously vindicated by Mr. Webster. A conservative may breathe freely in the North after this."[37]

The free-breathing, exhilarated conservatives of the North could hardly withhold their gratitude and appreciation. In New York, the "Union Safety Committee" was formed by one hundred of the state's leading mercantile figures to insure continued support for Henry Clay and his compromise provisions, and throughout Massachusetts "Union Meetings" were organized to demonstrate enthusiastic support for Daniel Webster and the Compromise of 1850. Eight hundred of Boston's most prominent citizens promptly rushed to place their signatures on a public letter addressed to Senator Webster.[38] Approving the Senator's actions and endorsing his opinions, the letter concluded: "In a time óf almost unprecedented excitement, when the minds of men have been bewildered by an apparent conflict of duties . . . you have pointed out to a whole people the path of duty, have convinced the understanding and touched the conscience of a nation." Merchants such as Lawrence, Appleton, Perkins, and Amory; lawyers such as Choate, Lunt, and the Curtises; scholars such as Ticknor, Everett, Prescott, and Sparks—all added their voices to the paeans of praise for the great man whose speech they regarded as a milestone on the road to intersectional harmony.[39] "I hope soon to hear of the settlement of the slavery question," wrote Abbott Lawrence from his new post in England, and added confidently: "I entertain no fears for the safety of the Union."[40] A month later the *Advertiser* could survey the national situation and confidently assure its readers that ". . . it seems to be admitted that this crisis is to be passed by judgment and reason instead of the old fashioned method of tomahawks and daggers."[41]

Just when the Cotton Whigs were making every effort to bolster their defenses in support of Webster and the compromise program, summer brought the tragic news of President Taylor's death. Abbott Lawrence called the President's death a "National calamity," and Robert C. Winthrop referred to the news as a "thunderclap."[42] "Poor old Zack!" Winthrop moaned irreverently. "He died in the best time for himself, but in the worst for everybody else."[43] Uncertain as to Vice-President Fillmore's exact sentiments, the Whigs waited nervously. "Fillmore is an amiable, excellent, conscientious fellow," wrote Winthrop to a friend. "What he will do remains to be seen."[44] The immediate grief of the Whig Party leaders was soon turned into joy, however, when Fillmore proved to be even more conservative than Taylor himself.[45] Daniel Webster was elevated to the post of Secretary of State in the new President's Cabinet, and Robert C. Winthrop was assigned to Webster's senatorial chair for the remainder of the summer. The fall elections in Massachusetts sent Samuel A. Eliot, a strong "compromise" man, to Congress; and he was joined the following year by William Appleton. Webster was pleased: "When Boston has been represented by commercial men, she has always been better represented than at any other time."[46] The New England statesman was placed in a stronger position than he had held for many years, and he expressed his pleasure at seeing the pendulum of public sympathy moving in what he considered to be the direction of compromise and unity.[47] To make matters even better, President Fillmore, who had been impressed by the arguments in favor of the compromise to which he had listened as presiding officer of the Senate, now came out in support of the compromise—to the disgust of the New York antislavery leaders, William H. Seward and Thurlow Weed, but to the delight of the moderate Whigs. Abbott Lawrence was now convinced that Fillmore's new Cabinet would "command the confidence of the Country" and would eventually settle the "agitating question."[48] Robert C. Winthrop assured Nathan Appleton that such "ultra" Southern senators as Alexander H. Stephens and Robert C. Toombs (the "duo fulmina belli") were certain to be recalled and repudiated; and he was quite convinced that "the Union is safe, notwithstanding the occasional gasconading of Ultra-ists at both ends of the Union."[49] Southern Whigs agreed with their Northern brethren as to prospects for the future. Judge Ogden of New Orleans congratulated old Amos Lawrence that "the danger with which we have been menaced

1. The interior of the Dean Mills, near Manchester, N.H., in 1851.

2. "Bell time" at the Washington Textile Mills, Lawrence, Mass., in 1868—a drawing by Winslow Homer.

4. Amos A. Lawrence.

3. Abbott Lawrence, a portrait by Chester Harding, 1832.

6. William Appleton.

5. Amos Lawrence, a portrait by Chester Harding.

7. "King Andrew the First," a Whig cartoon of the 1830's satirizing President Jackson's supposed dictatorial tactics.

8. "The Times," a cartoon of the Panic of 1837 by H. R. Robinson. The Whigs blamed unemployment and bankruptcy on the newly-installed Democratic administration of Van Buren.

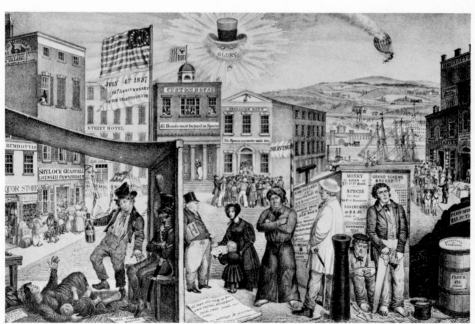

9. Whig supporters of William Henry Harrison rolled the tin-covered "election ball" from Cleveland to Columbus, Ohio, during the election campaign of 1840.

10. Ohio Whigs attend the wake of the "old Coon," in the aftermath of Clay's defeat and Polk's victory in 1844.

11. William Lloyd Garrison, about 1854. Garrison's *The Liberator,* first published in 1831, was a leading organ of Abolitionism.

12. A poster published by sympathetic Bostonians in 1851 to warn free Negroes against attempts to enforce the Fugitive Slave Act of 1850.

13. On-the-spot sketches of the dispute over slavery in Congress in 1858.

14. A cartoon
from *Harper's Weekly,*
published during
the Panic of 1857.

NEW YORK to PHILADELPHIA BANK. "Going to suspend yourself, eh? Is that your Brotherly Love?"

15. "The Panic in Wall Street," another *Harper's Weekly* cartoon of the Panic of 1857.

16. The last hours of Congress before adjournment in March 1859. A member pleads in vain for unity in an atmosphere of growing sectional bitterness.

17. John Brown and other prisoners are seized after the insurrection at Harper's Ferry—from *Frank Leslie's Illustrated Newspaper*.

18. Charlestonians go to the rooftops to witness the Confederate bombardment of Fort Sumter on April 12, 1861—from *Harper's Weekly* for May 4, 1861.

has passed"; and from Washington, D.C., Judge Bullard expressed similar sentiments of confidence.[50] "There is no serious agitation here," he confided to Lawrence. "The Administration is immensely popular, without, indeed, any formal opposition; and public affairs go on very smoothly and harmoniously."[51]

With the benediction of President Fillmore, the direction of young Senator Douglas from Illinois, and the loyal support of Northern and Southern Whigs, Clay's "Omnibus Bill" was finally passed. California was allowed to enter the Union as a free state; the principle of popular sovereignty was established in the territories of New Mexico and Utah; ten million dollars in claims was paid to Texas; the slave trade was abolished in the District of Columbia; and more effective fugitive slave legislation was provided. Clay, Douglas, Webster, and other moderates were convinced that they had averted secession by a narrow margin and that they had prevented the disruption of the Union.[52]

But the moderates had little time to bask in the glow of their recent triumph, for in Massachusetts an important contest of political strength was already shaping up, with the conservative advocates of compromise and concession pitting their strength against the radical proponents of Free-Soil and free men. Having finally abandoned any ideas they may have had of trying to resume their affiliations within the Whig Party, the Conscience Whigs now devoted themselves to carrying out the political goals of the Free-Soil Party and they prepared to make common cause with antislavery Democrats and anyone else who desired to prevent the expansion of slavery through political means.

For the Cotton Whigs it was Armageddon—the last desperate battle against the forces of lawlessness and greed, the last hope for peace and harmony. Anything less than victory at this crucial point, they feared, would mean the disappearance of those reasonable and objective men who were working to preserve the Union and prevent secession. Firmly convinced that a party system based on the slavery issue would lead to civil war, the Cotton Whigs saw that the subsequent withholding of cotton supplies, the disruption of credit, and the stock market collapse that would inevitably follow, would bring financial ruin to every textile mill in New England. Desperately, the chairman of the

Massachusetts Whig State Committee called upon every businessman in the area "to use all the influence he can over those in his
employ, or in any way under his control" to bring a crushing defeat down upon the heads of Free-Soilers and Democrats.[53]

The Cotton Whigs were doomed to disappointment in the fall
elections of 1850, however, as their opposition—"Conscience
Whigs," Free-Soilers, and Democrats—made good their threat to
join forces and pool their voting strength.[54] Ordinarily, although
they commanded less than 49 percent of the state vote, the Massachusetts Whigs had been able to control the State government
through the Boston delegation they sent to the legislature.[55] In
1850, however, the Anti-Whig "coalition," as it was called, united
on candidates for the legislature in practically every city and
town in Massachusetts and, as a result, overpowered the Boston
bloc. By informal agreement, the victorious Democrats took over
most of the State offices and put Robert Rantoul, Jr., into
Webster's unexpired Senatorship; while their Free-Soil partners
began their preparations to send Charles Sumner to the United
States Senate in the spring to take over Webster's seat on a
permanent basis.[56]

The Cotton Whigs were appalled at the prospect of this Abolitionist firebrand going to Washington to upset the national equi-
librium that Webster and Clay had worked so hard to maintain.
"For heaven's sake keep him home!" Congressman Samuel Eliot
pleaded with Amos A. Lawrence. "You can hardly imagine the
disgust and loathing with which such men as Sumner, Hale of
New Hampshire, Giddings and that set are looked upon by honest
men here."[57] Leading conservative Whigs of Boston, including
Lawrence, the Appletons, Robert Gould Shaw, George Lyman,
and others, needed little urging, and began to make elaborate
plans to defeat Sumner. The State Central Committee began
contacting the major manufacturing companies for contributions,
wards and districts were polled with expert care, and arrangements were made for a specific number of men "good and true"
in every town to hunt up all Whigs—and any man who could
cast a Whig vote—and "carry them to the ballot box."[58] Although
Amos A. Lawrence objected strenuously to the custom of exacting
political contributions directly from corporations, he took a

prominent role in the battle to defeat Sumner, conscious of the effect which such a defeat would have in Southern circles.[59] During the months of February, March, and April, 1851, Lawrence conducted numerous private subscription drives among the most prominent men of Boston in order to prevent Sumner from reaching Washington.[60]

In addition to economic pressures, the Whigs attempted a political coalition of their own by allying themselves with a small group of "old guard" Jackson Democrats to whom Sumner was loathsome, and who disapproved of the Free-Soil combination.[61] Convinced that Sumner's election would be a national catastrophe, the Democrat, Caleb Cushing, used all his influence against Sumner in the Democratic caucuses; and when he failed there, he took the fight to the floor of the House.[62] Between January 14 and April 24, 1851, political fortunes hung in the balance while 26 ballots were taken—until Charles Sumner was finally elected United States Senator by the margin of a single vote. The winners were jubilant, but the following day the Cotton Whigs appeared on the streets of Boston with wide bands of black crepe on their arms.[63] The coalition of antislavery Whigs and antislavery Democrats had jumped party lines to put into the Senate the thunderous orator who would lead the Free-Soil cause. But equally significant, in terms of local politics, the coalition had also succeeded in breaking the power of the Cotton Whigs. For the first time, the government of the State of Massachusetts was in the hands of a group of politicians who were openly and aggressively opposed to the principle of slavery.

Disheartened, but not discouraged, mindful of their solid core of political support in the city, the Cotton Whigs continued to fight—concentrating their efforts on developing a breach in the ranks of their combined enemies. The opposition press laughed openly at the picture of Abbott Lawrence "going about the State drenching his pocket-handkerchief with tears," and "dragging his wallet and contents out to 'feed' forty-one perambulating Whig orators"—but such canvassing was soon to produce results.[64]

In the year or so following the passage of the Compromise of 1850, a growing majority of the American people came to look upon that legislation as the only practical solution of a complex and otherwise insoluble problem.[65] By 1852 the Democratic Party itself had come to recognize this feeling, and the Democrats nominated the noncommittal and uncommitted Franklin Pierce of New Hampshire as their Presidential nominee, with a party program that formally accepted the Compromise of 1850 as the final settlement of the slavery problem. With something like a national sigh of relief, the bulk of the American people cast their vote for the Democratic Party as a means of pushing the extravagant slavery issue into the limbo of lost causes. Southern Unionists too, fearing that the Northern Whigs would all be converted to the "Conscience" cause, threw the weight of their votes to the Democratic ticket.[66] The New York "Barnburners" broke off their connections with the Free-Soilers and returned to their native Democratic Party.[67] And in Massachusetts, these latest developments caused almost immediate dissolution of the powerful anti-Whig coalition. The local Democrats could hardly take a stand different from that of their national party, and so had no alternative but to campaign for Pierce and the compromise. The Free-Soilers, on the other hand, could never bring themselves to accept the outrageous compromise plank—so the short-lived partnership was dissolved.[68] Although the local Whigs actually gained few additional votes, the breakup of the coalition meant that the Whigs could regain control of the State legislature with their solid Boston vote. With a majority of 10 votes the Whigs put in a slate of state officers and sent Edward Everett off to the United States Senate to offset Charles Sumner.[69] This action would show the South that "radicalism and rascality has [sic] not made so much progress here as the newspapers would have led them to believe," said Amos A. Lawrence happily; "the prospect is good."[70] But the opposition could hardly agree. "The coalition is dead . . . ," moaned a prominent antislavery journalist. "The Whig party remains in the complete control of Boston, and the money-bags of Boston rule the State."[71]

The Cotton Whigs were proud and happy at what seemed to them to be their present victory and their future hopes and dreams. For the present, they could disregard the one-sided defeat of the Whig Presidential candidate, General Winfield Scott, as being of little consequence (Winthrop dismissed it as "laughably overwhelming"), and they hailed the election of the New Hampshire Democrat, Franklin Pierce, as the start of a new era of national accord.[72] "Frank" Pierce was a relative and a close friend of Amos A. Lawrence, ever since he had taken the young Lawrence to see President Andrew Jackson when the Bostonian was on a tour of Washington during a summer vacation from Harvard.[73] Lawrence, now a wealthy and influential financier, immediately offered the new President-elect his services —"pecuniary or otherwise"—while his father, Amos Lawrence, insisted that the Pierce family come to Boston and accept his hospitality after the strenuous campaign.[74] Sensing the political opportunities which could be exploited because of his personal relationship with the President, young Lawrence urged his friend, Congressman William Appleton, to use his influence in Whig circles and play along with Pierce for the time being, while anticipating a break in the Democratic ranks. "If the conservative part of the Whig party will support him," he wrote, "it will make the sacrifice easier when he comes to make a break with some of his present supporters."[75]

Party alignments and political nomenclatures had ceased to have the same importance they once did, as far as the Cotton Whigs were concerned. They were more interested in issues and results than in party affiliations. Unmindful of the long-term consequences that their new political attitude foreshadowed, and apparently unaware of the fact that their own political structure was dissolving about them, the Cotton Whigs were happy in the confidence that they had just secured enough valuable time for the entire nation to become adjusted to the prospects of intersectional harmony and national accord. Having already repudiated the "ultra-ism" of such fanatical groups as the Abolitionists, the Liberty Party, and the Free-Soilers, the Cotton Whigs were sure that during the next four years the people of America would likewise repudiate the "ultra-ism" of Southern plans for nullification and secession. By the time that Franklin Pierce's term was over, then, this would mean that the people of the United States would be ready for a real "National" party—a party that the true Whig Party had represented all along—an American party— above sectionalism and localism—a party "knowing no North and no South."[76] Robert C. Winthrop felt that it augured well for the future that the electoral vote of the Whig candidate, General Scott, was divided between two widely separated sections of the Union—Massachusetts and Vermont; Tennessee and Kentucky. "Let us hope," he prayed earnestly, "we shall learn a little wisdom during the next four years."[77]

6

WAKE
THE SLEEPING TIGER

THE OPENING of the new adminis-
tration exceeded the fondest hopes of the Cotton Whigs as President Franklin Pierce, smiling, confident, looking younger than
his fifty years, assured the nation in his Inaugural Address that he
personally considered the Compromise of 1850 to be the final
settlement of the issue of slavery. "I fervently hope that the question is at rest," he concluded, "and that no sectional or ambitious
or fanatical excitement may again threaten the durability of our
institutions or obscure the light of our prosperity."[1] And at the
close of the year in his First Annual Message, the President again
promised the American people that "this repose is to suffer no
shock during my official term, if I have the power to avert it."[2]

Some called it another "Era of Good Feelings." The nation was
at peace, the administration had the support of both Houses, the
Treasury was full, foreign relations were relatively peaceful, and
business was getting better every day. The Compromise of 1850
had apparently solved all the political nightmares which had almost driven the country into a state of hysteria. North and South
congratulated each other on the future prospects for mutual
harmony and accord. Judge Ogden of New Orleans was convinced
that the danger of war had passed, and told Amos Lawrence of
Massachusetts that "the sterling intelligence, integrity and patriot-

93

ism of our countrymen will prevent any such suicidal madness as
secession or disunion."[3] Lawrence's old friend and long-time
Whig, Judge Henry Adams Bullard, had just been elected to
Congress and from Washington he assured Lawrence that affairs
in the nation's capital were proceeding "very smoothly and
harmoniously."[4] Nathan Appleton later recalled that as a result
of the Compromise of 1850, the free states were "satisfied and
content—in a state of perfect repose."[5] The slavery question
seemed virtually forgotten as the country plunged into a round
of building and spending.

In London, at the fabulous "Crystal Palace" Exhibition, Yankee
inventions were the talk of the town—from such prosaic exhibits
as picks and shovels to the more complicated intricacies of American sewing machines and mechanical reapers. The Ambassador to
England, Abbott Lawrence, had cooperated wholeheartedly with
his British hosts in the preparations for this great international
exhibit, and in his dispatches to the Department of State he had
urged that the United States be adequately represented. Euro-
peans were agog at the latest evidences of the material progress of
their trans-Atlantic cousins.[6] Not to be outdone, America held
its own industrial exhibition at New York's version of the "Crystal
Palace" during the steaming summer and fall of 1853.[7] Before
hosts of interested spectators, displays from Europe provided a
backdrop against which America proudly displayed its own amazing wares. For many, the exposition provided more evidence that
the United States was passing out of its adolescence of sectionalism
and parochialism and was beginning to forge an even more perfect Union.[8]

Restricted markets gave way to country-wide selling areas as
Northern manufacturers found customers all through the Middle
West and down into the Gulf States. McCormick reapers, Seth
Thomas clocks, and Colt revolvers became household words. Day
by day America was becoming more national in its transportation,
communication, and markets than ever before. The 1850's witnessed a tremendous expansion in the railroad system crisscrossing
the nation. One sad product of rail expansion was the list of sixty-
five fatal railroad accidents recorded during 1853 and the first
half of 1854.[9] Every morning an avid public eagerly read about

the latest records established by the new Yankee "Clipper" ships; by 1853 American ocean traffic surpassed British tonnage by 15 percent.[10] Newspapers everywhere testified to the increasing size and wealth of the nation. Capital invested in manufacturing had already doubled, and cotton growers were enjoying an unaccustomed prosperity as the price of cotton pushed upwards from its 1845 low of six cents a pound to over twelve cents during the early 50's.[11]

The same optimism and enthusiasm which marked the national attitude was reflected at the state and local levels. Proud residents of Massachusetts took delight in displaying the latest in local developments at a series of fairs and expositions. At the Boston Fowl Show in 1852, three Cochin Chinas sold for $100; and at the great Horse Show at Springfield the following year, sales of blooded horses varied between $500 and $1,500.[12] The Mechanics Fair at Faneuil Hall in September of 1853 drew thousands of excited spectators from miles around; and Robert C. Winthrop, who went to the Cattle Show at Lowell, expecting to hear yokels talking about "bullocks and manure" was amazed at what he classified as "a sort of miniature World's fair."[13]

The "Boston Association" by 1850 controlled one-fifth of the nation's cotton spindles, a third of the State's railroad mileage, and about two-fifths of Boston's banking capital as the value of Massachusetts manufacturing had risen to almost three hundred million dollars.[14] "We are all at work in New England, and now feel a twinge from too fast driving in some branches of business," reflected Amos A. Lawrence, "but in the aggregate, our country is rapidly advancing in wealth, power and strength. . . ."[15] With state-wide attention focused on local prosperity and national progress, reassured that the Compromise of 1850 had already destined freedom for the Western lands, Boston's Cotton Whigs relaxed in the firm belief that the possibility of sectional conflict had passed. "Since it has turned out that the whole of the vast territories hereafter to be admitted as States are to be free," wrote Lawrence in obvious complacency, "it seems most unwise to be quarreling about abstractions."[16]

"Men spoke softly not to rouse the sleeping tiger," Allan Nevins has dramatically written, "but in his sleep he stirred and

growled."[17] It would be absurd, of course, to suggest that every
vestige of the extreme bitterness which the slavery question had
engendered during the past two decades had completely died out.
The emotional response to the Fugitive Slave Act in Massachusetts alone provided evidence that sectional issues were not forgotten. First in February, and again in April, 1851, law enforcement
officials outraged the sympathies of Boston by trying to enforce
the obnoxious law. A Negro called Shadrach had the good fortune
to be rescued and spirited off to freedom by irate Bostonians; but
the next victim, a waiter named Thomas Simms, was not so
fortunate. He was marched off to a waiting vessel before daybreak
on the morning of April 12, 1851, with an armed escort of over a
hundred city police.[18]

The Fugitive Slave Law had been an integral part of the Compromise of 1850 and it had been reluctantly accepted by the
Whigs as the only alternative to nullification and secession. Local
Cotton Whigs put themselves on record as opposing this vicious
law as a matter of principle; they labelled it a "disgraceful act"
and worked constantly for its repeal.[19] Old Amos Lawrence condemned what he called the "skunk peculiarities" of the South in
having passed the Fugitive Slave Law in the first place, and insisted that the legislation was unconstitutional.[20] His son, Amos
A., declared with equal vigor that "Massachusetts never can be
made a hunting ground for masters to pursue their run-aways."[21]
And yet, although voicing almost unanimous disapproval of the
moral principles—or lack of them—upon which the law was
based, the conservative Cotton Whigs made every effort to abide
by the letter of the law in practice. Robert C. Winthrop assured
Senator Crittenden of Kentucky that although he himself never
regarded the Fugitive Slave Act as "a wise piece of legislation,"
the conservative North would support the law. "There is not an
agitator in the whole Whig Party here—no one who cares to disturb anything that has been done."[22]

In vain did Ralph Waldo Emerson hold his nose and complain
about the "poor smell" of Beacon and Mt. Vernon Streets, and
Theodore Parker express his contempt for the sleeping State of
Massachusetts, "her head pillowed on her unsold bales of cotton,"
dreaming only of "orders from the South."[23] With no result did

Wendell Phillips denounce the Fugitive Law as the means of determining whether "the mills of Abbott Lawrence make him worth two millions or one"; and to no purpose did the old Federalist, Josiah Quincy, shake his head sadly and think back to the Boston of 1775.[24] "Boston has now become a mere shop—a place for buying and selling goods; and I suppose," he added mournfully, "also, of *buying and selling men*."[25]

All of this had no effect. Boston's men of wealth refused to be stampeded into another serious breach with their Southern brethren like that which had occurred after the Mexican War. Although they made it clear that they did not like the Fugitive Slave Law, they made it equally clear that they considered themselves honor-bound under the Constitution to obey it to the letter until it was repealed. "It is lamentable to have such a triumph given to Nullification and Rebellion," wrote Robert C. Winthrop in reference to those who spirited Shadrach away; while Daniel Webster agreed that the Negro's rescue was, "strictly speaking, a case of treason."[26] "Revolution is a terrific remedy," cautioned Professor Packard of Bowdoin College. "I should never resist an unjust Law . . . until the proper method of repealing it had been long tried in vain."[27] Amos A. Lawrence summed up the uncomfortable Whig position by asking the crucial question: "Shall we stand by the laws or shall we nullify them? Shall we uphold the Union or shall we break it up?"[28] As if in answer to his own question, he went off to offer his services to the United States Marshal in Boston, to serve "in any capacity 'during the war'."[29] "If we must knock these fellows [Abolitionists] on the head (and it must be done)," he told Congressman Samuel Eliot, "we should prefer to do it according to law . . . ."[30] This was not a case, he emphasized, of loving the Negro less—but of loving the Union more. In replying to William Lloyd Garrison's charge that Congressman Eliot had supported the Fugitive Slave Act because he hated the Negro, Lawrence defended Eliot by saying "he loves the black race more than most men . . . . But he loves the perpetuity of this Government and the Union of these States (even under the present system)—better."[31] Rufus Choate told an audience that there was no one who mourned more than he did the fact that "there is a slave who needs to run, or a master who desires to pursue." Nevertheless, he declared that he had not "a shadow of a doubt" about the constitutional power of the Congress to pass such a law, and about the necessity that every citizen of the United States "assist . . . in its execution."[32]

The Cotton Whigs continued to hold the line, maintaining the same devotion to the Union and to the goal of intersectional harmony that had characterized their national attitude during the past twenty years. The Union was indivisible, the Constitution infallible, and the Compromise of 1850 indissoluble. This was the creed of those who hoped to escape the dire consequences of nullification and secession.

And then it happened: On January 4, 1854, the beautiful dream came to a sudden end. "We went to bed one night, old-fashioned, conservative, compromise, Union Whigs," wrote Amos A. Lawrence, "and waked up stark mad Abolitionists."[33] On that day, Stephen A. Douglas, Senator from Illinois, reported a bill into the Senate which called for the organization of the territorial government of Nebraska. Suggesting that the Compromise of 1850 had, for all practical purposes, superseded the Missouri Compromise of 1820 by granting popular sovereignty to New Mexico and Utah, the bill proposed that when Nebraska should be admitted to the Union, it should enter "with or without slavery" as fixed by its constitution at the time.[34] It was a simple statement—but one which was destined to have the most far-reaching consequences, as it brought virtually the entire North to its feet in indignant protest. "It aroused and alarmed the whole North," wrote Nathan Appleton to William C. Rives of Virginia, still unable to grasp what had happened.[35]

In short, the Nebraska Bill reopened the question of the expansion of slavery and immediately made it a red-hot political issue once again. As expected, leading antislavery men like Salmon P. Chase of Ohio, William Seward of New York, and Charles Sumner of Massachusetts led the attack upon the measure as providing further proof of an insidious conspiracy to extend the Slave Empire.[36] But among the groups in the North which set themselves against this "Nebraska infamy" none were more outraged and resentful than the Cotton Whigs. On February 23, 1854, they held a great protest meeting at Faneuil Hall, attended by some three thousand of the "solid" men of the city, and headed by Abbott Lawrence, Robert C. Winthrop, and Samuel Eliot.[37] These men of standing and property believed that they had shown their good faith by their support for the institution of slavery where it was sanctioned by the Constitution and by their accepting the Fugitive Slave Law in order to placate the South and preserve the peace. They expected that the South, in return, had guaranteed that the territories would remain free. Convinced that the Compromise of 1850 had unequivocally decided the future of the West and had ended the matter once and for all, Boston merchants and businessmen now felt cheated and ridiculed by what they considered to be the machinations of a cheap demagogue.[38] "If I could have prescribed a recipe for reinflating Free-soilism and Abolitionism, which had collapsed all over the country," Winthrop wrote in utter frustration, "I should have singled out this precise potion from the whole *materia medica* of political quackery."[39]

American business interests, which up to this point had deplored public antislavery agitation, now began to add their mighty influence to the ground swell of public opinion. Angrily, Amos A. Lawrence condemned the political stupidity that opened the great social gap once again. "Where is the spirit that led us to volunteer to shoot the abolitionists and free-soilers and support the Law . . . ?" he wailed, referring to the past history of the Cotton Whigs. "It's pretty much gone already: this will 'crush it all out'."[40] As he felt himself being borne along with the tide, Lawrence was apprehensive about the future of the Union. After all, if the large merchants and the "retired gentlemen who go into State Street for an hour or two every day" were being converted to the antislavery cause, then who else was left? "These constitute pretty much all the 'slave power' in this community," he confided to a friend, "and if *they* give up the Compromises and say that they have been cheated, we all know that sympathy for the South and their 'Institution' must be gone."[41]

There was only one thing to do—and that was to defeat Douglas and destroy his nefarious bill. To this end the Cotton Whigs directed their attention and their energies, assuring their close friends below the Mason-Dixon Line that the "Nebraska business"

would be a failure, and pleading with their Southern colleagues to
"pause before they proceed farther to disturb the peace which we
hoped the Compromise measure of 1850 would have made perpetual."[42] Constantly they urged their political representatives to
"pour in the vollies of red hot shot" upon the Nebraska Bill and
make sure that "Douglas' day is over!"[43]

As one practical means of demonstrating their new-found antip-
athy for Douglas and the party he represented, leading conservatives rushed off to offer their services and their wealth to aid
the Boston Negro, Anthony Burns, who had been seized as a
fugitive slave on May 26, 1854. Richard Dana, who had played a
prominent role in previous fugitive slave cases, was now amazed
to find conservative gentlemen stopping to converse with him on
the streets, and even more amazed to hear these gentlemen actually talking "treason."[44] Rufus Choate privately admitted to
Dana that he had been wrong in the past and that he was now
willing to do all in his power to help the cause of the fugitive
slave. Amos A. Lawrence called upon Dana in his office and,
representing a number of what he called "active 1850 men," he
offered "any amount" to provide the legal talent necessary to
defend Anthony Burns.[45]

Lawrence's stand on the Burns case was particularly startling,
since only three years earlier, at the time of the Simms trial, he
had volunteered his personal services to the United States Marshal
to assist in the return of the fugitive. Now, in 1854, Lawrence
angrily told the Mayor of Boston that he would rather see the
courthouse burned to the ground than have Burns returned to
slavery; and when he was finally forced to witness the victim's
tragic march to the dock, he told his brother that only the unusual
military safeguards that day "prevented the total destruction of
the U.S. Marshal and his hired assistants."[46] "The commercial
class of the city have taken a new position on the great question
of the day," reported the Boston *Times*, which noted that a number of prominent merchants "who have never before given their
influence on the anti-slavery side," had just signed a public petition calling for the repeal of the Fugitive Slave Act.[47] And this
was not an isolated instance of a development restricted merely
to the City of Boston. "You may rely upon it," Lawrence told a

friend, "that the sentiment at this time among the powerful and conservative class of men is the same as it is in the country towns throughout New England."[48]

The consummate political skill of Senator Douglas, however, proved more than a match for the irate protestations of his Whig opponents in the North. Borne along by the furious energies of the young Illinois politician, supported by administrative approval from the White House, and sustained by jubilant Southerners—Whigs and Democrats alike—the Nebraska Bill swept aside the Northern opposition and was signed into law by President Pierce on May 30, 1854. Providing for the new territory to be divided into two separate units, the Kansas-Nebraska Act called for the outright repeal of the Missouri Compromise and provided a clear-cut defense of the doctrine of popular sovereignty.[49]

With the passage of the Douglas bill, the whole question of the extension of slavery was broken wide open once again, leaving the moderates and conservatives of the North aghast. In bewilderment they desperately tried to think of a way to heal this latest breach of national unity in a manner which would be consistent with their policy of nonextension of slavery. This was precisely the dilemma in which the Cotton Whigs now found themselves: As realistic men of business and capital, the Yankee manufacturers felt obligated to retain the faith and goodwill of a Southern plantation economy whose production of cotton created personal fortunes already being reckoned in millions of dollars.[50] As men of political principle, the New England Whigs felt constrained to preserve the Union that Marshall had defined, and Webster had defended—the Union that the Whig Party had labored so hard and so long to maintain. But as men of honor and integrity, these keepers of the Puritan conscience felt themselves consumed by righteous wrath at what they considered the selfish designs of unscrupulous politicians who had gambled with the stakes of national unity for the sake of railroad ties and caucus votes.

The Cotton Whigs had pledged their word that they would never interfere with the South or any of its institutions where the Constitution provided sanctions; but they had also gone on record as opposing the extension of that "peculiar institution" beyond those prescribed constitutional limits. So, by God, Douglas or no Douglas, Bill or no Bill, the New Englanders determined that if population was to be the determining factor in deciding the fate of Kansas—then there would be a flood of "free citizens" to the new territories the like of which had not been seen since the waters of the flood overflowed the earth.

"Anger hath no mercy, nor fury when it breaketh forth. And who can bear the violence of one provoked!" states the Book of Proverbs. With all the fervor of an evangelistic crusade, the New England conscience went into action, with the battle cry of William Seward ringing out: "God give the victory to the side that is stronger in numbers, as it is in right!"[51]

The earliest response to the Kansas challenge centered about the Massachusetts Emigrant Aid Company, created early in the spring of 1854 by Eli Thayer of Worcester, a member of the Massachusetts legislature. Preparing a charter, Thayer obtained an act of incorporation in February, 1854, and after the legislature adjourned began stumping New England to sell stock in his enterprise, pointing out the dual opportunity of aiding the cause of free men, and at the same time making a sound profit.[52] Thayer proposed to preempt blocks of land with company funds, sponsor whole villages of settlers to develop the fertile soil of Kansas, and then divide up the profits between the homesteaders and the investors. On April 26, 1854, the Governor of Massachusetts signed a charter authorizing a capital stock of five million dollars, and Thayer was off to New York to convince other subscribers of the fabulous opportunities involved in making Kansas free.[53]

Assisted by the monetary support of such prominent men as Amos A. Lawrence and J. M. S. Williams of Massachusetts and John Carter Brown of Rhode Island, the association was successfully organized, and by the end of July, 1854, a company of twenty-four Free-Soil settlers had already arrived at Kansas City, Missouri.[54] Loading their tents, equipment, and baggage—including a printing press—onto wagons, the emigrants set off along the historic Sante Fe Trail for about fifty miles, until they came to an elevation of land, just south of the Kaw River, from which they could look out for miles in all directions. Here they pitched camp and decided to settle permanently on what they called Mount Oread, after Eli Thayer's well-known "castle" in Worcester. After setting up a collection of tents, thatched huts, and crude log cabins in the weeks that followed, the settlers named their new city Lawrence in honor of the New Englander who had invested so much of his personal income in their dreams of the future.[55] During the remainder of the summer of 1854, the Emigrant Aid Company sent out five more groups under the direction of Doctor Charles Robinson, an experienced colonist, a practicing physician, and an ardent Free-Soiler, who had been selected as the company's agent in Kansas. All in all, a total of some six hundred Free-Soilers had settled either in Lawrence, or in such nearby settlements as Osawatomie, Manhattan, and Topeka by the time the freezing winter closed in.[56]

Back in Boston, however, things were not going quite as smoothly. Hardly more than a month passed before Thayer's Emigrant Aid Company began to be labeled as a crass, money-making scheme, and the motives of its membership ascribed to selfish greed masquerading behind the glittering façade of humanitarianism. Amos A. Lawrence, already greatly disturbed by the various ugly rumors which he himself had heard, and hard pressed by many of the influential investors who had suddenly become fearful of the amount of liability they had incurred in Thayer's "harum scarum" project, demanded that Thayer reform the company or lose the support of his Boston subscribers.[57]

Learning of these developments in New York City, Thayer rushed back to Boston after hastily obtaining another charter of incorporation from the State of Connecticut apparently in order to hold firm his New York subscribers. Thayer's attempts to fight the Boston men proved fruitless. Lawrence was adamant, and threatened to withdraw his name and his money if a change were not forthcoming. Thayer yielded, and on July 24, 1854, a "voluntary association" was formed by which the subscribers associated themselves together into a non-corporate joint stock company to be known as "The Emigrant Aid Company." Management was vested in three trustees—Amos A. Lawrence, J. M. S. Williams, and Eli Thayer—with Dr. Thomas H. Webb as Secretary, and Lawrence acting as Treasurer.[58]

In February of the next year, the members of what was now commonly referred to as The New England Emigrant Aid Company applied to the Massachusetts legislature for a new charter, and on February 21, 1855, Governor Gardner signed the act authorizing incorporation "for the purpose of directing emigration Westward and aiding in providing accommodations for the emigrants after arriving at their places of destination . . . ." On March 5, a meeting was held, the charter accepted, and the organization crystallized in readiness for the struggle for Kansas during 1855–1856. John Carter Brown was elected President, Eli Thayer and J. M. S. Williams were chosen as Vice-Presidents, Amos A. Lawrence continued in his post as Treasurer, and Dr. Webb was kept on as Secretary.[59]

The new company was now established as a purely local organization, separate and distinct from similar emigrant organizations in other states, with wary investors assured of limited liability under the careful hand and expert eye of Mr. Lawrence. From now on "aid" would consist of free information and a 15 percent reduction in railroad and steamship fare through quantity purchase. No political questions were to be asked of the emigrants, since the avowed purpose of the organization was to get people to Kansas, and there let them make their own free choice—to oppose the establishment of slavery "by all legal and constitutional means."[60]

Amos A. Lawrence was particularly careful to make it clear that the reorganized company was not a speculative venture for profit. When two of the trustees proposed to buy real estate in Kansas, to the amount of twenty-eight million dollars, Lawrence vetoed the idea outright. Such a purchase, he wrote in a memorandum, "is for the purpose of speculating, to make a profit; and it is not necessary in order to accomplish the objects for which the Society was formed."[61] Although some members, especially Eli Thayer, continued to expect fabulous returns on their investments, Lawrence himself never expected that the company stock would pay dividends, or even that the stockholders would ever see their money again. He was, in fact, quite upset when the free settlers named their capital Lawrence, fearing that his motives in sponsoring the Emigrant Aid Society would be interpreted as an attempt to promote his own influence and make him a celebrity.[62] Writing to Senator Thomas Hart Benton of Missouri, Lawrence forcefully denied that the funds of the company were to be used for any other purpose than to provide for the basic needs of the emigrants; and he insisted that the company stock was worthless and meaningless. Furthermore, continued Lawrence, the emigrants were not Abolitionists—"so far as we know not one known to be of that stamp has gone in our parties. They are free to vote and do as they please. The Society has no agreement with them, nor pledge, nor are they asked any questions."[63] The Emigrant Aid Society was created solely for the purpose of promoting freedom—not money.[64]

With the Company reorganized, Lawrence not only received the additional backing of such men as his prominent uncle, Abbott Lawrence, and of William Appleton and Joseph Lyman, but was contacted by such leading New York businessmen as Moses Grinnell who sought to join forces with the New England group.[65] Collecting money, writing letters, encouraging friends and denouncing foes, Lawrence demonstrated the enthusiasm which motivated many Northern Whigs to work so zealously for a Free-Soil Kansas. He had letters sent to every minister in New England, explaining the nature and purpose of the Emigrant Aid Society and soliciting their support. "We beg you," he urged, "to consult with your most influential and patriotic parishioners and townsmen, and with them take such measures as shall carry forward this undertaking to a successful issue."[66] So convinced was he of the righteousness of his cause that Lawrence told Governor Gardner that if he were a member of the Massachusetts legislature he would go so far as to vote "in favor of placing at the disposal of the Governor and Council a liberal sum to be used in case an attempt is made to drive our people from the Territory [of Kansas] by force."[67] Assuming that there was no question as to the legitimate status of the Free-Soil inhabitants of Kansas, Lawrence formally requested the President of the United States to recognize the free settlers as the legally constituted government of Kansas.[68]

The New Englanders, however, reckoned without the hostile attitude of the pro-slavery settlers just across the border in Mis-

souri. Angered at what they considered to be an unwarranted
interference by outsiders in the normal course of events, Missouri
bordermen—bullwhackers, buffalo hunters, and Indian fighters—
prepared to take whatever steps were necessary to prevent Free-
Soil Yankee imports from creating an artificial free state next door
to them.[69] The first opportunity for such action came in the fall
of 1854 when the territorial Governor, Andrew Reeder, called
for elections for territorial delegates. Into Kansas swarmed a
roaring horde of Missouri ruffians to stuff the ballot boxes in favor
of slavery. When Reeder called for the election of a territorial
legislature the following March, the Missourians once again carried the day for pro-slavery candidates.[70]

Outraged at what he considered to be an unfair and illegal
interference with a constitutional procedure, Amos A. Lawrence
wrote directly to President Franklin Pierce. Informing him of the
activities of the Missouri agitators, Lawrence warned the Chief
Executive that if the United States Government did not take
immediate steps to protect the free settlers, the Kansans would
have to take matters into their own hands.[71] Against the current
accusations that the Free-Soil emigrants were traitors because they
refused to recognize the new territorial government of Kansas,
Lawrence condemned the pro-slavery government as fraudulent,
and flatly denied that the emigrants would ever resist or even
question the laws of the United States—when executed by "the
proper officers."[72] But, he concluded, the Free-Soil settlers would
never recognize the present pro-slavery legislature, "nor its enactments, nor its officers." Lawrence also took time out to write to
Senator Atchison, of Missouri, demanding that he see the contest
was conducted according to the rules of fair play. The Kansas-
Nebraska Act had decreed that the future of Kansas was to be
dependent on the factor of population, and it was to be a wide
open race—so let the best man win! The New England settlers,
Lawrence pointed out, were not Abolitionists, but continued interference on the part of the pro-slavery elements, he warned,
"may make them abolitionists of the most dangerous kind."[73]

Even as he wrote, threatened, and argued, Lawrence came to
the conclusion that stronger measures would have to be taken in
order to provide adequate protection for the emigrants. Charles
Robinson, the Free-Soil leader in Kansas had been pleading for

guns since the spring elections. "Cannot your secret society send us 200 Sharps rifles as a loan till this question is settled?" he begged of Eli Thayer on May 2, 1855; and a few days later, he sent a letter off to Edward Everett Hale urging that two hundred rifles and two fieldpieces be sent to Kansas.[74] Not content with waiting, Robinson sent George Washington Deitzler to New England to obtain as many weapons as possible for the Free-Soil cause. A month later Robinson was in possession of a letter signed by Thomas H. Webb, Secretary of the Emigrant Aid Society, acknowledging the arrival of Deitzler, and assuring Robinson that one hundred "machines" were on their way.[75] The first shipment of "machinery" arrived at Lawrence, Kansas, in the middle of May, and when the emigrants tore open the crates variously stamped "hardware," "machinery," or "books," they found themselves in possession of a hundred of the latest and most advanced type of breech-loading weapon—the Sharps rifle.[76] With increased firepower and accuracy, the Free-Soil settlers of Lawrence, for the first time, were in a position to offset the numerical superiority of the hostile Missourians across the border, most of whom were still armed with antiquated muzzle-loaders and buffalo guns.

Until recently Amos A. Lawrence had refused to consider sending weapons to the emigrants, but after the fraudulent elections and the attacks of the "border ruffians" he had changed his mind. Writing to Robinson, Lawrence told him of his decision. "You must have arms, or your courage will not avail," he admitted. "We must stir ourselves here tomorrow and see what can be done."[77] But Lawrence did not wait for the next day to "stir" himself, for on the same day he sent out a letter to the Secretary of the Emigrant Aid Company, ordering: "Write to Hartford and get their terms for one hundred more of the Sharps rifles at once." As far as the Yankee industrialist was concerned, the course was clear—"when farmers turn soldiers, they must have *arms*."[78] "Up to this time," he wrote to President Pierce accusingly, "the government has kept so far aloof as to force the settlers to the conclusion that if they would be safe, they must defend *themselves*, and therefore many persons here who refused at first (myself included), have rendered them assistance by furnishing them means of defense."[79]

Encouraged by the generous assistance they were receiving from their patrons in the East, the free settlers of Kansas took things into their own hands, and followed the precedent recently set by California, of establishing a state government in advance of Congressional permission. They elected delegates to a constitutional convention at Topeka, October 23, 1855, and proceeded to draw up a free-state constitution. Submitted to a totally Free-Soil electorate, the constitution was adopted, Charles Robinson was named "Governor," and a Free-Soil legislature was elected. Congress was formally requested to admit Kansas as a free state.[80]

The question was now thrown into the lap of official Washington. Which was the lawful government of Kansas? Which votes were legitimate and which were fraudulent? Who would make the final decision? President Pierce personally denounced the action of the Free-Soil settlers as treason, and declared that the Government of the United States would support the pro-slavery territorial government as the only lawful government of Kansas.[81] Senator Stephen A. Douglas of Illinois sharply denounced the action of Pierce, however, and argued that it was not a question for Congress to decide—the question would have to be settled in the territories themselves; and on this point he was supported by Senator John J. Crittenden.[82] Congress itself could not arrive at any decision, and in March, 1856, the Representatives sought to clarify matters by appointing a three-man committee to investigate conditions in Kansas. In midsummer this committee only confused the issue further with a majority and minority report, adding more tension to already strained tempers. As the debate on the Kansas issue reached its climax in the Senate in May, 1856, Charles Sumner rose to give his famous speech, "the Crime against Kansas." Infuriated, a Representative from South Carolina, Preston Brooks, lashed the Yankee unmercifully with his cane and left him lying on the floor of the Senate, unconscious and bleeding.[83]

Possibly there was no more striking example of the powerful psychological reaction which the attack upon Sumner produced in the North than Amos Lawrence's invitation to Sumner to rest at his Cottage Farm home on his way back to Boston—this from one of Sumner's greatest political foes and the man who had tried so hard to defeat him in 1850–1851. "You may prefer to be with some one of those who agree with you in regard to party politics," wrote Lawrence to the injured Senator; "but I assure you that no one will give you a more cordial welcome."[84] Sumner accepted the invitation, and on his triumphal return to Boston, spent the weekend at the Lawrence house.[85] So far had Lawrence's attitude toward Sumner changed that in 1859 he suggested that it was "high time" that Sumner be given an honorary degree by Harvard College![86]

Violence begat violence, for while blood began to flow in the nation's capital, the situation among the factions in Kansas had degenerated from opposition of legislatures and constitutions to the crack of rifle fire and the hiss of bowie knives. Even as Sumner was sent crashing to the floor of the Senate, a pro-slavery "posse" of about a thousand men came riding into the "Boston abolition town" of Lawrence, Kansas, arrested "treasonous" free-state leaders, and sacked the town.[87] Three days later, a ranger named John Brown struck at Pottawatomie Creek, murdering five pro-slavery settlers to avenge the five free men already killed. The lid was off, and the "little civil war" was on in Kansas.[88]

In Boston, supporters of the freedom struggle shipped out more rifles, wrote more checks, called for more action—and gave only one warning: Avoid trouble with the Federal authorities! Kick "Calhoun [pro-slavery Surveyor General] and his adherents out of the territory," "put an end to their operations at once," don't let your "boys" permit a "handful of scoundrels" to embarrass the Government and breed ill will throughout the country, urged Mr. Lawrence.[89] *But*—and this was a large "but"—this violence must be employed by "volunteers" who have no connection with the free-state government—and never, under any circumstances, must it be directed against the Federal authorities.[90] Lawrence repeated this again and again in his personal correspondence with Governor Charles Robinson. "We would be pleased to hear to their expulsion in any *informal* [sic] way, by the action of independent corps of men and not of the free-state Government or any of its members."[91] Lawrence was prepared to sanction any activity as long as it did not impugn "the direct authority of the Federal Government."[92]

In this respect, the only danger that Lawrence could see was the unpredictable and irresponsible actions of John Brown, and he cautioned Robinson to keep a close watch on him. "Old Brown will be your humble servant and an efficient one," he wrote, "but he requires some coaxing, as well as some controlling power near him."[93] See to it that Brown reports to you regularly, the New Englander urged. "It is bad policy to have a ranger like him with money and arms at his disposal, and only accountable to people here."[94]

Even in the midst of riot and bloodshed, Amos A. Lawrence clung steadfastly to what he felt was a strictly constitutional position. A man was free to act on slavery in the territories, as long as he did not transgress the authority of the National Government, or infringe upon the rights of Southern states where they were protected by the Constitution. It was the only way to obey the letter of the Compromise of 1850 and still prevent the territorial expansion of slavery. This was a supreme effort to make freedom in Kansas consistent with the national unity of the States.[95]

Against this background of tension and violence the national elections of 1856 were conducted, and the new President was the Democratic candidate, James Buchanan. Anxious to quiet the fearful Kansas uproar as soon as possible, the President appointed Robert J. Walker of Mississippi to the post of Governor, and promised administrative support of an impartial settlement.[96] Walker called for a constitutional convention and urged settlers of both local parties to cooperate in electing delegates. The free-state men, however, suspicious of the administration's motives, refused to participate in the convention; and as a result, in the fall of 1856, the pro-slavery delegates at Lecompton were able to draft a constitution which guaranteed the protection of slave property in Kansas.[97] It was decided that the entire constitution would not be submitted to the people. Instead, the Kansans would be given the opportunity to vote either for "the constitution with slavery" or for "the constitution with no slavery." Even if the free-state party voted for "no slavery," the resulting constitution would provide for the protection of all the slaves who were already in the Territory.[98]

Amos A. Lawrence was loud in protest against this latest action. "The whole country has become tired and disgusted with the perpetuation of frauds," he complained, and he denounced the pro-slavery party: the "principles of Constitutional liberty" had been "crushed down by those who have destroyed the elective franchise in Kansas." "The time for keeping the settlers out of their Constitutional rights is past. Any attempt at coercion will result in disastrous defeat to the Government, and will bring on a crisis such as we never have seen!"[99] "All reasonable measures for ridding the Territory of the renegades who have disgraced it will be sanctioned by the people of the country," he wrote to Robinson.[100]

Governor Walker himself was outraged at this flagrant political trickery and announced that he would have no part in such a stratagem. "I consider such a submission of the question a vile fraud, a base counterfeit and a wretched device to prevent the people from voting," he declared—and then was promptly removed from his office by President Buchanan.[101] The pro-slavery plan went into effect according to schedule: In the voting of December 21, 1857, the pro-slavery voters pushed through their "with slavery" clause with little difficulty as the indignant Free-Soilers refused to participate in what they regarded as a fraud. The victory was short-lived, however, for two weeks later the newly elected Free-Soil legislature resubmitted the entire Lecompton Constitution to the people of the Territory, and it was rejected by a Free-Soil vote of well over 10,000 ballots. Popular sovereignty had spoken![102]

But President Buchanan would not have it. Announcing his unqualified support of the Lecompton Constitution, the Chief Executive urged Congress to accept the pro-slavery document.[103] Again in February, Buchanan personally relayed a copy of the Lecompton Constitution itself to the Congress and requested that Kansas be immediately admitted to the Union as "an independent State."[104]

Hardly had the President made his position clear when Senator Stephen A. Douglas arose to attack the administration policy and condemn the pro-slavery Lecompton Constitution as a violation of popular sovereignty. Again supported by Senator Crittenden who condemned the constitution as "a gross violation of principle and good faith," Douglas demanded an honest vote on the *entire* constitution.[105] From Boston, Amos A. Lawrence sent a letter to Crittenden, congratulating him upon his forthright stand. "Permit me to express my gratitude for the important part which you have taken in opposition to the Lecompton scheme," he wrote. "In doing so, I am impelled by the natural desire which every Northern man has, to prevent the extension of slavery over Territory which we have always considered devoted to free labor."[106]

Although Buchanan was able to secure the support of the Senate, Douglas brought about the defeat of the Kansas Admission Bill in the House; and the issue was deadlocked.[107] A House-Senate compromise, known as the English Bill, was adopted on May 4, 1858, as a means of fulfilling the technical requirements of popular sovereignty while at the same time assuring passage of the Lecompton Constitution.[108] The people of Kansas were to vote for a third time on the constitution. If a majority accepted it, the State would be admitted to the Union immediately. If the constitution were voted down, then Kansas would have to wait until its population was large enough to justify admission through the normal processes—the obvious expectation being that the voters of Kansas would be so anxious for Union status that they would swallow the otherwise unpalatable features of the pro-slavery document.[109] In this respect, however, the administration plans were thwarted, as the Kansans overwhelmingly rejected the compromise in August, 1858, and voted to remain a territory. Although slavery continued to remain legal in Kansas for the time being, the Free-Soilers kept control of the legislature; and it was apparent to all that slavery would be abolished as soon as Kansas achieved statehood on its own terms.[110]

For all practical purposes, the battle for Kansas had been won, and the Cotton Whigs in New England congratulated themselves upon achieving a moral and political victory in the territories, without damaging the authority of the Federal Government or infringing the constitutional rights of the Southern states.[111]

The various participants in the struggle to make Kansas free were certain in their own minds that they had preserved the Union, and were convinced that it was the Emigrant Aid Company which had turned the tide. Eli Thayer took pride in recalling a meeting with Congressman Henry J. Blow of St. Louis in 1862, when the Missourian introduced himself and enthusiastically hailed the consequences of the Kansas victory which he obviously regarded as having held the Border states in check. "Your success in making Kansas a free state has kept Missouri in the Union," said Blow, pumping the New Englander's hand warmly. "If she had seceded, Kentucky and Tennessee would have gone also . . . . Your Kansas work has made it possible to save the Union!"[112] Governor Charles Robinson, in reviewing the success of the free-state movement, said that "the people of Kansas almost made the Republican Party. They have furnished most of the material to make it what it now is . . . ."[113] Robinson was especially expansive in his praise of the role of Amos A. Lawrence. "Without your name," he told the Yankee financier, "the Emigrant Aid Company would have been a cipher, and without your encouragement, courage and support, what little I have been able to do would have been left undone."[114] Lawrence, too, felt confident that the crisis of the Union was over, and that the work for which the newly created Republican Party had been formed had already "been effectually accomplished" by the Emigrant Aid Company. As Lawrence saw it, Charles Robinson, Eli Thayer, and all the other Free-Soil leaders in the Kansas crusade had "in reality carried off the day, and all real danger of the extension of slavery had passed."[115]

Now, reflected the Whig leadership, there was only one other thing to do—and that was to return the political system of the United States to men of goodwill: men of wealth, property, standing, and intellect, whose principles had not been compromised by the petty jealousies of party politics and selfish interests. The Cotton Whigs now went in search of a political party which would represent the interests not of a section, nor of a cause, nor of an individual, but a party which represented the interest of the nation as a whole. In short, they were looking for an "American" party.

7

COTTON WHIGS
IN SEARCH OF A PARTY

DURING the years when Amos A. Lawrence and his colleagues were expending their money and their energies to make Kansas free, the same Cotton Whigs were also hard at work seeking to create a new, moderate, and truly national political party in the United States.

The Kansas-Nebraska Act not only produced bloodshed and violence on the plains of Kansas, but it also acted like a bombshell on the traditional balance in the nation's political power structure. Not only did it cause widespread havoc, but it also made any kind of a *status quo ante* arrangement a practical impossibility. The most badly damaged of all the political groups were the Whigs who saw their organization twisted and broken as a result of Douglas's bill. The Southern branch of the Whig Party, which had already leaned dangerously in the direction of the Democrats in 1852 when party leaders insisted upon General Winfield Scott as the Whig candidate, went over completely in 1854 by siding with Senator Douglas on overthrowing the Missouri Compromise and upsetting the Compromise of 1850.[1] When it became known that prominent Southern Whigs had contributed their support to the Kansas-Nebraska Act, Horace Greeley concluded: "It was clear enough to all discerning vision that old party distinctions were superseded and meaningless!"[2]

Northern Whigs were even more uncertain about their political future. Midway between the extreme pro-slavery forces of the South and the extreme antislavery forces in the North, the conservative Whigs had stood firm for some twenty years, remaining aloof from the unsavory controversy and refusing to permit their party to become embroiled in the political aspects of the issue. Despite their relatively small numbers, their social status and their political influence allowed them to maintain their strategic center position between the feuding forces as a respected element of calm and neutral detachment—an island of logic in a turbulent sea of emotional upheaval.

Once they had given money, guns, and personal commitment to the Free-Soil cause in Kansas, the theoretical principles and the practical politics of the Cotton Whigs were no longer as clear as they used to be. They were still *not* Abolitionists—that was perfectly clear; and they were not really "antislavery" men in the accepted use of the term. Although they had come dangerously close to going over to the side of the young Conscience Whigs whom they had drummed out of the party six years earlier, they still could not bring themselves to make common cause with those whom they regarded as reckless and self-seeking agitators.

For all practical purposes, Thomas Jefferson's dreaded "firebell in the night" had sounded the death knell of the old Whig Party. Split asunder, their program repudiated, their principles now ridiculed, and their influential leadership fast dying off (Daniel Webster, Henry Clay, Harrison Gray Otis, Samuel Eliot, John Davis, old Amos Lawrence, Samuel Appleton—all gone), the old-line Whigs were in a panic of uncertainty. Upon what terms could they justify a separate political existence now that they had come out so openly in the struggle for Kansas? Would they be able to preserve their own identity and political independence? Where could they go? With whom could they ally themselves? Certainly not with the Democrats! Any vestige of integrity that party had possessed the Whigs considered completely dissipated by the Democrats' continued pro-slavery position and their gross misconduct in supporting Douglas and his Nebraska Bill.[3]

For some distraught Whig leaders, the only apparent alternative to political oblivion was fusion with the new party which was even now rising out of the rubble and debris of the Kansas debacle—the Republican Party. Already there was an alarming movement of former Whigs into the ranks of this new organization, and a series of "union" and "fusion" conventions throughout the Northern states had begun as early as 1854 to establish party tickets and even win local victories.[4]

In Michigan, Whigs had already begun moving into the Republican ranks; and in New York, Thurlow Weed was hard at work during 1854 gathering antislavery elements under a single banner. Although the Whig Party and the Republican Party had decided to hold separate conventions at Syracuse in September, 1855, the reports of the invasion of Kansas by Missourians produced such an indignant reaction throughout the North that at convention time Weed was able to march his Whig followers over to the Republican hall where they agreed to the appointment of a single central committee, settled on a joint Republican ticket, and formed one party. The conservative "mercantile" Whigs from New York City were enraged over this surrender of the Whig Party to the forces of "sectionalism," condemned the action of the Syracuse convention, and voted to hold a separate Whig convention the following month—but it was no use. It was clear that most of the Whigs, especially upstate, supported fusion with the Republicans as the only effective means of stopping the expansion of slavery and of checking the power of the Democrats.[5]

In Massachusetts, the Nebraska Bill had hardly passed into law when Charles Sumner began going around the state trying to use the high emotionalism of the moment to form a new party out of the antislavery forces. It was time to forget about tariff disputes, internal improvements issues, and all those other controversies which had kept parties divided in the past. Now was the time to form "a *Grand Junction* party" in the North, argued Sumner, which could effectively "take control of the Government."[6]

Not only did Sumner lack the political finesse and the broad base of party support of a Thurlow Weed, but there were certain specific reasons why his fervent appeals for fusion went unheeded, and why the Republican Party took such an unusually long time to develop solid political roots in the Bay State. For one thing, influential Cotton Whig leaders were adamant in their refusal to accept the principle of fusion. Although the Whig Party had not always been the best, the wisest, or the most discreet political party in American history, admitted Robert C. Winthrop, it *had* been "more pure, more patriotic, more faithful to the principles of the Country and the true principles of the Constitution."[7] Republican Party leaders regarded Winthrop as the most influential Whig leader and they asked him to lead a fusion ticket in Massachusetts, but Winthrop stoutly defended the Whig Party as a constitutional party pledged to uphold law and order, the constant advocate of national prosperity and welfare. Winthrop contrasted the recent Free-Soil-Democratic coalition which had sent Charles Sumner to the Senate in 1851, to the Whigs who had never stooped to any "bargain" and tolerated "no traffic as a means of securing office." Above all, Winthrop concluded, his was a party which "deplores the existence of domestic slavery within the limits of the American Union," and would "omit no legal effort to arrest and prevent its extension"; but at the same time, it was a party which scrupulously "abstains from all unconstitutional and illegal interference with it whatever."[8]

It is clear that beyond Winthrop's political and constitutional reasons for refusing, he felt the deep and smouldering animosity of the old Cotton Whigs toward those Conscience Whigs who had broken away from the party for the sake of Free-Soilism. "We are urged to abandon our old colors, and rush wildly into the promiscuous ranks of a one-idea party in order to promote some grand result connected with human liberty," sneered Winthrop sarcastically. "Let us look at the new party . . . and see what claims it has to our confidence." In the analysis of the Republican Party that followed, it was obvious that Winthrop's principal objection to the party was the people who led it—those "ultra," "radical," and "reckless" Free-Soilers who had "usurped a lead which belonged to others and gave an odor of abolition to the whole movement."[9]

As long as such extremists were allowed to operate at both ends of the Union, declared Winthrop, such elements would inevitably involve the nation in a "never-ceasing series of mischievous and deplorable measures." As far as he was concerned, he was determined to remain faithful to his own party—the Whig Party—

a party that once made it possible for Massachusetts to be called the "model State" of the Union. "If that title is ever to be regained," wrote Winthrop, "it will be under something less speckled and motley than a Fusion flag!"[10] In a similar vein, T. D. Eliot wrote to Charles Sumner declining an invitation to come over to the Republican Party and informing him that he felt he could do his duty more efficiently and sincerely "as a Whig than in any other way."[11]

Sumner's great expectation, therefore, that all the antislavery elements would want to join the ranks of the new Republican Party were quickly shown to be premature. Not only did the conservative Cotton Whigs take a dim view of making common cause with unstable agitators, but the Massachusetts Democrats, too, faithfully obeyed the stern dictates of their own leader, Caleb Cushing, and remained true to their traditional party loyalties. Even more significant, many Free-Soilers could not be persuaded to accept the Republican Party as the only road to political salvation. Under Henry Wilson's leadership they were already experimenting with the possibilities offered by the newly created "American" Party.[12]

For some time there had been developing a school of thought that focused attention upon the rapid growth of foreign immigration into the United States. Many people of English Protestant background feared that immigration carried a new Roman Catholic threat. Pledging themselves to the work of isolating and suppressing these dangerous and undesirable imports—particularly those of Irish and German extraction—local societies with elaborate names sprang up throughout the country. By 1852 and 1853, various local Nativist groups had combined in a single political party, known officially as the "American" Party—and unofficially as the "Know-Nothing" Party because of the lack of information which could be elicited about its organization and its membership.[13]

Seeing a ready-made political organization with a high emotional content and considerable national support, many factions sought to take over the new structure and to move into the political vacuum which had suddenly been created by the collapse of the Whig Party and the temporary eclipse of Democratic power in the North. In New York City, a number of "mercantile" Whigs, still disgruntled over the fusion of their party with the Republicans, supported the Know-Nothing ticket as the only practical way to preserve "a great Union party in opposition to abolition and sectional names." In Massachusetts, the well-known Free-Soiler, Henry Wilson, swiftly took the opportunity to join the Know-Nothing organization. Hoping to win enough political support to send him to Washington as Sumner's antislavery colleague in the Senate, Wilson came out in support of Henry J. Gardner, the Know-Nothing candidate for governor.[14]

Although an old-time Whig like Rufus Choate might complain disgustedly that history had never seen "any thing more low, obscene, or feculent" than this new party ("We shall come to the worship of onions, cats, and things vermiculate!" he growled),[15] many of his Cotton Whig friends and associates were not so critical. Indeed, they could see distinct tactical possibilities in a prefabricated political machine as a practical alternative to surrendering to Republican principles without a fight. In many instances there is little doubt that the strong anti-foreign, anti-Catholic planks of the American platform were quite appealing to the type of conservative persons who composed the hierarchy of the industrial and commercial classes of the Northeast. But for many people attracted to the American Party, nationalistic and religious prejudices were essentially a secondary issue when compared with the political and constitutional potential of the party. Many conservatives saw no reason why they could not move into control of the new party, deprive it of its more obnoxious social characteristics, and use it as a political wedge to splinter and destroy the existing parties. "The leaders of the American party are neither my friends nor acquaintances," said Amos A. Lawrence when he first became associated with the party; and J. V. C. Smith, the Know-Nothing Mayor of Boston in 1854, not only continued to maintain close business relations with his Irish-Catholic friends, but as an amateur sculptor, executed a fine bust of his friend, John Bernard Fitzpatrick, Catholic Bishop of Boston.[16] As Henry Wilson explained, "hundreds of thousands" did not actually believe in the principles or the purposes of the American Party, but were "willing to use its ma-

chinery to disrupt the Whig and Democratic parties. . . ."[17] Time
was of the essence, and this was one practical way of bypassing
the necessity of organizing and developing an entirely new
political party with a minimum of effort.

In addition to the organizational factor, the basic tenets of the
American Party offered the possibility of a national appeal which
might drive the divisive elements of sectionalism and slavery back
into the obscurity of forgotten causes. Conjuring up a national
platform of peace, prosperity, Protestantism, and no-Popery, many
Cotton Whigs felt they could envision the possibility of a new
basis of understanding with their Southern friends. With a united
North-South crusade to fight the terrifying spectre of foreign-bred
Catholicism, possibly the immediate menace of the slave problem
might be lost in the shuffle.[18]

Almost overnight, the Whig power in such urban centers as
Boston, New York, Philadelphia, Baltimore, and St. Louis, took a
sudden and decided swing toward the policies and the politics of
the American Party. Spring of 1854 saw a Know-Nothing sweep
in Pennsylvania; New York was estimated to have upwards of
seventy thousand registered "American" voters by fall of the same
year; and in Massachusetts, the newly formed American Party
came out of nowhere and ran away with the State by an overwhelming margin. In less than a year the party had been able to
absorb enough power to poll over 80,000 votes—which put it
50,000 votes ahead of its nearest rival.[19]

The following year, Know-Nothing forces and their conservative Whig allies were able to hold the line once again against
Republicanism. In New York, the businessmen of the city polled
enough votes to bring about the defeat of the Republican candidate, and expressed the hope that the following year might see a
revival of the old Whig Party.[20] And in Massachusetts, thanks to
the encouragement and support of such prominent Cotton Whigs
as Amos A. Lawrence and Robert C. Winthrop ("the Rip Van
Winkles of our politics," snorted Sumner), the Know-Nothings
were able to sweep to victory again in the state elections. At
this point Charles Sumner was ready to give up all hopes for the
success of Republicanism in Massachusetts. Bay State politics, he
moaned, were "in a perfect muss!"[21]

But the triumph of the Know-Nothing Party in the United States, although swift and substantial, was remarkably short-lived. The cause was nebulous, the issues artificially contrived, and the attempt to establish a broad base of political power on religious prejudice collapsed of its own weight. In the South, the cause of Nativism sputtered violently and died quickly due to the fact that the total number of foreign immigrants below the Mason-Dixon Line was comparatively small and their political influence trifling. The terrors which the spectre of Irish politicking and Papal domination could arouse in the Southland were nothing, compared with the immediate and all-consuming preoccupation with the institution of slavery and its future prospects.[22]

Throughout the Northern states, too, the American Party steadily lost adherents after its brief and gaudy triumph. For one thing, religious bigotry proved a poor cement for the foundations of a truly national political organization. In Massachusetts, especially, a farcical series of investigations of convents and nunneries by Know-Nothing leaders brought such ridicule and discredit upon the whole Nativist movement that its political underpinnings crumbled almost immediately.[23]

Then, too, national events during the early part of 1856 brought the controversial issue of slavery back into prominence with such dramatic force that all other movements and activities were practically forgotten. Any hopes that conservative elements in New York and Boston may have had that 1856 would see a revival of the old Whig Party were crushed with appalling finality. Reports of the sack of Lawrence, Kansas, by pro-slavery forces, the news of John Brown's massacre at Osawatomie, and especially the horrifying details of the beating of Senator Charles Sumner in the halls of the Senate provoked such violent reactions among Northerners everywhere that the final fusion of Whigs and Republicans began to appear a foregone conclusion. "It looks as if Brooks's bludgeon has given a sort of *coup de grâce* to the Whig party," Robert C. Winthrop acknowledged as he read the handwriting on the wall.[24]

The violence of 1856 placed conservative Whigs in a peculiar quandary in terms of the upcoming Presidential election. With no candidate of their own, the Whigs were forced to make a choice between the three in the field—James Buchanan, the Democratic candidate; John C. Frémont, the Republican nominee; and Millard Fillmore, the choice of the American Party. Sensing the imminent collapse of the whole Know-Nothing movement, many Whigs wrote off Fillmore and spent their time debating whether a Democrat or a Republican President would be the lesser evil.

The Republican nomination of John C. Frémont, instead of William H. Seward, presented the electorate with what was generally regarded as a more moderate and less militant standard-bearer; yet most conservatives could not be persuaded that the election of *any* Republican candidate would not present a menace to the Union. For this reason, many Northern Whigs felt they could best help the cause of sectional accord by defeating the "sectional" Republican Party, and they came out in support of the Democratic candidate. In August, for example, Rufus Choate announced in a public letter that he had made up his mind to vote for James Buchanan. It was the "first duty" of all Whigs, he insisted, "to defeat and dissolve the new geographical party," and there were many of his friends and associates in the North who agreed with him.[25]

There still remained, however, a hard core of old-time Whigs who, despite constant appeals and pressures from their friends in both parties, doggedly clung to the resolution that the only real hope for true intersectional peace lay in a third party which avoided the extreme regionalism becoming characteristic of the two major parties. "Choate has swallowed Buchanan," said Robert C. Winthrop, "but I could not do it." But, on the other hand, he was forced to admit that "all my convictions are opposed to a sectional party under Frémont." "Nothing remained," he concluded, "but to support Fillmore" and the American Party; and he indicated that fellow-conservatives like Edward Everett, Nathan Appleton, William Appleton, and George S. Hillard felt the way he did.[26] Amos A. Lawrence believed so strongly in the need for keeping a third party movement alive that he turned down an offer to become a Frémont elector, raised a "Fillmore" flag beside his house in Brookline, and accepted the nomination to run as the American Party candidate for Governor of Massachusetts although he was certain of defeat.[27]

In a campaign speech at Faneuil Hall shortly before the election, Winthrop repeated his opinion that the future of the nation would be seriously endangered by the victory of either the Democratic or the Republican Party, and that "the best safety of the Union is to be found in the defeat of both of them." Describing a vigorous third party with strength enough to step between two hot-tempered fighters before they actually came to blows, Winthrop made an eloquent appeal for the American Party as the only way to keep the political party system in the United States from being completely divided along geographical lines. "When a party composed of only half the States in the Union shall assert its title to the name of a national party, and shall be claimed and recognized as such," he warned prophetically, "it will not be long I fear—it will not be long—before half the States will claim to be recognized as a nation by themselves."[28] And in New York City, an old-line Whig, Luther Bradish, echoed Winthrop's sentiments in calling for support of the American candidate as the only way to keep the Whig banner "still floating in the breeze." If you want to call this "Old Fogeyism," he challenged, "Be it so!"[29]

Although Fillmore ran a poor third in the elections of 1856, receiving only the 8 electoral votes of Maryland, his 874,534 popular votes undoubtedly helped to provide Buchanan with sufficient political momentum to defeat Frémont in the Republicans' first attempt to capture the Presidency. With Buchanan polling 1,838,-169 popular votes to Frémont's 1,335,264, it was obvious to the leadership of both parties that the movement of the votes of those who had supported Fillmore could be a crucial factor during the next four years.

Despite the defeat of Fillmore, however, conservative Whigs in the North still refused to give up their determination to keep alive a third party as an alternative to intersectional warfare; and they obviously felt that a peaceful administration under a conservative Democrat like James Buchanan offered valuable working time for such a development. In New York City, the remnants of the influential "mercantile" Whigs continued to oppose fusion with both Democrats and Republicans; and in Massachusetts, Amos A. Lawrence continued to announce himself an "American" stalwart even after the election had clearly demonstrated the weakness of the Know-Nothing cause.[30]

In a letter written to Moses G. Cobb in July, 1857, Lawrence continued to stump for the third party, outlining the advantages to be gained in fighting for an independent existence. The American Party, argued Lawrence, cherished a "purer nationality," and although it would certainly assure toleration for all citizens, it would "never allow the diversion of the public funds for the support of sectarian schools" because "we love the Protestant religion." It would be the policy of the American Party to refuse foreigners the right to choose the rulers and the right to make the laws. Foreigners had never enjoyed those rights in their own countries and should not be entrusted with them in America, said the industrialist. That power belonged to "those alone who [were] educated to exercise it." In this way, those principles of the Fathers of the Republic, as handed down by George Washington and as carried on by the Whig Party, might be perpetuated by the American Party.[31]

Of more immediate importance, of course, was the critical issue of slavery. Here again, said Lawrence, the American Party was prepared to make a truly unique political contribution. The Democratic Party could offer no real solution, because it was "indifferent" to the moral issues involved in the institution of slavery. The Republican Party, on the other hand, was equally useless, he argued, since it was essentially "sectional," its organization and membership being limited to those states north of the Mason-Dixon Line. Echoing the sentiments which Winthrop had expressed the previous year, Lawrence emphasized the fact that the two sections were currently in the process of producing two separate parties—two parties so hostile and so distinct that they would inevitably create a dangerous crisis in the American political system.[32]

Only the American Party was willing and able to take a clear-cut stand on slavery which was consistent with both moral law and constitutional principles. "I believe it should be treated like a polite highwayman," wrote Lawrence. "We must ride along with him, always keeping an eye out, and when we see he meditates an overt act, then seize him by the throat and down with him!" Then, as if suddenly realizing that his vehemence might alarm his correspondent, Lawrence continued in a more affable vein. He did not mean that Southerners themselves were highwaymen, he hastily assured Cobb. "They are members of the same family with ourselves and we must live on good terms with them; in order to do so we must use kindness, we must feel it, and we must not irritate them by words." At the same time, he concluded, we must not "let them bully us."[33]

Dedicated as they were to the cause of reviving Whiggism, however, Northern conservatives found that they had little time to reflect upon the election of 1856, the plans of President Buchanan, or the complexities of the political structure. Another problem had suddenly appeared which put the issue of slavery and the fear of sectionalism into a secondary position for the time being. Disaster had struck—in the form of a financial collapse, the Panic of 1857.

Already American economic development demonstrated a cyclical pattern, and the 1857 crisis showed a dangerous downward curve in the cycle. The Panic was the product of numerous forces. Overexpansion of railroads, overproduction of manufactured goods, overspeculation, together with an unstable banking system —all these factors had served to inflate the economy unhealthily. With the crash of the Ohio Life Insurance and Trust Company, the panic was on, as good businesses followed bad ones into bankruptcy and ruin. Although the immediate financial crisis itself was soon ended, the economic reverberations continued for several years, as depression, unemployment, and financial indolence provided ample evidence of how seriously the economy had been disrupted.[34]

Northern capitalists, manufacturers, industrialists, merchants, and investors—and the Cotton Whigs of Massachusetts in particular—were transformed in the Panic of 1857. Preoccupation with their immediate financial and industrial affairs now forced them to relegate their political interests to a secondary position until such time as they should once again regain some measure of stability and security.[35]

"Commercially, we have been so distressed as hardly to be able to consider anything deliberately, but how to save ourselves from total prostration," wrote Amos Lawrence to "Governor" Charles Robinson in Kansas.[36] The situation was decidedly worse than the panic of '37, the New Englander explained, and "the financial derangement in the country now absorbs everything. Here it has spread ruin over every interest . . . . Our manufacturing interest is for the present completely broken down and discredited."[37]

As a result of the financial upheaval, and the necessity of having to plunge once again into the economic complexities of supply and demand, the Cotton Whigs found it necessary to take stock of their position with regard to their Southern brethren. In the years following the introduction of Douglas's Nebraska Bill back in 1854, the Northern business interests had grown highly critical of and intensely hostile to the aims and the institutions of the Southern states. Business opposition to Douglas, its outright support of Free-Soil in Kansas, and its growing approval of Senator Sumner were all indications of a much more outspoken and independent attitude than the financial North had ever before dared to express.

The Panic changed all this. The cotton belt had not been as seriously affected by the crisis as had been the industrial areas of the East, and the wheat belt of the West.[38] With industrial production falling off alarmingly, and with Western markets drying up everywhere, Northern manufacturers realized that they had no alternative but to rely upon the relatively prosperous markets of the South as the only means of weathering this serious financial storm.[39] The South realized this too, however, and took full advantage of her momentary position of power to demand a "new deal" for the Southern planter from the financial interests of the North. Denouncing the "money changers" of Wall Street who were bleeding the planters of their just profits, the South called for a complete readjustment of financial policies—or else![40] The North, the Southerners said, could not possibly survive without Southern markets, and unless changes were forthcoming, the South would boycott "any article or merchandize [sic] or manufacture, purchased directly or indirectly in any of the Northern States."[41] Furthermore, not only would the North find itself shut out of Southern markets, but it would also find itself cut off from the precious bales of Southern cotton—until it was willing to come to satisfactory terms. "What would happen," asked Senator Hammond in a speech on the floor of the Senate, "if no cotton was furnished for three years?" Conjuring up the awful possibilities of idle mills and empty spindles, Hammond hurled defiance at the Northern states. "Cotton is King!" he cried exultantly, as the Southland applauded his battle cry.[42]

The dire threats of the South were not lost upon the business interests of the North. In haste, indeed, in panic, they tried to disassociate themselves from those political connections which the South might construe as hostile to its interests, and once again began to assure the Southerners of their good intentions. The cry of the New York *Herald,* that people must forget about "Bleeding Kansas" and the "Nigger Agitation," was taken up in earnest by the manufacturers of New England.[43] "Will the vast commercial manufacturing interests of the North indorse this horrible and suicidal war on the South?" asked the Boston *Post.* Such an "irrepressible conflict" can bring no good to our New England manufactures. *"Vote* it down!"[44] "I shut my eyes and ears to politics, sick of the very sound of brawling and bickering about slavery," complained Robert C. Winthrop, who announced his intention of stopping the Abolitionist Republicans by voting Democratic in the elections of 1858.[45]

Winthrop was not the only Whig who was apprehensive about the growing power of the Republican Party during 1858 and who was ready to resort to practically any political means in order to check its rapid growth. The Panic of 1857 had not only produced financial dislocation and intersectional stresses for the Northern businessman, but had created one more pressure which, in addition to its purely economic effects, nudged hesitant conservatives closer to the ranks of the Republican Party. Playing skillfully upon the economic depression as a political instrument with which to lure the business and commercial interests, Republican leaders blamed the panic upon the actions of a Southern-controlled Democratic administration in Washington. The financial welfare of the nation, they claimed, was being weakened by the administrations of Pierce and Buchanan whom they accused of working against good business practices by failing to pass an effective tariff bill, by refusing to make grants available to railroads, and by neglecting to provide adequate bankruptcy laws.[46] There was the clear and persuasive suggestion that the only way in which the businessmen of the North could secure a National

Government sympathetic to their desires and responsive to their needs would be by supporting the Republican Party. Observing so many of his Whig and American friends going over to the Republican Party, Amos A. Lawrence complained that the Republicans were "stealing all our American doctrines." They have almost abandoned completely the cry of "no more slave states," and are emphasizing such things as "home protection, extended period after naturalization before voting, etc., etc."[47]

In 1858, Lawrence himself was again approached by the Americans and the Republicans to run on a ticket either for Congress or Governor. Lawrence still could not stomach the Republicans and their "slogans" about ending slavery and their policy of "crying and abusing the South," and so he refused their support— "I cannot desert my friends," he told Governor Charles Robinson.[48] Thinking over the American offer, Lawrence was faced with a choice of two evils. Although he had a greater chance of winning a congressional seat, he would be forced to go off to Washington and spend his time and energy in functions in which he had little interest.[49] If he ran for the Governorship, on the other hand, Lawrence was certain he would be defeated.[50] Nevertheless, so strong was his belief in traditional Whig principles and so great was his conviction that a Republican victory would endanger the Union that he swallowed his pride and reluctantly offered to run as the American candidate for Governor in 1858.

Not only did Lawrence commit himself to the task of keeping the Americans from being absorbed by the Republicans, but he also kept a wary eye out for any indications that Americans were drifting toward the camp of the Democrats. When George Lunt and George S. Hillard, editors of the Boston *Courier*, expressed an interest in supporting the Democrats in order to halt the progress of the Republicans in the Bay State, Lawrence spoke out sharply and warned his friends that the Democrats had nothing whatever in common with the "National Americans and Old Whigs." The Democrats, he pointed out, were against extending the terms of naturalization; they were opposed to registry laws; they were committed to lowering the tariff, a position dangerous to the interests of American manufacturers; they were in favor of indefinite territorial expansion; they were responsible for the repeal of the Missouri Compromise; and they were the perpetrators of unjust and disgraceful acts in the Kansas Territory. Seen in the light of these factors, noted Lawrence, the program of the Democrats was diametrically opposed to that of the Americans.[51]

Although, he admitted, these differences might not seem terribly significant on the local scene (which was where the editors of the *Courier* suggested cooperation with the Democrats), Lawrence expressed his opinion that it would be wiser "to keep an eye on National affairs." The state of the nation demanded solid opposition to the policies of the Buchanan administration. By surrendering to the Democrats at this particular time, even in a local election, the American Party would be seriously compromised and would not be strong enough to contest the Democrats in 1860. "Is the *Courier* prepared to surrender the Government to a party whose policy it has always opposed and does now, in perpetuity?"[52]

The results of the election of 1858 justified the fears of Northern conservatives that the Republican Party had made remarkable gains in the course of the last two years, and that all hopes of reviving the Whig Party "as it used to be" were doomed to failure. Except for the States of Illinois and Indiana, the Republicans had swept every Northern state—including Buchanan's home-state of Pennsylvania. In New York, a coalition of Republicans and anti-administration Democrats won an impressive victory; and in Massachusetts, Republican Nathaniel Banks won the Governorship by over 30,000 votes. As he had expected, Amos A. Lawrence was swamped, and his defeat brought the sarcastic comment by Greeley's *Tribune* that "Amos A. Lawrence, the 'American' candidate, is left so out in the cold that he will one day be obliged to procure affidavits that he was ever a candidate at all."[53]

But Lawrence could look philosophically upon his personal defeat. It was more important he thought, that every individual throw whatever influence he had against the progress of a political party that Lawrence regarded as promoting disunity and provoking sectionalism. In fact, he expressed relief when the news from Illinois recorded the reelection of Stephen A. Douglas. Lawrence felt that this Democratic victory in the West had served the overall purpose of offsetting the Republican victory in Massachusetts.[54] Like many others, Lawrence could see that the election of 1860 was to be the crucial—and perhaps the final—test of whether or not the political structure of the nation would become divided along strictly geographical lines. He was still most anxious to establish a means of providing the voters with an alternative to either Southern Democracy or Northern Republicanism. Anything less than this, he was convinced, would ultimately lead to disunity and civil war.

Lawrence's reluctant acknowledgment that the American Party was dead and his fears about the election of 1860 were drawn out in a letter he wrote to a conservative associate in Washington, D.C., the chairman of a convention of conservative "Americans" who were making preparations for the coming Presidential election. After apologizing for not being able to attend this convention, Lawrence informed his correspondent realistically that the number of men in Massachusetts who still held "American views" was by this time so small that they could well be "left out of the account without being missed." Lawrence had come to the conclusion that the American Party had no chance whatsoever of political survival and that some other means of establishing a third party had to be devised as soon as possible.[55]

In this respect he was undoubtedly reflecting upon the letter which Eli Thayer of Worcester had written to him the previous month. Expressing his fears that the Republican Party would not be able to sustain the margin it had achieved in 1858 and that the Democrats would make a dramatic comeback in 1860, Thayer confided to Lawrence: "We must now look for some original and comprehensive policy which will commend itself to the patriotism and good sense of the people and shall be in accordance with the origin and spirit of our government."[56] Only a few days after Thayer's letter, Lawrence had received a letter from Edward Jay Morris of Pennsylvania asking about the possibilities of his forming a new fusion party with the Republicans in Massachusetts. Republicans and Americans, he said, were waiving their distinctive organizations and forming a new "People's Party" in Pennsylvania, New Jersey, Delaware, and Kentucky, assuming all the elements of a national organization. "Would it not be well to start such a movement in Massachusetts?"[57]

It was precisely this idea of an "original and comprehensive policy" that Lawrence himself was speculating about during the months after the election of 1858; and the only practical alternative he could see (and the one suggested by Morris) was a new "fusion" party made up of conservative Republicans who had become dissatisfied with the radicalism of the leaders, moderate Democrats who had become disenchanted with their national program, along with old-time Whigs and recent members of the American Party. "God grant," he fervently prayed, that such a fusion would be possible—"that the national strife may cease while a union is made of the opposition all over the country, that our people may learn to discriminate between hatred of slavery and hatred of the South; and that Southern men may cease to brand as incendiaries all those who will not bow to their Baal."[58] The time was short and the chances slim; but Lawrence was determined to work with every resource at his command over the next two years to see that the electorate would have at least one national party representing the interests of moderation and compromise as an alternative to those which appealed to sectionalism and violence.

8

THE ELEVENTH HOUR

"WE ARE ready for any sort of combination that will unite the opposition," Amos A. Lawrence wrote to Governor Robinson of Kansas in January, 1859.[1] Convinced that a new conservative coalition of nationwide proportions was the way to avoid disunion and civil war, Lawrence worked energetically to construct the framework of an organization. He pressed into service many of his closest friends and associates—the cotton manufacturer Nathan Appleton and his cousin William Appleton; George Peabody, famous merchant and financier; Benjamin F. Butler, lawyer and investor who was one of the largest stockholders in the Middlesex Mills of Lowell; as well as such prominent Cotton Whig political stalwarts as Robert C. Winthrop, George S. Hillard of the *Courier*, George Ticknor Curtis, and Rufus Choate.[2]

Throughout 1859, Lawrence tried to pull together the nucleus of a strong party to insure the defeat of the Democrats in 1860, and also to drain off the extremism of the Republican Party. He insisted that any real hope for a successful third party lay basically in "American" ideals, and in October, 1859, he told former Governor George N. Briggs that he had sent a man into Essex County to sound out "American" sentiment in that area, or, as he put it, "whether there *was* any."[3] Since he admitted that by this time most of Massachusetts was in basic agreement regarding slavery, he felt that the main reliance of the new ticket would have to be based upon the principles of the religion and the

132

institutions of the Puritans, and against Romanism, atheism, rum, and the graded school system which forced all pupils to proceed at the same pace.[4] Although Lawrence was obviously preparing to present the same program to the electorate in 1860 that had already been soundly repudiated in the past, he apparently felt that the national issues of the moment left him no other alternative.

Lawrence was encouraged in the fall of 1859 because it appeared that relations between the North and the South were beginning to readjust to a more normal and peaceful pattern. The effects of the Panic of 1857 still led Northern businessmen to profess extreme tolerance for the South and its local institutions, political disagreements had been pushed somewhat into the background, and old friendships were being renewed.

One rather surprising demonstration of the new spirit of tolerance and conciliation in the business community may be seen in the enthusiastic reception given to Jefferson Davis during the autumn of 1858. Returning from a visit to Maine, the Davis family was forced to remain in the city of Boston when their baby came down with the croup. Never had Boston extended a more gracious welcome. Mrs. Harrison Gray Otis came over in person to nurse the infant through the night, while the prominent citizens of the city prepared a public ovation for their unexpected visitor from Mississippi. On October 11, 1858, Faneuil Hall was packed —standing room only—while on the platform men like Edward Everett, Robert C. Winthrop, and Caleb Cushing took pleasure in introducing their guest as the personification of "intellectual cultivation and of eloquence, with the practical qualities of a statesman and a general." The audience was completely captivated; and when Davis made his appearance, the audience rose en masse to give the Southern statesman a deafening ovation.[5]

When Mr. John Henry Vessey of England was dining with the Lawrence family in their Beacon Street home in the spring of 1859, he was amazed to find both Mrs. Lawrence and her husband expressing "their sympathy with the Southerners on the slave question"—a subject, he added, "I should never have dreamt of mentioning in Boston which I had always considered to be the very hotbed of abolition."[6]

Just when Lawrence was piecing together the basic elements

of his new state organization, and just when the absence of explosive incidents might have allowed a realignment of the political structure, John Brown launched his famous attack on Harpers
Ferry, October 19, 1859. Although the ill-planned invasion ended
in failure, it sent a shiver of horror throughout the length and
breadth of the Southland. It was not so much that Brown had taken
up arms against the Federal Government, but that he had actually
tried to incite a slave revolt. All their lives, Southern men, women,
and children had lived under the spectre of a slave uprising, and
now a Northern man, a white man, had threatened to make it a
reality!

A panicky South was put on a virtual war footing. Rigid cur-
fews were established everywhere and increased appropriations
were demanded for local defense measures. Southerners angrily
blamed the entire North for making such an undertaking possible,
and leading Congressmen from the Cotton Kingdom insisted upon
a full-scale congressional investigation in order to discover exactly
how John Brown had received money, guns, and support.

"Mr. Brown, who sent you here?" "How many are engaged with
you in this movement?" "Have you had any correspondence with
parties at the North on the subject of this movement?" "Who are
your advisers in this movement?" Again and again the prosecution
demanded that the prisoner tell them who in the North had
conspired with him. They wanted names, dates, places, sums—but
Brown would give them nothing. About himself, he admitted
everything; but he would implicate no one else. Silent, grim, de-
fiant, the wounded prisoner refused to speak.[7] The South refused
to accept his silence. There *must* have been others. Any such
project involved a great deal of expense, and Old Brown was
known to be virtually penniless.

Although it was over four hundred miles from Harpers Ferry,
Virginia, to Boston, Massachusetts, John Brown's raid made that
distance seem considerably shorter. A number of prominent New
Englanders had associated with John Brown over the course of the
last three or four years, and now it began to look as though these
persons might be considered accessories in a plot involving such
charges as murder, inciting slaves to rebellion, and treason against
the United States.

Merchants and industrialists like Amos A. Lawrence of Boston and John Carter Brown of Providence, serving as officers of the Massachusetts Emigrant Aid Society, had sent money, guns, and frequent encouragement to "Captain" Brown during his exploits in the Kansas Territory. George L. Stearns, another successful Boston merchant, had constantly made almost unlimited funds available to the man and his cause. Dr. Samuel Gridley Howe, noted for his work among the blind, had turned from the struggle for Greek independence to take up the fight for Negro freedom, and had become one of Brown's closest associates in the East.[8]

Preachers like Theodore Parker and Thomas Wentworth Higginson continued to rage against slavery, pounding their pulpits in Boston and Worcester, demanding an end to man's inhumanity to man. Wendell Phillips, representing one of Boston's oldest families, had become the "golden trumpet" of Garrison's abolition movement and a staunch backer of John Brown. In Concord, young Franklin B. Sanborn, just out of Harvard, left his post as schoolmaster to devote all his time to the antislavery crusade, and soon found himself one of the leading disciples of the "old man" from Kansas.[9]

It was one thing to be snubbed for associating with Abolitionists, for reading the *Liberator*, or for sending aid out to the free settlers of Kansas Territory. But it was quite another matter to find oneself implicated in a plot which involved the invasion of a state, the murder of a number of citizens, and an attack upon property and forces belonging to the United States of America!

The Senate had appointed a special investigating committee, headed by Senator James Mason of Virginia and Senator Jefferson Davis of Mississippi, in order to uncover the "higher and wickeder" villains in this nefarious scheme and make them share in the punishment of John Brown. At this point, many Bostonians, once fearless in their support of John Brown, now blanched as they faced the possible loss of their good names, their businesses, their wealth, their property—and, perhaps, their freedom.

There were, of course, those who remained steadfast in their beliefs, who acknowledged their part in Brown's plans, and who defied the South to do its worst. Theodore Parker was in Europe at the time of the raid, but he wrote back his approval of what

Brown had tried to do, and warned that this was only the beginning. In Worcester, the tall Unitarian minister, Thomas
Wentworth Higginson, admitted his complicity with John Brown
and dared the Southern senators to call him to the witness stand.
Wendell Phillips continued to applaud the deeds of Brown, and
together with William Bowditch and others tried to develop a
fantastic plot to rescue the old man from his Virginia prison.[10]

For the most part, however, reaction in Boston took the form of
hysterical denials and rapid excursions out of the city "for reasons of health." Franklin Sanborn, one of Brown's most ardent
followers, thought that he would head for Canada to "try a change
of air for my old complaint" shortly after the old man was captured. Dr. Samuel Gridley Howe, a close associate who undoubtedly knew much about Brown's secret plans, vehemently
denied all knowledge of the raid, and then left for a tour of
Canada. George L. Stearns, another gentleman who had become
intimately connected with Brown's project, similarly insisted
that he knew nothing whatsoever about the invasion plans—and
then he, too, departed for Canada.[11]

Conservatives throughout the city of Boston were appalled at
the news of John Brown's raid, and the Cotton Whigs, particularly
conscious of the effect of this explosive incident upon their
political plans, threw up their hands in despair. Mournfully, Edward Everett warned Robert C. Winthrop that this event would
surely pave the way for the "final catastrophe."[12] Fearing that
the South would interpret Brown's ill-timed attack as proof that
the entire North had turned "abolitionist," the business community desperately sought a way out by trying to convince the
leaders of the South that this was the work of a single, unsup-
ported madman, and was in no way sanctioned by the conservative
gentlemen of the North.

Writing to William W. Seaton, co-editor of the influential *National Intelligencer*, Amos A. Lawrence labeled Brown as an unfortunate "monomaniac" who was not mentally responsible,
dismissed the attack as "quixotic," and pleaded with the leaders
of the South not to create a martyr out of a madman.[13] Seeing
the obvious implications not only to himself but to the new
political organization he was trying to organize in the Bay State,

Lawrence reacted in alarm at the news that a special congressional investigation was afoot. To Senator Jefferson Davis of Mississippi, Boston's guest of the previous year, Lawrence sent personal assurances that neither he nor his associates had ever been connected with any of Brown's plans outside of the Kansas Territory; and to Governor Wise of Virginia, Lawrence issued a direct plea for a fair trial, saying that Brown's mind had obviously "become disordered by hardship and illness."[14]

In New York John Brown's raid had the peculiar effect of causing such widespread discouragement among the mercantile groups that they momentarily withdrew from all political activity in "complete apathy,"[15] but Boston's reaction was markedly different. Fearing that this latest catastrophe might well wreck his well-laid plans for a third party and that it might eliminate any possibility for intersectional peace, Lawrence worked at fever pitch to organize his program in the Bay State as quickly as possible. "In view of the present disturbed condition of public sentiment and dangers which threaten our Union," he issued a clarion call to those "who honor and cherish that Union—who mean to maintain the Constitution of the United States and faithfully to carry out all its requirements and obligations."[16]

Meeting at Faneuil Hall on December 8, 1859 (only five days after John Brown was hanged), conservatives officially formed the "Constitutional Union Party" with Levi Lincoln, former Cotton Whig Governor of Massachusetts, as president and George Peabody as vice-president.[17] The delegates adopted resolutions expressing sympathy for the people of Virginia as a result of their frightening experience, and lamented the existence of those circumstances which had led to such a violent upheaval. The members of the new party formally pledged themselves to support an unchangeable Union which they regarded as indispensable to the prosperity of all citizens and "to our existence as a civilized nation," and they proposed to use every means to maintain amicable relations between the peoples of the United States.[18]

Within a matter of days, Lawrence was busy contacting such leading unionists in the South as John J. Crittenden of Kentucky and John Bell of Tennessee, seeking to form political connections with compromise movements in other states so as to organize the

Constitutional Union Party on a national scale before the elections of 1860. Lawrence particularly singled out Senator Crittenden to be the national figurehead of the new party. A close
friend of the famous Abbott Lawrence, long-time supporter of
Whig principles, outspoken opponent of the Kansas fiasco, Crittenden was considered to possess all the necessary personal and
political qualifications to capture the votes of responsible, thinking moderates, North and South. "What is wanted is a pro-
gramme," Lawrence wrote to the Kentuckian, urging hasty action.
"If you will send me two notes of three lines each in your own
handwriting, asking me whether the Union-loving men of Massachusetts are ready to unite with the opponents of the Democratic
party in the other States for the defeat of that party and of all
extremists, I will promise to organize this whole State in eight
weeks."[19]

It was John Crittenden himself, emphasized Lawrence, who
would be the new party's biggest asset; and he assured the Senator
from Kentucky that if he would agree to be the party's Presidential
candidate (Lawrence brushed aside the suggestion of General
Winfield Scott), even the conservative Republicans of Massa-
cusetts would be won over to the Union ticket—especially since
the party's platform was already calculated to appeal to the
wealthy industrialists of the North. He expressed regret that so
many Southerners whom he felt should be supporting "American"
principles had deserted to the Democratic Party which had
cursed the country with its "agitation for slavery . . . . free trade,
and foreigners."[20] Given a leader like Crittenden, however, and
assurances that a "reliable organization" existed in other states—
and especially in the South—he felt certain that those conservatives who had left the party to vote for Frémont in 1856 would
be happy to come back to the fold in 1860. This was unparalleled
opportunity for the manufacturing classes of the North to join
with the slaveholders of the South to ward off the "irrepressible
conflict."[21]

For a short time, hopes ran high as prospects for North-South
accord seemed to be taking a turn for the better. The "Union of
the States" was more important than anything else, said Rufus
Choate, who insisted that all America's troubles would be ended

when union was preserved.[22] Amos A. Lawrence himself took a brief tour through the South early in 1860, and upon his return to Boston confidently assured his apprehensive neighbors that he had incurred no risk whatsoever. "How mistaken this opinion is of the two sections of the country in regard to the feelings of each other," he philosophized. "May God make them more friendly and more emulous and excel in promoting the great cause for which our government was made."[23] Seeking to impress his Southern friends with the need for a united opposition against the inroads of the Republican Party, Lawrence continued to plead the cause of national unity. "However badly we think of slavery (and the Northern sentiment is pretty much alike on that subject)," he wrote to Emerson Etheridge, Whig Representative from Tennessee, "we cannot jeopardize the Union of the States by strengthening a sectional organization."[24]

The appeal for national harmony was echoed, in a more formal and public manner, by Lawrence's friend and fellow-manufacturer, Nathan Appleton. Appleton had just read an article in the Richmond *Whig* by the Honorable William C. Rives of Virginia, and he was so impressed by the peaceful sentiments and reasonable approach of the Southerner that he immediately wrote an "open letter" to Mr. Rives, reviewing the mutual problems of the North and South, and pleading that the Union be preserved.[25] Addressing himself to his fellow-Northerners, Appleton asked them to give up their attempts to abolish slavery. Amalgamation was impossible, emigration was impractical, and annihilation was unthinkable. Since this exhausted the possibilities of any probable solution to the slavery problem in the United States, further actions, he concluded, were "utterly idle and futile."[26]

Turning to the Southerners, Appleton made a similar appeal to reason and forbearance. "Why continue this useless agitation on mere abstractions?" argued the manufacturer, when the South already *had* possession of all the land where slavery can be profitably employed. Why discuss theories of political power when the North was already outstripping the South in terms of population? Why discuss the possibilities of secession when the South could not even control a Presidential election? The time had come to face cold, hard facts. "Your true palladium is the Constitution of the United States," stated Appleton. "This is your ark of safety .... there is in reality nothing between the North and the South to quarrel about."[27]

W. C. Rives, former Representative, Senator, and Minister to France, was delighted to find that his own expressions of sympathy and affection had produced such a responsive reply from the Bay State, and immediately had copies made of the lengthy letter from Appleton for distribution to prominent men and newspapers throughout the State of Virginia.[28]

Despite all the expressions of friendship being exchanged between reasonable gentlemen of the North and the South, and despite all the fanfare of enthusiasm which accompanied the initial appearance of the Constitutional Union Party on the political scene in Massachusetts, there was really little hope for eventual success—and the leaders began to realize it. Lacking grass-roots support, bitterly assailed from all sides as "simpleminded snobs" and mercantile "Brahmins," the Unionists could not even prevail upon Senator John J. Crittenden, their trump card, to accept the nomination for the Presidency. Instead they had to settle for John Bell of Tennessee and Edward Everett of Massachusetts as their standard-bearers, much to the disgust of Amos A. Lawrence who considered the talents and national reputation of Crittenden indispensable to the cause of unionism.[29] Standing foursquare at their March convention upon "THE CONSTITUTION OF THE COUNTRY, THE UNION OF THE STATES, AND THE ENFORCEMENT OF THE LAWS"—as Everett expressed it, "without note or comment"—the new party based whatever hopes it had on drawing off the moderates and conservatives from the other parties with a deliberate noncommittal position on the slavery question.[30]

The political threat posed by the new party was not lost upon opposition leaders, and Constitutional Union adherents came under fire from two sides. Boston Democrats declared that *their* party was the only true "Constitutional Union Party" and appealed to the third party leaders to throw in their lot with the Democrats in order to defeat the Republicans and put the slavery question to rest forever. "Why turn weapons against each other," asked the Democratic *Post*, "that should be leveled against that bane to the country, the geographical party?"[31]

Using a combination of ridicule and bombast, the Republicans struck from the other side. "Its ticket is universally respectable. It is worthy to be printed on gilt-edged, satin paper, laid away in a box of musk and kept there," sneered the *Springfield Republican* as it surveyed the prominent Bay Staters who made up the leadership of the Constitutional Union Party. "It might as well have taken the multiplication table and the decalogue for its platform as the Constitution and the Union."[32] Blaming the Democrats for the past history of sectional agitation, the Republicans attempted to persuade Union leaders not to engage in competitive campaigning which would not only help the "common enemy" but which might well deprive the voting public of the right to decide the Presidential election.[33]

Before long, however, it became clear to practically everyone that with its lackluster candidates, its meaningless platform, its Whig antecedents, and its discredited Know-Nothing associations, the Constitutional Union Party had very little appeal in Massachusetts except for isolated pockets of conservative resistance in the industrial cities and towns. When Abraham Lincoln of Illinois was nominated by the Republican Party at its Chicago convention on May 16, 1860, Robert C. Winthrop was forced to admit, grudgingly, that the new man did have some "ability and amiability";[34] and even Amos A. Lawrence was ready to concede that *"Old Abe* and his split rails" had already won the public support of Massachusetts. Looking back over the hard work of the previous months, he denounced the timidity of his erstwhile friends who had promised so much and had done so little—"the intelligent conservative men, the great merchants and manufacturers"—who had expressed elaborate approval of the Union ticket, and then went out and voted for someone else.[35]

The only other measure Lawrence could think of to avoid having to accept a Republican candidate of Abolitionist leanings would be for conservatives to come together and agree upon some Republican whose views were moderate and acceptable. Toward this end, he offered an interesting proposition to Emerson Etheridge, a prominent supporter of the Constitutional Union Party. He recommended that the Southern opposition to the administration in Washington give solid support to Edward L. Bates, a moderate Republican and an old-time Whig, as the opposition candidate. The next step would be to urge that there be only one electoral ticket in each state for candidates opposed to the Democratic administration in power. If these proposals were carried out, Lawrence suggested there would be no need of a convention in Baltimore, and the Republicans would have to accept Bates—thus assuring the election of a conservative.[36] Nothing came of the plan, however—except for the unusual coincidence that both Amos A. Lawrence and Horace Greeley supported the same man for the Presidency!

It is ironic to observe that at the very time that the businessmen of Boston were giving up hope for the success of their Union Party, the merchants of New York had come to life again and were working for a coalition of all anti-Republican forces in the State. Realizing that New York's 35 electoral votes, together with the 135 electoral votes of the Southern states, might make it possible for the Empire State to prevent the election of a Republican candidate, the New York merchants worked energetically through the summer and fall of 1860 to effect a merger of the Douglas, Breckenridge, and Bell-Everett forces in the state.[37] For some reason, there seems to have been no attempt at coordination —indeed, no communication at all—between the New York businessmen and those in Boston with regard to joining forces or pooling their political resources. The New Yorkers appear to have ignored political developments in the Bay State; and while the Bostonians communicated frequently with political leaders in Virginia, Kentucky, Tennessee, and Pennsylvania, they indicated no particular desire to associate themselves with developments in New York. What would have happened if both New York and Massachusetts had been able to coordinate their activities and had denied the Republican candidate a total of 46 electoral votes is a matter of academic, but certainly fascinating political speculation.

In any case it was a losing cause. Although he failed to secure the vote of a single Southern state, Abraham Lincoln carried eighteen free states and he collected a total of 180 electoral votes. The Unionist candidate, John Bell, came in a disappointing third, with only 39 electoral votes representing three border states. Although New York City itself had supported the anti-Republican

Union ticket, the effects of the city vote were negligible compared with the Republican performance through the Empire State at large. And in Massachusetts, except for those isolated pockets of resistance in the industrial and commercial areas of the east, the Constitutional Union Party suffered a crushing defeat as the Bay State supported Lincoln for President and placed Republican John A. Andrew in the Governor's chair.[38]

The first reaction of the Northern manufacturer was to heave a disgusted sigh, shrug his shoulders in annoyance, and then proceed to endure life under a Republican administration with stoic calm and a philosophical outlook. After all, he rationalized, it *had* been a fair election, and under the circumstances it was a part of American political tradition to cooperate with a duly-elected Government—regardless of who was running it.[39] Besides, Lincoln himself had been a loyal Whig before he turned Republican! He was said to be a man of conservative tendencies and reflective instincts. "It is too early, as yet, to judge of the result," wrote Robert C. Winthrop, "but as Mr. Lincoln is a much more moderate person than any of the leaders of his party, I hope for the best."[40] There was no great cause for alarm; so why not wait and see what developed? Anxiously, the Northern conservatives pleaded with their Southern neighbors to adopt the same attitude.[41]

The South, however, could not look upon the election of Abraham Lincoln with such calm indifference. As soon as the results were known, the South Carolina legislature called a state convention which promptly adopted an Ordinance of Secession on December 20, 1860. Before the end of February, 1861, six other states of the lower South had marched defiantly out of the Union and had organized themselves into the "Confederate States of America."[42]

The North was stunned at the swiftness with which these events had taken place, and outraged at the idea of secession. Lawrence's friend John Bell condemned the idea in no uncertain terms: "By no principle of public law, by no code of morals, by no law of earth or heaven," he declared, "would Mississippi or any other State be justified, under existing circumstances, in withdrawing from the Union."[43] The Union was "a government of the people, instituted by the people of all the States," stated Boston's conservative newspaper, the *Advertiser*, and not a compact between the states which any state might rescind at pleasure.[44]

Appreciating the seriousness of the crisis, and realizing how little it would take to tip the balance in the direction of civil war, conservatives, North and South, anxiously sought some solution to the problem. From Kentucky, Crittenden wrote to Lawrence and suggested that if he could somehow bring pressure to bear upon the Massachusetts legislature to repeal the state's Personal Liberty Laws, this would be a tangible gesture which might "contribute materially to soothe and quiet the South."[45] While Lawrence promised to do what he could about the Personal Liberty Laws, in his response he tried to impress upon Crittenden the importance of avoiding any act of violence against the Federal Government—any incident, any blow, any shot—which, at this particular time, would "arouse and unite the whole Northern people." Nobody in the North or in the West had even thought about war or violence, he wrote. Nine out of ten people in the North would laugh if they were told that blood must be shed. "Not a musket or a pistol has been *bought* or *sold* for any civil strife," he concluded in an effort to emphasize the need for that atmosphere of reason and calm in which the search for a peaceful solution could be found.[46]

Of special concern to industrial Massachusetts, of course, was the initial impact of secession upon the Bay State economy. As early as December, 1860, an agonized wail went up from the manufacturing centers throughout the State as North-South trade came to an abrupt halt—and all for what Nathan Appleton contemptuously referred to as "an impracticable idea, a nonentity, connected with the institution of slavery."[47] Charles Eliot Norton commented upon the "universal alarm, general financial pressure, and great commercial embarrassment" which resulted from numerous business failures and factory shutdowns.[48] "Our money people here have been badly frightened," wrote John Murray Forbes to Charles Sumner, "and many decent-looking men . . . would try to have a kind of compromise made that would promise to patch up difficulties and their pockets."[49]

In southern Massachusetts, reports told of "hundreds" being

thrown out of work; and in the western counties observers predicted that the mills would shut down completely in ninety days.[50]
The *Courier* reported that the "Boston streets today are full of
discharged workmen," as the number of business failures began
to mount up.[51] The manufacturing interests, now badly frightened, watched the average prices of a share of stock in cotton
sheeting drop from $518.34 to $304.22, while stock sales were falling off at an alarming rate.[52] Some measure of the hysteria grip-
ping Boston may be seen in the frenzied way the popular wrath
was turned upon local abolition groups who were blamed for
having forced the slavery issue to such a critical and uncompro-
mising state of affairs. On December 3, 1860, a howling band of
businessmen and office clerks, "solid and respectable men," burst
into Tremont Temple and broke up a meeting commemorating
the execution of John Brown.[53] Wendell Phillips lashed out at
this "broadcloth mob" the following month, and in a thinly
veiled reference to the younger Lawrence, condemned the "snob-
bish sons of fathers lately rich, anxious to show themselves rotten
before they are ripe."[54] So great was public reaction against the
orator at this point, that it took the combined efforts of regular
Boston policemen, special detectives, and his own private body-
guard to keep the Abolitionist from being lynched as he left the
lecture hall.[55]

But this was a situation that demanded steady hands and
clear minds. Once again the Cotton Whigs of Massachusetts were
caught up in a frenzied effort to forestall bloodshed and restore
harmony to the Union. While compromise proposals were being
presented to the Congress by such men as William H. Seward of
New York in the Senate and Charles Francis Adams of Massachusetts in the House of Representatives, Union Meetings were
once again being held in Faneuil Hall in an attempt to arrive
at some point of mutual understanding with the alienated South.[56]

In the midst of these activities, William Appleton, the manufacturer, hurried down to the nation's capital in the middle of
December, 1860. He not only desired to find out firsthand just
how serious the political situation actually was, but he also hoped
to use his influence as an outstanding industrialist and former
congressman to foster the cause of intersectional peace. Despite

his seventy-five years, the slender old gentleman received numerous callers, visited both Houses of Congress, had dinner with President Buchanan, and discussed national affairs with his business colleagues from various parts of the country. The prospects, he was forced to admit, were not bright, and he was disturbed by what he saw—although he was not yet certain what it all meant. "No parties of any kind, all anxiety and gloom," he wrote in his diary, as he tried to fathom the strange mood of the city; "yet not without hope, but no present light."[57]

Reports of the growing seriousness of the situation convinced Appleton's fellow manufacturers back in New England that greater efforts were demanded of them if peace were to be preserved. A committee of leading conservatives in Massachusetts, headed by Amos A. Lawrence, William Appleton, Edward Everett, Benjamin Curtis, and George Ticknor Curtis, all former Constitutional Union supporters, circulated a petition through the State calling for the passage of the Crittenden Compromise. "If we have to go to battle," asked the Boston *Advertiser*, "will it not have been well for us to be able to say that we acted magnanimously, and did all that was possible for conciliation?" One petition, drawn up by the conservatives but designed to appeal to moderate Republicans, was phrased in general terms and merely called for a concerted effort directed at the "pacific settlement of our present difficulties."[58] Another petition, sarcastically labeled by its critics as the "Doughface Petition," and described as about a hundred yards long and a foot in diameter when rolled up, specifically endorsed the Crittenden Compromise and gathered over twenty-two thousand signatures when it was circulated throughout the Massachusetts communities. Both these documents were roundly denounced by Bay State Republicans as containing fraudulent signatures of persons whom they described as thoughtless, ignorant, and uninformed.[59]

Despite these barbs by local critics, a group of conservative "Union-Savers" led by Amos A. Lawrence, Edward Everett, and Robert C. Winthrop departed for Washington, D.C., bringing with them their highly touted petitions.[60] The Bay State leaders went to work with hopeful vigor although they were only a small part of the gigantic wave of business delegations which poured into the nation's capital during the last week of January, 1861 (leading Philip Foner to suggest that this might have been called "Businessman's Week"). The New York *Times* reported the arrival of the Boston group in the capital on January 24, and stated the assertion of the Bay State delegation that "a large number of the people of Massachusetts are in favor of the Crittenden resolutions."[61] The newspaper also reported that shortly after the arrival of the peacemakers, some "verbal sparring" took place between Lawrence and Charles Sumner who accused the conservatives of going far beyond the Breckinridge platform which had already been condemned by the American people when they elected Abraham Lincoln as President. The whole purpose of the delegation, said the Massachusetts Senator, was "all wind." Lawrence immediately snapped back that it was the "object of the Committee to prick a bag of wind and produce a collapse for their country's good."[62]

The bitter exchange between Lawrence and Sumner was undoubtedly heightened by developments in Boston. The Massachusetts conservatives staged a public demonstration at Faneuil Hall on February 5, 1861, in an effort to display their willingness to accept concession. As one Boston newspaper expressed it, the purpose of the meeting was "to expose the determination of the people of Massachusetts to override all questions of party and to subordinate all platforms in deference to the one great duty of preserving the Union."[63] Among those at the meeting who came out in favor of compromise, there were some who actively supported the Crittenden program. Charles A. Welch, for instance, voiced his "confidence that the North would make the necessary concessions . . . to preserve the Union"; and Nathaniel B. Shurtleff, Jr., announced that he would rather see all the " 'mementoes of the Revolution' swallowed up by the earth than have our soil deluged with our brothers' blood." As far as he was concerned, the question was not one of compromise, "but of showing the South some spirit of reconciliation."[64]

Despite the pleas for concession, however, the meeting itself was ineffective, largely because none of the resolutions proposed ever expressly endorsed the Crittenden plan. Indeed, the Compromise was "virtually ignored" by those present who expressed their willingness to sacrifice much for the sake of peace but were not prepared to go to the length of "endorsing a demand for the future perpetuation of the political power of slavery."[65] Although the compromise convention, therefore, was of little or no consequence in the city of Boston itself, many residents felt it was possible to convince other Northerners that Massachusetts was ready to support the pro-slavery resolutions of the Crittenden plan. As the *Journal* expressed it:

> There may be those abroad in other states who will only learn that a large meeting was held in Boston endorsing the pro-slavery demands of the Crittenden proposition and who will infer from this that the people of New England, willingly, yes eager, to go so far, are ready for any recreancy from their hitherto avowed principles.[66]

Undoubtedly hoping that the widespread reports of the compromise meeting would enhance the possibilities of their peace mission, Lawrence, Everett, and Winthrop passed along their huge petitions to Senator Crittenden who formally displayed them to the Senate on February 12, 1861. Here, he said, was overwhelming proof that a significant number of persons in the North desired a peaceful solution to the slavery problem according to the ideas which he had proposed in his compromise reestablishing the old Missouri Compromise and extending the 36° 30' line westward to the Pacific.[67]

Hardly had Crittenden stopped speaking when Senator Charles Sumner got to his feet, denouncing the petitions as meaningless. Either the signatures themselves were fraudulent, he charged, or else the citizens of Massachusetts had been completely hoodwinked —they didn't know what they were doing when they signed the documents![68]

In a masterpiece of sarcastic response, Crittenden asked his colleagues in the Senate whether or not they could believe Mr. Sumner any longer. For years, he pointed out, Sumner had continually boasted to the Senate of the high level of literacy among the people of his home-state. If the citizens of Massachusetts were so well educated, asked Crittenden, how then could they possibly be so ignorant of the petitions which they had signed?[69]

While the debate continued in the Senate, the "Union Savers" were hard at work trying to get further support for the Crittenden Compromise and their own peace petitions. They called on President Buchanan, Vice-President Breckinridge, General Winfield Scott, Governor Seward, Senator Sumner, and practically any other prominent political figure who would listen to them. Desperately they tried to impress the leaders of the Government with the urgency of their appeal for national unity and intersectional harmony.

But it was a losing battle. The delegates from the Bay State found hospitality and sympathy—ex-President John Tyler offered "sincere sympathy" with their mission, and Millard Fillmore prayed that "you will do all you can to save the Union"—but there was no promise of action.[70] Perhaps Senator Sumner expressed the cold realities of the situation best when he told the crestfallen committeemen, with a cynical smile, that their efforts were "of no more use than a penny whistle in a tempest."[71]

Their mission a failure, Everett and Lawrence were forced to make their way back to Boston in the face of laughter and ridicule. "Only think of it!" crowed the *Springfield Republican,* "the great Boston petition has come to naught. The mission of Everett has failed; Lawrence hasn't saved the Union. And why? Simply because their petition didn't mean anything. Just imagine Mr. Everett administering a bread-pill to the invalid Union; and Amos Lawrence carrying a pint of cold water to extinguish the great conflagration which is already licking the pillars of the grand Temple of Liberty."[72]

It seemed that the only remaining hope of averting war rested with the "Peace Convention" that was assembling at Willard's Hotel at the corner of Fourteenth Street in Washington, even as the despondent businessmen were packing their bags and preparing to return to Boston. First suggested by the State of Virginia as a means of averting hostilities, the Peace Convention received a favorable response from a number of Northern and Border states, and it was scheduled to begin its deliberations early in February, 1861.[73]

Governor John A. Andrew of Massachusetts, long a bitter foe of slavery, was reluctant to give any official sign of support or even recognition to a movement which he regarded as foolish and futile. On the other hand, however, he feared that men like Lawrence and Everett might "volunteer" their own services in the name of the Bay State, and so he sent a group of prominent anti-slavery Republicans to join the delegations from fourteen other states in this late attempt to stop the clock. Andrew took this action over the outraged protests of antislavery leaders like Charles Sumner so that Massachusetts would not later be accused of having failed to work for the maintenance of the Union through peaceful means. "I am a little afraid," he mused, "that absence would confirm the charge of indifference which is much used against us."[74]

Hopes began to run high. In business circles, stocks started to rise and financial journals reported the disappearance of "panic" and the quieting of "commercial fears." The "political diffi- culties," readers were assured, would soon be settled and the crisis would be ended "within a short time."[75] The momentary optimism that war might be averted was further reflected in the upward swing in New England textile sales during late February and early March, 1861, while the Peace Convention was holding its meetings.[76]

It was no use. A meeting with President Buchanan yielded noth- ing. Perhaps a session with the President-elect would offer more. Less than twenty-four hours after Lincoln arrived in Washington, delegates of the Peace Commission called on him in an attempt to get some positive commitment on his future policies. The reception in Parlor Number 6 of Willard's Hotel was quite in- formal, as the delegates gathered around the strange, tall figure, anxious to get a close look at the rail-splitter from Illinois, strain- ing to hear any word or phrase that would give the slightest hope for a peaceful compromise.[77]

Everything went quietly for a while, with Lincoln chatting affably with the delegates, moving quickly from one to another, shaking hands, renewing old acquaintances, making new ones. To all queries and questions Lincoln held out no other course than that supplied by the Constitution itself. "My course is as plain as a turnpike road," he told William C. Rives. "It is marked out by the Constitution. I am in no doubt which way to go."

The civility of the discussions was suddenly broken by James

A. Seddon of Virginia (later to be Secretary of War in the Confederate government) who charged the Republican Party with having encouraged John Brown and William Lloyd Garrison in their attempts to provoke slave insurrections in the South. When Lincoln dryly observed that Brown had been hanged and that Garrison was in prison, Seddon blasted the Northerners for not having carried out the statutes calling for the return of fugitive slaves. Again Lincoln quietly parried by pointing out that fugitive slaves *had* been returned—from the very shadow of Boston's Faneuil Hall, in fact. Although people in the North were required to observe the letter of the law, he said, there was nothing in the law which forced them to enjoy their work.

"Your press is incendiary!" cried Seddon, suddenly changing his attack; and he went on to accuse the newspapers of the North of promoting slave uprisings and murder in the South.

At this point Lincoln's smile faded and his tone became sharp. "I beg pardon, Mr. Seddon," he replied. "I intend no offense, but I will not suffer such a statement to pass unchallenged, because it is not true. No Northern newspaper, not the most ultra, has advocated a slave insurrection or advised slaves to cut their masters' throats. A gentleman of your intelligence should not make such assertions. We do maintain the freedom of the press—we deem it necessary to a free government. Are we peculiar in that respect? Is not the same doctrine held in the South?"

Passing on to other members of the delegation, Lincoln greeted each one and chatted pleasantly about personal affairs. As he mingled with the New York group, William E. Dodge raised his voice so that he could be heard throughout the room. Dodge hoped to get a preview of what Lincoln intended to say in his inaugural address, and he asked whether the President-elect expected that grass would grow in the streets of the commercial cities of the nation?

Lincoln, however, had maintained his silence all the way from Springfield and had no intention of letting down now. As far as he was concerned, he replied with a disarming smile, hoping to brush the question aside, the only place grass would grow was in the fields and meadows where it always grew.

But Dodge was on him like a tiger. "Then you will yield to

the just demands of the South?" "You will admit slave states into the Union on the same conditions as free states?" "You will not go to war on account of slavery?"

As the room suddenly quieted and the delegates waited in silence for Lincoln's reply, the tall man slowly answered in tones that were stern and measured and thoughtful. He said evenly,

> I do not know that I understand your meaning, Mr. Dodge, nor do I know what acts or opinions may be in the future, beyond this. If I shall ever come to the great office of President of the United States, I shall take an oath. I shall swear that I will faithfully execute the office of President of the United States, of all the United States, and that I will, to the best of my ability, preserve, protect, and defend the Constitution of the United States. . . . It is not the Constitution as I would like to have it, but as it *is*, that is to be defended. The Constitution will not be preserved and defended until it is enforced and obeyed in every part of every one of the United States. It must be so respected, obeyed, enforced, and defended—let the grass grow where it may.

No one could answer. No one could think of anything to say. The determined words and the unquestionable tone of authority with which they had been delivered stunned the delegates. The new man was prepared to give one promise, and only one, relating to his future conduct as President: He would obey the Constitution of the United States.

From this point on, the situation became more depressing behind the doors of the conference room as it became evident, day after day, that it was impossible to arrive at any satisfactory grounds for compromise. Every attempt to bring up the Crittenden proposals was fought down by Northerners as outright "surrender," while the Southern representatives were determined that they would accept nothing less. "The Peace Congress," observed John Murray Forbes, "was slowly talking against time, and coming to no conclusions."[78] Somewhat less kindly, the New York *Tribune* referred to the gathering as "a convocation of old hens sitting on a nest of eggs, some of which would hatch out vipers, while most were addled."[79]

Just before March 4, 1861, the ineffectual convention concluded its sessions, with most of the departing members convinced that all hopes of reconstructing the Union were gone and that civil war was imminent. With the news that the main purposes of the Peace Congress had failed, the stock market collapsed and sales in New England plummeted to an appalling new low.[80] By Inauguration Day, the mood of the nation matched the raw, biting chill of that memorable day in March when the new President promised no conflict, unless the South provoked it—a promise that left everyone as tense and as uncertain as before.

9

THE POINT OF NO RETURN

ABRAHAM LINCOLN had been in office less than a month when he received word from Major Anderson, commander of Fort Sumter, that his garrison must either be supplied with food by April 15, or be withdrawn. The Federal Government regarded Fort Sumter, located in Charleston harbor, as United States property which must be maintained and defended. The Confederate States regarded it as the property of a foreign power—a potential threat which must be removed. If the President sent a relief vessel to the fort, he would be accused of an act of aggression that would undoubtedly touch off a full-scale civil war. If he did not send relief, he was failing in his duty as President and Commander in Chief, and would be giving tacit recognition that the Union was, in fact, broken.[1]

Even as the new President was pondering his deadly dilemma, and as the nation watched and waited, William Appleton was sailing out of New York harbor aboard the steamer *Nashville*, bound for Charleston, South Carolina.[2] This trip to the South, insisted the elderly industrialist, was for "reasons of health," but there were many of his Bay State neighbors who accused him of other motives in going to South Carolina at such a critical moment. Convinced that Appleton intended some kind of an eleventh-hour attempt at compromise, Charles Hale, editor of the Boston *Daily Advertiser*, publicly criticized Appleton's visit on the grounds that it would "cruelly deceive" the South into believing that they would find any kind of "active sympathy" in the North.[3]

On the evening of Thursday, April 11, 1861, the *Nashville* lay off the Bar outside Charleston harbor, awaiting the turn of the morning tide. About four o'clock the next morning, the crash of cannon fire brought startled passengers rushing from their cabins in their nightclothes. Peering through the darkness before them, they watched with amazement as the guns of the Confederate shore batteries opened fire on the federal fort. Lincoln had finally decided to supply Sumter with the needed provisions, and the booming guns of Confederate shore batteries proved to be South Carolina's answer to what it regarded as an invasion of its soil. "Every flash we could see," wrote Appleton, breathless with excitement, "then the smoke; then followed the report; the bombshells we saw ascend and would anxiously watch whether they fell in Fort Sumter."[4]

As soon as he could reach shore, the old gentleman elbowed his way through the cheering crowds and the marching squares of the "seven or eight thousand troops in this vicinity," and telegraphed the electrifying news to his colleagues back in Massachusetts.[5] The guns of Sumter had spoken.

There was no doubt at all in the minds of the cotton manufacturers of Massachusetts that their place was with the Union— "We must stand by our country," John Whitin, manufacturer of textile machinery, told a customer somewhat ruefully.[6] Robert C. Winthrop could see no alternative but to "support the powers that be . . . in their measures for defending the Capital and upholding the Flag of the Country."[7] Amos A. Lawrence assured William Appleton that in the North there was now a "unanimity of sentiment about sustaining the government." "There will be no difficulty in obtaining men if the means of supply and transportation are at hand," he said, and promptly went off to offer his own services to the state.[8] Turning all his resources over to the Federal Government, Lawrence now devoted all his extra time to drilling regiments of local volunteers and instructing young Harvard undergraduates in the manual of arms. The manufacturer had become as enthusiastic in the cause of winning the war as he had been in working to preserve the peace—indeed, he expressed disappointment that Lincoln had only called for 75,000 volunteers—500,000 would be more like it, he told William Appleton.[9] A short time later he offered his services to Secretary of the

Treasury Salmon P. Chase who was trying to work out a plan to move Southern staples to Northern markets. Pointing to his years of experience as a large buyer in Southern markets for manufacturing purposes, Lawrence offered to serve the Government without pay "at any personal inconvenience and risk on any part of the Atlantic coast."[10]

And yet, although civil war was an accomplished fact, and he had made his own position clear, Lawrence felt morally bound to make at least one last effort to preserve what was left of the Union. In hopes of prevailing upon his friends and acquaintances in the Border states to remain loyal, Lawrence dispatched a flood of letters, stressing the factor of unanimity in the North and emphasizing the determination of its war effort. "The North is becoming one great army," he told his old friend, John J. Crittenden of Kentucky. "Every man is for supporting the government at all hazards, and there will be no delay in moving vast masses of fighting-men down to the border." It would be very sad if the Union men in the Border states would not stand up for their country. "Cannot you rally them?" he appealed.[11]

To another Unionist in Kentucky, the Reverend Robert Jefferson Breckinridge, a longtime opponent of slavery, Lawrence directed a similar plea. If Kentucky would send even a single regiment of Union men to defend the capital, it would be enough to change the attitude in the North which he described as being bent upon a gigantic invasion of the South and the Border states and the destruction of slave property. Reminding Breckinridge that he himself had been opposed to the election of Abraham Lincoln, Lawrence now insisted that the Republican administration was not determined upon a war of aggression—"Its struggle now is only to sustain the existence of the government." Blaming the South and its belligerent attitude for causing the present crisis, Lawrence emphasized his belief that the "North has been growing more and more conservative since December, and the South had nothing to fear, absolutely nothing." It was the bombardment of Fort Sumter and Jefferson Davis's "piratical proclamation" which had aroused the North to arms, said Lawrence, and he predicted that there would be a great Northern tide of sentiment that would produce a large army ready to invade the

South and crush out the institution of slavery. "Your property is
doomed to certain destruction unless some portion of your people
march to the present relief of the Government."[12] Letters of a
similar nature were sent to the Honorable James Guthrie of
Louisville, a prominent Unionist legislator and railroad promoter,
and to George William Brown, mayor of the City of Baltimore.[13]
Lawrence also made efforts to help influence friends in Virginia.
"We have bad accounts from Virginia," he wrote to a friend,
Robert Ridgeway, in Richmond shortly after Anderson's sur-
render. "Why cannot the Union men stand by the Government?"
he asked as he tried to dramatize the fact that the people in the
North were highly indignant over the attack on Fort Sumter and
determined to vindicate the honor of the Federal Government.
"Business and pleasure are forgotten, and every man is a volunteer.
Party lines are blotted out; we all stand together." He ended this
letter with the question: "Who will rally the Union men of
Virginia?"[14]

While Maryland and Kentucky continued to remain with the
Union, Virginia and Tennessee decided to join their embattled
sisters in the Confederacy. When Tennessee seceded, John Bell,
a native son and the candidate of the constitutional Union Party
in 1860, followed his State into secession. This was a particularly
bitter blow to Northern conservatives in general, and to Amos
A. Lawrence in particular, and he quickly wrote a personal letter
to Bell in hope that the first reports were incorrect: "Permit me
to ask you to relieve your friends here from the unpleasant position in which we are placed by the information which comes to
us in the newspapers that you have advised the people of Tennessee 'to form a military league with the other Southern States
against the common invading foe.' " Lawrence could not believe
it possible that the candidate of the Union Party who went into
the campaign under the banner of "The Constitution, the Union,
and the enforcement of the laws," had now abandoned the flag
in the hour of its greatest trial. "Is it possible," he wrote, "that
our Constitutional Union leader is giving aid and comfort to
traitors, while the Democrat Andrew Johnson of Tennessee is
suffering obloquy at the hands of a mob?" All the Union men of
Massachusetts, Lawrence proudly asserted, remained faithful to

the government, the Constitution, and the laws of the country. He closed his letter with the personal hope that Bell would not, "at this late hour," mar the beauty of a long and consistent public career by "aiding a sectional party to overthrow the grandest Government on earth."[15]

While the textile manufacturers had determined upon their own political positions and responsibilities, their economic future was in a state of grave uncertainty now that civil war had become a reality. What could be done? Their factory workers were either going off to the front in large numbers, or else they were leaving the mills to take higher paying jobs in defense industries.[16] Hundreds of millions of dollars owed by Southern merchants could no longer be collected, and staggering business losses were being written off by Northern wholesalers. Reports from the South pointed out that most merchants and planters "seemed to delight in the fancied release from their obligations secession gives them."[17] But the most serious threat was the lack of raw cotton. The proposed Union blockade was sure to cut off the export supply of cotton; the Confederacy insisted that it would produce no more; and Great Britain was already bidding lavishly for the reserve stocks held by various New England mills.[18] Behind closed doors in every textile factory, worried groups of men held worried conferences in a frantic effort to hammer out some solution. What should they do? What *could* they do?

The only possibility which offered any hope at all to the distraught manufacturers was that the war would be a short one; and with almost childlike naiveté they clung fiercely to this comforting thought—the dream of "peace in ninety days." The shameful Federal rout at Bull Run in July, 1861, rocked the North back on its heels and sent cloth sales to unprecedented lows by the close of 1861; but the news of Grant's capture of Fort Donelson in February, 1862, the victory of the *Monitor* over the *Merrimac* in March, and then the occupation of New Orleans in April, restored a large measure of confidence in the North. An anxious New England relaxed again, sat back complacently and waited for the news of the Confederate surrender. Oliver Wendell Holmes confided to his friend John Motley, the historian: "The almost universal feeling is that the rebellion is knocked on the head," and Amos A. Lawrence assured his sister that the Union would be maintained, and that the "stars and stripes" would wave over the entire seaboard "before New Year's and over the whole country before another New Year's after that," adding with finality: "There is no more doubt about it than that the sun will rise."[19] Newspaper readers were informed that the "rebellion is crumbling" and that the "backbone of the rebellion is broken." Although, it was admitted, there might be a *little* more fighting, the final "subjugation of the enemy will be comparatively easy."[20]

Once again convinced that the war would be a relatively short one, some textile companies, tempted by the profits offered by the high price of cotton, decided to shut down their operations completely and sell off their raw cotton at a handsome profit—all in the expectation that it would be "business as usual" after a brief but inconvenient interlude. Lowell was the classic example: In that city the Merrimack Manufacturing Company, followed by eight or nine others, closed down their plants, sent their workers home, took their profits on the sale of raw cotton—and plunged their community into years of tragic depression.[21] Other companies, with sufficient capital reserves and a moderate supply of cotton on hand, decided to stay in operation on a reduced scale, employ a skeleton force, and use the idle time to rebuild and enlarge their manufacturing facilities. Philosophically, these owners prepared themselves for the period of great activity which they felt must inevitably follow the end of this "short war" when cotton would once again be plentiful. Still other plants, however, determined to keep their skilled personnel intact and their mills running at full blast. Sparked by the prospect of lucrative government contracts and orders from the Army for uniforms, tents, and other military equipment, directors of these factories bought up as much cotton as possible and hoped to reap a brief but highly profitable harvest while other plants were idle.[22]

But the idyllic dreams of a swift Union victory and a catastrophic collapse of the rebellion came to a sudden end. In June, 1862, General George B. McClellan started off on his much-heralded Peninsular Campaign—and then all was strangely silent. For five days, even official Washington did not know the whereabouts of the Army of the Potomac. When the truth finally reached the North during the first week in July—over fifteen thousand men killed, wounded, or missing, millions of dollars worth of lost stores, the incredible tales of the bloody "Seven Days' Battle"—it was apparent to everyone that this was not going to be a "short war" and that the Confederacy was not about to collapse of its own weight. Wall Street reacted in panic. Textile sales dropped 75 percent in a single month; and the mill owners of Massachusetts, having already dumped most of their cotton reserves on the open market in exchange for short-term profits, could only look on in helpless frustration at empty factories and idle spindles. With a long war in sight, and the possibilities of obtaining raw cotton from a belligerent South terribly remote, the Cotton Whigs of Massachusetts suddenly found themselves, as Amos A. Lawrence expressed it, "looking forward into empty space . . . ."[23]

But their great political dilemma was now over. The era of compromise, concessions, Faneuil Hall meetings, elaborate programs, and complicated petitions, was a thing of the past. Although the Cotton Whigs would have to work out their individual financial arrangements during the course of the war itself, to resort to almost fantastic lengths to obtain their precious cotton supplies in order to run their factories and meet their contracts, their immediate purpose was now clear and their goal was self-evident: The Union must be saved.

War had come to New England. It was a war that many prominent and influential New Englanders had long feared, and a war that many of them had worked long and hard to avoid. Although the specific efforts of the Massachusetts Cotton Whigs ultimately proved to be unsuccessful and futile, the very *fact* of their efforts is historically significant. That these New Englanders were willing to go to such extremes in order to avert a conflict which they considered to be both political and economic suicide, shows quite clearly that at least one influential portion of the North did *not* regard the economic differences between the North and the South as essentially divergent or necessarily antithetical.

On the contrary, the cotton textile interests of the Bay State consistently regarded the economy of the South as a basic supplement and, above all, a necessity to the economy of the North. While it is true that these men showed moral aversion to the institution of Negro slavery, time and time again they demonstrated their willingness to forego their personal convictions in order to maintain the political unity and economic stability of the nation.

The motives of the cotton manufacturer of Massachusetts in pursuing his course of action were not due solely and exclusively to reasons of economic self-interest, but to an overwhelming desire to preserve the constitutional structure of the American Union—as he saw it. Contrary to traditional stereotypes of the antebellum businessman, this attitude was no haphazard rationalization of political views periodically adjusted to suit the temporary financial situation; rather, it was a coherent, consistent, and logical pattern of constitutional belief. In the interests of national unity, the Northern industrialist, as typified by Amos A. Lawrence, showed himself ready and willing to compromise with the South on matters of economic policy. He gradually lessened his insistence on a high protective tariff, and even indicated a cooperative attitude with regard to efforts of the South to become industrialized. Regardless of his personal dislike of slavery, the manufacturer went out of his way to denounce and attack the Abolitionists who sought to tamper with the "peculiar institution" where it was already established under the protective sanction of constitutional law.

The Northern industrialist did have moral scruples about the continued existence of slavery in the United States, however, and when the course of national expansion threatened to take the institution far beyond established constitutional limits he saw it as his right and his duty to work against this development. His opposition to the annexation of Texas and his bitter denunciation of the Mexican War attested to the violence of his opinion on this score. And his acceptance of the Compromise of 1850 came only after he was morally convinced that the geography and topography of the Western lands involved would automatically prohibit the importation of slaves. In return for granting the South the principle of extending slavery into the Western territories, the Northern manufacturer felt assured that his Southern brethren would not resort to its practice. In the year 1850, many a mill owner of the Bay State considered his constitutional position justified in theory, and also workable in practice. The constitutional privileges of the South had been upheld; but slavery in the territories had been prevented.

The Kansas-Nebraska Act upset the delicate political balance the Cotton Whigs had worked so hard to achieve by throwing the lands in the Middle West open to slavery. Despite the sense of personal outrage which characterized the violent reaction of the cotton men of the North, they still continued to operate within the rigid framework of constitutional procedure. The Emigrant Aid movement, designed to populate the Kansas Territory with Free-Soil settlers, was carefully conducted by Lawrence and his associates in the states of the Northeast as an exclusively volunteer and unofficial enterprise, disassociated from all contact with the Federal Government. Even while they made every effort to establish free government in Kansas, the Cotton Whigs continued their efforts to impress the South with the honesty of their intentions and the sincerity of their purpose.

But while the conservatives themselves could find ways to make elaborate mental distinctions between what their activities in Kansas meant and what they did not mean, most of these theoretical niceties were lost upon the greater part of the American public. Northerners rejoiced that the businessmen of the nation had seen the light and had joined in the antislavery crusade, while Southerners could only regard this as further evidence of the growing Northern conspiracy to destroy their traditional way of life. Not only did the reaction of the Cotton Whigs to Douglas and his Kansas-Nebraska Act make it impossible for them to maintain their separate political status much longer, but it brought a new dimension to the nationwide controversy over slavery. For the first time in more than twenty years, the business community of the Northeast had departed from its traditional position of strict neutrality to take a direct and active part in the struggle to prevent the expansion of slavery into the territories.

Unaware of the broader meaning of their activities in opposing the Kansas-Nebraska Act, the apparent success of their Emigrant Aid ventures convinced the Cotton Whigs that they had discovered a sound and workable political formula by which they could continue to maintain friendly relations with the South and with Southerners while at the same time working effectively toward the gradual containment and eventual elimination of slavery. They soon found, however, that their ideals were almost impossible to implement because of the rapidly shifting political situation. Having lost the support of the young Conscience Whigs, and with their old leaders dying off, the old-line conservatives were already fighting for their political lives when the Kansas-Nebraska Act precipitated the crisis that was so painfully imminent. At this point Lawrence and his colleagues had one major objective in mind as they struggled to remain alive amid the rubble and debris of their splintered party—to prevent a clear-cut victory by either the Democratic Party which they regarded as increasingly Southern and pro-slavery, or by the newly created Republican Party which they considered to be controlled by fanatic Conscience Whigs and Abolitionists, until such time as the old Whig Party could be reorganized and revived again as a major national force.

Toward this end, the Cotton Whigs fought desperately against the "fusion" movement in Massachusetts as Republicans tried to gather dissident elements for the new party. In the temporary political vacuum which was created when the Whig Party moved out and before the Republican Party actually moved in, the "American" Party appeared with an explosive force that was startling to everyone. The social basis of the Know-Nothing Party was a violent anti-Catholic, anti-foreign bigotry which continued to make its presence felt during the 1850's, but the political force welding together a motley collection of local nativist groups into a national organization of unusual proportions was the Kansas-Nebraska Act and the political realignments which it produced.

Dissatisfied with their own parties, and not yet certain about the future political prospects of the newly established Republican Party, conservative Whigs, antislavery Democrats, and ardent Free-Soilers quickly moved into the ranks of the American Party with the hope of taking over its organization for their own purposes. But the "American" experience was as brief as it was un-expected; and by 1856 its moment of glory had already faded away. Its conservative programs, its varied membership, and its reactionary ethnic appeals could not keep pace with the rush of national events. Bloodshed in Kansas, the sack of Lawrence, John Brown's raid at Osawatomie, and the beating of Senator Charles Sumner, all contributed to the overwhelming defeat of Fillmore and the American Party in 1856. Slavery was still the most pressing issue facing the American electorate by the mid-1850's, and the voters would not be distracted by issues not connected with slavery.

Despite the collapse of the American Party in 1856, the Cotton Whigs still persevered in their determination to keep alive a third party—a truly conservative party. They saw—perhaps more clearly than any other single group in the United States at that time—that the critical issues of the 50's were forcing the nation toward accepting a two-party system that was not based upon political ideologies but upon geographical divisions. The Demo-cratic Party more and more appeared a distinctly pro-slavery party, a "Southern" party, while the Republican Party was looked upon as an antislavery party, an exclusively "Northern" party. The conservatives consistently pointed out that such a polarization of political views would lead not only to national division but to eventual civil war, and they made every effort to provide a con-crete political alternative to what they regarded as the movement toward political suicide and national destruction.

For a brief time, especially when the Panic of 1857 forced con-servatives and businessmen throughout the North to take stock of their political attitudes toward the South, it looked as though there might be a possibility for some measure of reconciliation, and during 1858 the Cotton Whigs of Massachusetts worked furiously to establish a new "fusion" party of their own made up of hard-core Whigs, former "Americans," and moderate Demo-crats. But John Brown's raid at Harpers Ferry in October, 1859, destroyed whatever chance this new organization had for national survival. The hysterical excitement which this latest incident produced made party lines more rigid than ever before and brought the hopes of conservatives crashing down upon their heads.

But a last remaining hope that the spectre of disunion and civil war might shock the American public into rejecting the extremist positions of both sectional parties prompted the Cotton Whigs into a final try at political action—the Constitutional Union Party. By linking together the conservatives of New England with the conservatives of such Border states as Kentucky and Tennessee, Lawrence and his friends in Massachusetts hoped to offer the voters of the North and the South a national ticket based upon reason and moderation, a party that avoided the uncertain prospects offered by the Democrats and the Republicans. Pleading the cause of national unity and constitutional law, studiously avoiding the controversial slavery issue, seeking to make common cause with the moderates in every section who might be searching for a middle road to peace and mutual understanding, the Cotton Whigs attempted to provide the electorate with an alternative.

Once again, however, it was a losing cause. Voters, both in Massachusetts and throughout the nation, overwhelmingly rejected what they considered the shopworn and reactionary platform of old-line Whigs who had retreated into the politics of the past and blinded themselves to the realities of the moment. The election of the Republican candidate, Abraham Lincoln, in November of 1860, touched off a train of events which the Cotton Whigs had tried to prevent and could not stop. Despite frantic efforts at compromise, elaborate petitions, personal appeals, and eleventh-hour conferences, the guns of Sumter spoke and the nation plunged into civil war.

As far as the cotton manufacturer was concerned, the Civil War came about *despite* his efforts—certainly not because of them —and in this point lies the historical significance of such a study. If, as Philip Foner has demonstrated in his *Business and Slavery*, the New York City merchants and financiers were unalterably opposed to war between the North and the South; and if, as this study has attempted to show, the Massachusetts cotton manufacturers and industrialists assumed a remarkably similar position —then what Northern economic forces *did* desire an intersectional conflict? Indeed, it might be pointed out that rather than a deliberate and concerted effort by Northern Capitalism to force such a war upon the agrarian South, one of the main reasons for the failure of political conservatism in the 1850's to provide an effective alternative to the political crisis was the fact that there was practically no contact between the capital interests of the North in pursuing objectives of common interest. Noticeable by its very absence is the lack of any extensive correspondence between the Cotton Whigs of Boston, the Hunkers of New York City, or the industrial interests of Philadelphia during the 1840's and 1850's concerning either national affairs or local developments. Although there are occasional references to the Texas question, the Mexican War, the Compromise of 1850, the fusion movement, the Presidential elections, and the Crittenden proposals, there is no evidence at all that conservative Whigs in one state made any serious or sustained efforts to work in close cooperation with groups in other states to achieve political ends. Even during the creation of the Emigrant Aid societies, which marked an unusual degree of interregional cooperation between Northern financial capitals during the Kansas crisis, close association was kept to a minimum and Amos A. Lawrence kept a careful eye on the Massachusetts organization to see that it did not become involved with those in other states. "We are of the opinion that our efficiency will be increased by confining our operations to a small sphere," he wrote to a friend in Washington, D.C., in August, 1854, "and that we should embarrass ourselves by forming any connection with any other society."[24]

Throughout the late 1850's, conservatives in Boston, New York, and Philadelphia engaged in extensive correspondence with conservative leaders in the Southern states and in the Border states— but they did not communicate with each other! Conservative political reactions and movements in New York City were almost identical with those of Boston during the same period of time, and yet there is no indication that any effort was made to coordinate these efforts toward a common goal through the use of common means. It seems, therefore, that contrary to the traditional stereotype of the capitalistic "juggernaut" making war upon a passive and unresisting South, Northern capitalists failed to maintain the peace and stability which they desired for economic prosperity because they did not make common cause, pool their economic interests, or coordinate their political forces during the critical years.

As more evidence comes to light regarding the economic policies, the political beliefs, and the personal convictions of the
American businessman before the Civil War, it is more difficult
than ever to sustain the thesis that the Civil War was the product
of an "inevitable" clash of two separate and divergent economic
systems. On the contrary, the American manufacturer was among
the most powerful and influential forces consistently working to
prevent the disruption of the Union and energetically seeking to
establish harmonious relations between the North and the South.

Notes

⚜ INTRODUCTION

1. Philip Foner, *Business and Slavery* (Chapel Hill, 1941), 318–22.
2. Charles and Mary Beard, *The Rise of American Civilization* (2 Vols., New York, 1927), II, 6–7.
3. *Ibid.*, 10.
4. Thomas J. Pressly, *Americans Interpret Their Civil War* (Princeton, 1954), 208.
5. Vernon L. Parrington, *Main Currents in American Thought* (3 Vols., New York, 1927–30), III, xxiv.
6. *Ibid.*, xxiii, 3.
7. Frank L. Owsley, "The Fundamental Cause of the Civil War: Egocentric Sectionalism," *Journal of Southern History*, VII (1941), 4–6.
8. Frank L. Owsley, "The Irrepressible Conflict," *I'll Take My Stand* (New York, 1930), 91.
9. Kenneth Stampp, *And the War Came* (Baton Rouge, 1950), 2.
10. Roy Nichols, *The Disruption of American Democracy* (New York, 1948), 24.
11. Charles W. Thompson, *The Fiery Epoch, 1830–77* (Indianapolis, 1931), 25; Henry H. Simms, *A Decade of Sectional Controversy, 1851–61* (Chapel Hill, 1942), 187.
12. Avery Craven, *The Repressible Conflict, 1830–61* (Baton Rouge, 1939), 96–97.
13. Avery Craven, *Democracy in American Life* (Chicago, 1941), 13, 111–12.
14. Charles Grier Sellers, "Who Were the Southern Whigs?" *American Historical Review*, LIX (1954), 333–46.
15. B. C. Forbes, ed., *America's Fifty Foremost Business Leaders* (New York, 1948); Frank Taussig and Carl Joslyn, *American Business Leaders: A*

Study in Social Origins and Social Stratification (New York, 1932); William Henry, "The Business Executive: The Psychodynamics of a Social Role," *American Journal of Sociology*, LIV (1949), 286–91; William Miller, "American Historians and the Business Elite," *Journal of Economic History*, IX (1949), 184–200.

16. Dexter Perkins, "We Shall Gladly Teach," *American Historical Review*, LXII (1957), 306.
17. Allan Nevins, *John D. Rockefeller: The Heroic Age of American Enterprise* (2 Vols., New York, 1940); George Gibb and Evelyn Knowlton, *The Resurgent Years: History of the Standard Oil Company, 1911–27* (New York, 1957).
18. Evelyn H. Knowlton, *Pepperell's Progress* (Cambridge, 1948); Thomas R. Navin, *The Whitin Machine Works Since 1831* (Cambridge, 1950); George S. Gibb, *The Saco-Lowell Shops: Textile Machinery Building in New England* (Cambridge, 1950).
19. See Louis M. Hacker, review of Gibb and Knowlton, *Resurgent Years*, in *The New York Times Book Review*, January 27, 1957.
20. Glyndon Van Deusen, "Some Aspects of Whig Thought and Theory in the Jackson Period," *American Historical Review*, LXIII (1958), 305–22.
21. Thomas Cochran, "The Social Sciences and the Problem of Historical Synthesis," *The Varieties of History*, ed. Fritz Stern (New York, 1957), 356–57.
22. Parrington, *op. cit.*, I, 3–4.

1 ⅍ THE MERCHANT AND THE MILLER

1. Louis M. Sears, *Jefferson and the Embargo* (Durham, North Carolina, 1927), 145; Ruhl J. Bartlett, "Commerce and Industry," *Commonwealth History of Massachusetts* (5 Vols., A. B. Hart, ed., New York, 1929), III, 533–34.
2. Sears, *op. cit.*; Samuel Eliot Morison, *Maritime History of Massachusetts* (Boston, 1921), 191.
3. Sears, *op. cit.*, 152–53. Sears gives a list of over five thousand signatures on Massachusetts petitions during the months of March and April, 1808.
4. Edward F. Humphrey, *Economic History of the United States* (New York, 1931), 167–68; Glenn Tucker, *Poltroons and Patriots* (2 Vols., New York, 1954), I, 45.
5. Bartlett, *op. cit.*, III, 543–44.
6. Tucker, *op. cit.*, I, 23; Claude M. Fuess, "Massachusetts in the Union," *Commonwealth History of Massachusetts*, 435–36; Morison, *op. cit.*, 195–98.
7. Comparative banking statistics are provided in *Niles' Register*, VII (December, 1814), 195–96.

8. Morison, *op. cit.*, 207–09.
9. Gardner W. Allen, "Massachusetts in the War of 1812," *Commonwealth History of Massachusetts*, III, 496–97; Norman S. B. Gras, *The Massachusetts First National Bank of Boston* (Cambridge, 1937), opp. p. 38, has a graph which vividly illustrates the rise and fall of specie on hand in Massachusetts.
10. Nathan Appleton, *The Introduction of the Power Loom* (Lowell, 1858).
11. Caroline F. Ware, *Early New England Cotton Manufacture* (Boston, 1931); Melvin T. Copeland, *The Cotton Manufacturing Industry in the United States* (Cambridge, 1912), 4–6; Samuel Batchelder, *Introduction and Early Progress of the Cotton Manufacture in the United States* (Boston, 1863), 5–6.
12. New York *Spectator*, June 29, 1812; Connecticut *Herald*, July, 1813.
13. Morison, *op. cit.*, 211–12; Robert G. Albion, *The Rise of the New York Port* (New York, 1939), 9–10; Henry Adams, *History of the United States During the Administration of James Madison* (4 Vols., New York, 1930), IV, 96–97.
14. George Dangerfield, *The Era of Good Feelings* (New York, 1952), 78; Morison, *op. cit.*, 213–14; Bartlett, *op. cit.*, III, 545; Albion, *op. cit.*, 60–61.
15. Adams, *op. cit.*, IV, 97–98; James Ford, "Social Conditions and Social Changes," *Commonwealth History of Massachusetts*, III, 510–11. Edward Stanwood, *American Tariff Controversies in the Nineteenth Century* (2 Vols., Boston, 1903), I, 131, reports the value of gross imports in 1814 as $12,965,000; in 1815, $113,000,000; and in 1816, $147,000,000—with the value of net imports ($130,000,000) almost doubled that of any year preceding the war. See also *Annals of Congress*, 14th Congress, 1st Session, 1651–56.
16. *Niles' Register*, IX (January, 1816), 265.
17. Thomas Jefferson to Benjamin Austin, January 9, 1816, *The Writings of Thomas Jefferson* (18 Vols., Memorial Edition, Washington, 1903), XIV, 392; James D. Richardson, comp., *Messages and Papers of the Presidents* (11 Vols., Washington, 1896), I, 567, Seventh Annual Message.
18. Pointing to the fact that it was the Republican Congress which ordered Hamilton's *Report on Manufactures* to be reprinted, Stanwood concludes: "The Republican party, as a whole, stood forth as the champion of manufactures." See Stanwood, *op. cit.*, I, 136; and Edward Young, *Special Report on the Customs-Tariff Legislation of the United States* (Washington, 1874), 37–40.
19. Stanwood, *op. cit.*, I, 142. Stanwood feels that this is the first recorded instance of parties going in person to Washington to promote the passage of a particular tariff schedule.
20. *Annals of Congress*, 14th Congress, 1st Session, 1348, 1351–52. See also Frank W. Taussig, *Protection to Young Industries* (Cambridge, 1883), 34.

21. *Annals of Congress, op. cit.,* 1269, 1315, 1327. Also see *ibid.,* 1137–38, 1257–58, 1269–73.
22. Harold U. Faulkner, "Political History of Massachusetts," *Commonwealth History of Massachusetts,* IV, 76. "Moneyed Massachusetts began to split between manufacturers and shippers, and hence between those favoring high tariffs and internal improvements, and those opposed."
23. Dangerfield, *op. cit.,* 178; Frank W. Taussig, *Tariff History of the United States* (New York, 1931), 19–20.
24. Taussig, *Protection to Industries,* 24–25, 34–35.
25. *Ibid.,* 27; Stanwood, *op. cit.,* I, 179–80.
26. *Annals of Congress,* 16th Congress, 1st Session, 1916–46, 1952–63, 2115–2135, 2137–40, 666–72.
27. Taussig, *Protection to Industries,* 34–36; Batchelder, *op. cit.,* 70–71; Perry Walton, *The Story of Textiles* (Boston, 1912), 194–95; Appleton, *op. cit.*
28. *Niles' Register,* XXI (1821), 39.
29. Edward C. Kirkland, *A History of American Economic Life* (New York, 1949), 334–35; Louis M. Hacker, *The Triumph of American Capitalism* (New York, 1940), 261–62. Caroline Ware, in her *Early New England Cotton Manufacture,* records the fact that in Rhode Island during the 1830's, the average plant was capitalized at not much more than $30,000.
30. Kirkland, *op. cit.,* 332–33; Walton, *op. cit.,* 200–03, 205–06.
31. Victor S. Clark, *History of Manufacturing in the United States* (2 Vols., New York, 1929), I, 450; Hacker, *op. cit.,* 262. Arthur B. Darling, *Political Changes in Massachusetts, 1824–1848* (New Haven, 1925), 11, estimated a total investment of capital in the late 1830's of about $12,000,000.

2 ✻ THE COTTON ARISTOCRACY

1. Sarah Forbes Hughes, ed., *Letters and Recollections of John Murray Forbes* (2 Vols., Boston, 1889), I, 116–17.
2. Store goods could also be used in payment of wages to employees of factories. See Kirkland, *op. cit.,* 337.
3. Darling, *op. cit.,* 11.
4. Nathan Appleton, *Speech on the Bill to Reduce and Otherwise Alter the Duties on Imports, January, 1833* (Washington, 1833), 22. Also see Susan Loring, ed., *Selections from the Diaries of William Appleton, 1786–1862* (Boston, 1922), 40–41.
5. Abbott Lawrence to Amos Lawrence, February 2, 4, 8, 14, 1828, Amos Lawrence Letters, Massachusetts Historical Society, I, 30; Robert Means to Amos Lawrence, September 24, 1828, Amos Lawrence Papers, Massachusetts Historical Society, Box 1.

6. Claude M. Fuess, *Daniel Webster* (2 Vols., Boston, 1930), I, 376–77; Hamilton Hill, *Memoir of Abbott Lawrence* (Boston, 1883), 29.

7. See Amos Lawrence Letters, II, 222 (1837), for statistics on Lowell manufactures and a list of major factories in the area.

8. Hill, *op. cit.*, 23–26. Almost all the private papers and correspondence of Abbott Lawrence were destroyed in the great Boston fire of 1872. An imaginative German author named Ralph Anders wrote a fictionalized account of the "secrets" of Abbott Lawrence's success in *Der Weg zum Glück, oder die Kunst Millionär zu Werden* (Berlin, 1856).

9. *Hunt's Merchants' Magazine*, XLIV (1861), 173–76. See also Vera Shlakman, *Economic History of a Factory Town: A Study of Chicopee Massachusetts* (Smith College Studies in History), XX (1934), 35 ff.

10. *Hunt's Merchants' Magazine*, XLV (1861), 114–30; Boston *Daily Atlas*, October 6, 10, 16, 1835.

11. Sister M. Grace Madeleine, *Monetary and Banking Theories of Jacksonian Democracy* (Philadelphia, 1943), 147–51; Davis R. Dewey, *State Banking before the Civil War* (Washington, 1910), 82–96.

12. Amos Lawrence to Abbott Lawrence, September, 1832, Amos Lawrence Papers, Box 1; Kenneth W. Porter, *The Jacksons and the Lees* (2 Vols., Cambridge, 1937), I, 88 ff.; Ferris Greenslet, *The Lowells and Their Seven Worlds* (Boston, 1946).

13. Robert M. Lawrence, *Old Park Street and its Vicinity* (Boston, 1922), 79–80.

14. William R. Lawrence, *Extracts from the Diary and Correspondence of the Late Amos Lawrence* (Boston, 1855), 184–86. In his study of Unitarianism, Edward Everett Hale, "Religion and Social Reforms," *Commonwealth History of Massachusetts*, IV, 254, accepts the view that the Unitarians were "the liberal, often the radical, members of the ecclesiastical body, differing with their more conservative and reactionary brethren on many subjects . . . ." Arthur B. Darling, however, in his *Political Changes in Massachusetts 1824–1848*, p. 25, provides a contrary interpretation, stating that "Paradoxical though it may seem, Unitarianism was not a movement toward radicalism; on the contrary, it was a development toward conservative rationalism."

15. T. L. Nichols, *Forty Years of American Life, 1821–1861* (New York, 1937), 84–85; William Lawrence, *Life of Amos A. Lawrence: With Extracts from His Diary and Correspondence* (Boston, 1888), 59–60; Morison, *op. cit.*, 239–40; Sarah Hughes, ed., *Letters and Reflections of John Murray Forbes*, (2 Vols., Boston, 1900), I, 6–7; William Lawrence, *Memories of a Happy Life* (Boston, 1926), 4–6.

16. Hill, *op. cit.*, 56–58.

17. Amos Lawrence to Amos A. Lawrence, January 16, 1831, Lawrence, *Diary*, 103–04. See also Loring, *Diaries of William Appleton*, 38.

18. Faulkner, *op. cit.*, IV, 79–80; Darling, *op. cit.*, 56–59.

19. *Ibid.*, 85–89; Faulkner, *op. cit.*, IV, 81–83.
20. *Ibid.*, Faulkner. Arthur M. Schlesinger, Jr., *The Age of Jackson* (Boston, 1945), 83–85, 145–46, has some brilliant character sketches of the leading Massachusetts statesmen of the period.
21. Amos Lawrence to Amos A. Lawrence, January 16, 1831, Lawrence, *Diary*, 103–04.
22. Boston *Post*, September 7, October 9, 1832.
23. Faulkner, *op. cit.*, IV, 84; Darling, *op. cit.*, 115–18.
24. Judge Henry Adams Bullard to Amos Lawrence, December 6, 1834, Amos Lawrence Letters, III.
25. Abbott Lawrence to Amos Lawrence, June 2, 6, 9, July 2, 1832, Amos Lawrence Papers, Box 1. Also see Amos Lawrence Letters, IV, for a lengthy appraisal of the Jacksonian economic program, written by Abbott Lawrence, March 27, 1837.
26. Appleton, *et al.*, to Board of Directors of the United States Branch Bank at Boston (draft), June 21, 1834. Also see Appleton to Nicholas Biddle (draft), July, 1834, Appleton Papers, Massachusetts Historical Society.
27. Boston *Daily Atlas*, July 17, 19, 21, 1832.
28. Amos Lawrence to his sister, March 16, 1835, Lawrence, *Diary*, 130.
29. Lawrence, *Diary*, 141. See also James Means to Amos Lawrence, May 15, 1837, Amos Lawrence Papers, Box 1.
30. Darling, *op. cit.*, 203–04, 236–37.
31. *Ibid.*, 224–26.
32. Boston *Daily Atlas*, November 17, 1838; Faulkner, *op. cit.*, IV, 88–94.
33. Amos Lawrence to Jonathan Chapman, November [ ], 1844, Lawrence, *Diary*, 192.

3 ⚑ YANKEE MILLS AND DIXIE COTTON

1. Samuel Eliot Morison, *The Life and Letters of Harrison Gray Otis, Federalist, 1765–1848* (2 Vols., Boston, 1913), II, 259–61.
2. *Ibid.*, 261–62.
3. Wendell Phillips Garrison and Francis Jackson Garrison, *William Lloyd Garrison, 1805–1879: the Story of his Life told by his Children* (4 Vols., New York, 1885–89), I, 224; *Liberator*, No. 1, January 1, 1831.
4. Boston *Daily Atlas*, December 7, 1835; *Life of Garrison*, II, 238, 242.
5. Russell Nye, *William Lloyd Garrison and the Humanitarian Reformers* (Boston, 1955), 31–32. Also see Ralph Korngold, *Two Friends of Man* (Boston, 1950), John Jay Chapman, *William Lloyd Garrison* (New York, 1913), and Arthur Y. Lloyd, *The Slavery Controversy: 1831–1860* (Chapel Hill, 1939).
6. Lawrence, *Diary*, 317–18. Also see Amos Lawrence Letters, VII, for an

exchange of letters relating to Liberia during August and September of 1846. For a similar interest on the part of Lawrence's son, see Lawrence, *Amos A. Lawrence*, 53–54.

7. Philip Foner, *op. cit.*, 4; Albion, *op. cit.*, 98–99.

8. William Sparks to Amos Lawrence, October 17, 1835, AL Letters, IV.

9. David Cohn, *The Life and Times of King Cotton* (New York, 1956); Broadus Mitchell, *The Industrial Revolution in the South* (Baltimore, 1930); Emory Hawk, *Economic History of the South* (New York, 1934), provide a general background of Southern economy.

10. In 1825, the year of Whitney's death, the United States had raised three-quarters of the 228,000,000 pounds of cotton imported by Great Britain. See Jeanette Mirsky and Allan Nevins, *The World of Eli Whitney* (Cambridge, 1952), 91. Comparative statistics relating to cotton production and British consumption may be found in Copeland, *op. cit.*, 8 and Thomas P. Kettell, *Southern Wealth and Northern Profits* (New York, 1860), 30–33.

11. Copeland, *op. cit.*, 4–6. Amos A. Lawrence estimated the amount of cotton consumed by New England alone, by 1850, at about 150,000,000 pounds. Lawrence to R. J. Ward, February 10, 1851, AAL Letterbook, I, 264. Also see Albion, *op. cit.*, 98–99; Foner, *op. cit.*, 4; Morison, *Maritime History*, 299.

12. Evelyn Knowlton, *op. cit.*; Dane Yorke, *The Men and Times of Pepperell* (Boston, 1945), 30–31, reproduces examples of correspondence between this particular textile firm and its cotton buyers in New Orleans.

13. Amos A. Lawrence to Amos Lawrence, October 23, November 18, December 15, 1836, AL Papers, Box 1. Also see Joseph W. Patterson to Amos Lawrence, December 21, 1836, AL Letters, II, 138.

14. Amos A. Lawrence to Amos Lawrence, December 22, 1836, AL Papers, Box 1. Also see Henry Adams Bullard to Amos Lawrence, January 25, 1837, AL Letters, II, 196.

15. Amos A. Lawrence to Amos Lawrence, January 7, 11, 1837, AL Papers, Box 1.

16. Robert Means to Amos Lawrence, March 10, 1823, *ibid.*; Henry Adams Bullard to Lawrence, January 28, April 5, 1838, AL Letters, III; John L. Toomer to Lawrence, June 24, June 28, 1840, *ibid.*, IV; William Sparks to Lawrence, November 1, 1841, August 29, 1842, *ibid.*, V.

17. Adam Hodgson, *Letters from North America during a Tour in the United States and Canada* (London, 1824), I, 51.

18. Samuel Eliot Morison, *Three Centuries of Harvard* (Cambridge, 1946), 198; David D. Wallace, *South Carolina, a Short History* (Chapel Hill, 1951), 476; William C. Bruce, *John Randolph of Roanoke* (2 Vols., New York, 1922), II, 603; Edmund Quincy, *Life of Josiah Quincy* (Boston, 1868), 267, 342.

19. Robert Means to Amos Lawrence, November 3, 1831, AL Papers, Box 1.

20. Morison, *Otis*, II, 265–66. Otis also wrote an essay in the Boston

Courier, February 16, 1832, under the pseudonym of "Suggestor" calling for a national program of Negro colonization.

21. Fletcher Webster, ed., *The Writings and Speeches of Daniel Webster* (18 Vols., National Edition, Boston, 1903), VI, 12.

22. Amos Lawrence to Robert B. Rhett, South Carolina, December 12, 1849, Lawrence, *Diary*, 274–76. Also see Lawrence, *Amos A. Lawrence*, 53, 73–74, for the views of young Lawrence on slavery.

23. Morison, *Otis*, II, 262–63.

24. Cited in Darling, *op. cit.*, 152. Also see Boston *Daily Atlas*, September 30, 1835, for an article urging Northerners to see the Southern point of view regarding Abolitionist agitation.

25. *Liberator*, XIV, February 22, April 12, May 24, 1844. See also William and Jane Pease, eds., *The Antislavery Argument* (Indianapolis, 1965), lix–lxii, 343–94.

26. *Life of Garrison*, III, 96–133.

27. Boston *Daily Atlas*, August 22, 1835; *Life of Garrison*, I, 495. Also see George Benson to George W. Benson, August 7, 1835, and J. Farmer to Francis Jackson, August 21, 1835, Garrison Papers, Rare Book Department, Boston Public Library, V, 36, 41; and Curtis to George Ticknor, August 23, 1835, B. R. Curtis, *A Memoir of Benjamin Robbins Curtis* (2 Vols., Boston, 1879), I, 72.

28. Morison, *Otis*, II, 271–72; William Lloyd Garrison to Henry E. Benson, August 29, 1835, Garrison Letters, Boston Public Library, I, 65.

29. Boston *Daily Atlas*, October 17, 1835, reprinted a portion of an editorial by a New Orleans newspaper which praised most highly the speech of Harrison Gray Otis and indicated that it was universally commended throughout the South.

30. William Lloyd Garrison to Henry E. Benson, August 25, 1835, Garrison Letters, I, 64.

31. Boston *Post*, October 22, 1835; George W. Lyman to Rev. Benton Smith, June 30, 1879, Miscellaneous Manuscripts, Massachusetts Historical Society.

32. Boston *Post*, October 23, 1835. William Lloyd Garrison to George W. Benson, October 26, 1835, Garrison Letters, I, 76; George Thompson to Garrison, October 22, 1835, and George W. Benson to Garrison, October, 1835, Garrison Letters, V, 60, 62; Garrison to Samuel E. Sewall, October 24, 1835, Grenville H. Norcross Papers, Massachusetts Historical Society.

33. *Life of Garrison*, II, 30.

34. Wendell Phillips, *Speeches, Lectures and Letters* (Boston, 1892), 214.

35. T. L. Nichols, *op. cit.*, 84–88.

36. Nye, *op. cit.*, 79–80; Lloyd, *op. cit.*, 114; Dwight Dumond, *Antislavery Origins of the Civil War in the United States* (Ann Arbor, 1939), 58; Dwight Dumond, *Letters of James Gillespie Birney* (2 Vols., New York, 1938), I, 342–43.

37. *Life of Garrison,* I, 185; Wendell Phillips, *op. cit.,* 1–10; Korngold, *op. cit.,* 107–33.

38. Hughes, *op. cit.,* I, 100; Oswald Garrison Villard, "The Anti-Slavery Crisis in Massachusetts," *Commonwealth History of Massachusetts,* IV, 324–25.

39. Greenslett, *op. cit.,* 253–54; Korngold, *op. cit.,* 17–18.

40. Edward L. Pierce, *Memoirs and Letters of Charles Sumner* (4 Vols., Boston, 1877–1893), I, 173.

41. *Life of Garrison,* II, 200–02; *Liberator,* December 15, 1837.

42. Nye, *op. cit.,* 125–31; Villard, "The Anti-Slavery Crisis," IV, 335–36.

43. Amos A. Lawrence to Amos Lawrence, Washington, January 7, 8, 1836, AAL Letters, Massachusetts Historical Society, I.

44. J. W. Patterson to Amos Lawrence, London, December 1, 1840, AL Letters, V.

45. Robert C. Winthrop, Jr., *A Memoir of Robert C. Winthrop* (Boston, 1897), 24–25, 25–26. A candidate for Congress in 1840, Winthrop was surprised to find himself the recipient of a questionnaire demanding to know his position on various aspects of the slavery question.

46. Amos A. Lawrence to Amos Lawrence, Cambridge, England, July 29, 1840, AL Papers. Although young Lawrence expressed satisfaction with immediate political developments in the Bay State, he pointed out the potential dangers of the Abolition movement. Also see Amos A. Lawrence to Amos Lawrence, Liverpool, September 15, 1840, *ibid.*

4 ❦ COTTON VERSUS CONSCIENCE

1. William Sharp to Amos Lawrence, January 25, 1844, AL Letters, VI.

2. Samuel G. Brown, ed., *The Works of Rufus Choate, with a Memoir of his Life* (2 Vols., Boston, 1826), II, 274.

3. Amos Lawrence to a friend in South Carolina, June 12, 1852, Lawrence, *Diary,* 317–19. Also see William Sharp to Amos Lawrence, January 25, 1844, AL Letters, VI, for a letter indicating Southern appreciation of the position of Northern conservatives.

4. John D. P. Fuller, *The Movement for the Acquisition of all Mexico, 1846–48* (Baltimore, 1936), 15–16.

5. *Liberator,* XIV, April 12, 19, 1844. See William Lloyd Garrison to John Farmer, June 6, 1837, and Garrison to George W. Benson, June 14, 1837, Garrison Letters, II, 59, 60.

6. William Ellery Channing, "A Letter to the Hon. Henry Clay," August 1, 1837, Channing, *Works* (Boston, 1875), 773.

7. Lawrence to friends, March 25, 1837, Hill, *op. cit.,* 21.

8. Amos Lawrence to Jonathan Chapman, November [ ], 1844, Lawrence, *Diary,* 192.

9. Henry Adams Bullard to Amos Lawrence, January 25, 1837, AL Letters, II, 196.

10. Webster, *op. cit.*, II, 193–230.

11. Winthrop, *Memoir*, 38.

12. Boston *Daily Atlas*, December 25, 29, 1835.

13. J. W. Patterson to Amos Lawrence, December 1, 1840, AL Letters, V, 185.

14. Amos A. Lawrence to Amos Lawrence, September 15, 1840, AL Papers, Box 1, folder 3.

15. Abbott Lawrence to John J. Crittenden, January 7, 1841, Crittenden Manuscripts, Library of Congress, Washington, D.C.

16. William Sparks to Amos Lawrence, November 1, 1841, AL Letters, V, 391.

17. Abbott Lawrence, "Letter to the Whigs of Essex County," August 20, 1844, Hill, *op. cit.*, 76–77.

18. Abbott Lawrence to John J. Crittenden, April 5, 1844, Crittenden Manuscripts.

19. Lawrence, "Letter to Whigs," *op. cit.*, 76. See Kinley J. Brauer, *Cotton Versus Conscience: Massachusetts Whig Politics and Southwestern Expansion, 1843–1848* (Lexington, Ky., 1967), 77–80.

20. Lawrence, "Letter to Whigs," *op. cit.*, 77–78. Also see Abbott Lawrence to Amos Lawrence, May 12, 1844, AL Papers, Box 1, folder 3.

21. Abbott Lawrence to John J. Crittenden, April 5, 1844, Crittenden Manuscripts.

22. Brown, *op. cit.*, I, 98–100; Winthrop, *Memoir*, 35; Boston *Daily Advertiser*, February 21, 1845.

23. Lawrence, *Diary*, 192. Also see Abbott Lawrence to John J. Crittenden, April 5, 1844, Crittenden Manuscripts.

24. Boston *Daily Advertiser*, February 27, March 1, 1845. *Ibid.*, January 25, 27, 30, 1845.

25. *Ibid.*, March 3, 1845; Boston *Post*, March 3, 1845.

26. Lowell *Courier*, April 11, 1845.

27. Boston *Daily Advertiser*, March 15, 1845; Boston *Daily Atlas*, June 16, 1845.

28. Boston *Post*, March 14, 18, 1845.

29. Henry Wilson, *History of the Rise and Fall of the Slave Power in America* (3 Vols., Boston, 1874), II, 123–25.

30. Pierce, *Sumner*, II, 341–56; Charles Sumner, *Complete Works* (20 Vols., Boston, 1900), I, 28 ff., 52 ff.; Boston *Daily Advertiser*, March 13, 1877.

31. George F. Hoar, *Autobiography of Seventy Years* (2 Vols., New York, 1903), I, 24–28.

32. *Ibid.*, 134; E. W. Emerson and W. E. Forbes, eds., *Journals of Ralph Waldo Emerson* (10 Vols., Boston, 1903–14), VIII, 13.

33. Winthrop, *Memoir*, 31.

34. Pierce, *op. cit.*, II, 332; Brauer, *op. cit.*, 160.

35. Hughes, *op. cit.*, I, 118.

36. Emerson, *op. cit.*, VII, 232.

37. John C. Calhoun to Abbott Lawrence, May 13, 1845, "Correspondence of John C. Calhoun," *Annual Report of the American Historical Association*, 1899, II, 654–56.

38. "When that is accomplished," wrote Calhoun, "all conflict between the planter and the manufacturer would cease . . . ." Calhoun to Abbott Lawrence, May 13, 1845, *ibid.*, II, 655.

39. Abbott Lawrence to Calhoun, July 14, 1846, *ibid.*, 1086–87. Calhoun's fears of political repercussions were borne out by the fact that Charles Sumner, having heard rumors that the loan had actually gone through, was charging Lawrence and the Cotton Whigs with corrupting the politics of the nation with their gold. See Brauer, *op. cit.*, 163.

40. Edward Everett to Calhoun, April 6, 1846, *ibid.*, 1080–81.

41. Abbott Lawrence to Nathan Appleton, August 4, 1846, Hill, *op. cit.*, 32.

42. Broadus Mitchell, *William Gregg, Factory Master of the Old South* (Chapel Hill, 1928), 21. See Eugene D. Genovese, *The Political Economy of Slavery* (New York, 1965), 180–208, for a recent analysis of the pervading influence of slavery upon the life and society of the South. Genovese cautions against exaggerating the influence of the Southern industrialists as a stabilizing factor, noting that their political views coincided with those of their slaveholding colleagues on the plantations and that they supported the cause of the Confederacy into civil war.

43. Henry H. Simms, *op. cit.*, 23–24. Also see Hudson Strode, *Jefferson Davis: American Patriot* (New York, 1955), 214.

44. *De Bow's Review of the Southern and Western States*, V (1847), 182–85.

45. R. S. Allen to Amos Lawrence, January, 1849, AL Letters, IX, 463.

46. *Hunt's Merchants' Magazine*, XXI (1849), 492–502.

47. Lawrence, *Amos A. Lawrence*, 23–24. See Rt. Rev. William Lawrence, "The Relation of Wealth to Morals," *World's Work*, I (January, 1901), 286–92, for a classic statement regarding the relationship of personal wealth to the common welfare.

48. Lawrence, *Amos A. Lawrence*, 57–58.

49. *Hunt's Merchants' Magazine*, XXII (1850), 26–35.

50. Amos A. Lawrence to N. Silsbee, November 19, 1849, AAL Letterbook, I, 15.

51. Lawrence to William Gregg, August 21, 1850, *ibid.*, 174.

52. William Gregg to Amos A. Lawrence, September 2, 1850, AAL Letters, VIII, 120.

53. Amos Lawrence to Robert B. Rhett, December 12, 1849, Lawrence, *Diary*, 274–76.

54. Hill, *op. cit.*, 32–34. The formal invitation was transmitted to Lawrence through the Hon. William S. Archer, U.S. Senator from Virginia.

55. James D. Richardson, comp., *op. cit.*, IV, 437–43; *Congressional Globe*, 29th Congress, 1st Session, 796–804.
56. Charleston *Mercury*, May 25, 1846. See Wilson, *op. cit.*, II, 11; Fuller, *op. cit.*, 35–36.
57. Wilson, *op. cit.*, II, 7–17; Darling, *op. cit.*, 334.
58. Abbott Lawrence to John J. Crittenden, April 5, 1844, Crittenden Manuscripts.
59. Webster, *op. cit.*, IV, 31–32.
60. *Congressional Globe*, 29th Congress, 1st Session, 796–804. See Brauer, *op. cit.*, 186–87.
61. Darling, *op. cit.*, 334–35; Faulkner, *op. cit.*, IV, 95–96.
62. Amos Lawrence to Mark Hopkins, July 19, 1848, AL Letters, IX; Lawrence, *Diary*, 236.
63. Winthrop, *Memoir*, 58–59, "Speech on the War with Mexico," January 8, 1847.
64. Robert C. Winthrop to John P. Kennedy, January 21, 1848, *ibid.*, 79–80.
65. Boston *Whig*, July 3, 1846; H. V. Ames, ed., *State Documents on Federal Relations* (Philadelphia, 1906), 241–42.
66. Ray A. Billington, *The Far Western Frontier, 1830–60* (New York, 1956), 174–75; Justin Smith, *The War with Mexico* (2 Vols., New York, 1919) I, 194–95; Fuller, *op. cit.*, 35–36.
67. Winthrop, *Memoir*, 51.
68. *Ibid.*, 58–59.
69. Charleston *Mercury*, February 1, 1847; Arthur C. Cole, *The Whig Party in the South* (Washington, 1913), 104–34.
70. Winthrop, *Memoir*, 61–62. Also see Diary Fragment, January 19, 1848, Winthrop Papers, Massachusetts Historical Society, XXXVI, 118.
71. See Smith, *Mexico*, II, 127–39, 233–40; R. L. Rives, *The United States and Mexico, 1821–1848* (2 Vols., New York, 1913), II, 423 ff.
72. Allan Nevins, ed., *Polk: The Diary of a President, 1845–49* (New York, 1952), 308–15. See United States Senate, 30th Congress, 1st Session, *Senate Executive Document*, No. 52, passim, for debates over the Mexican Treaty.
73. William Sharp to Amos Lawrence, October 1, 1845, AL Letters, VII.
74. Amos Lawrence to Mark Hopkins, July 19, 1848, *ibid.*, IX, 257.

5 ❦ GENTLEMEN'S AGREEMENT

1. Abbott Lawrence to John J. Crittenden, September 18, 1848, November [ ], 1848, Crittenden Manuscripts.
2. John J. Crittenden to A. T. Burnley, July 30, 1848, Chapman Cole-

man, *The Life of John J. Crittenden: With Selections from his Correspondence and Speeches* (2 Vols., Philadelphia, 1871), I, 322–23.

3. Wilson, *op. cit.*, II, 138.

4. *Ibid.*, II, 136–38. See John J. Crittenden to Moses H. Grinnell, December 9, 1848, Coleman, *op. cit.*, I, 329–30.

5. Wilson, *op. cit.*, II, 138.

6. Winthrop, *Memoir*, 90–91; Hill, *op. cit.*, 78–79. See Abbott Lawrence to S. Draper, S. Loudon, and R. M. Blatchford, May 12, 1848, Amos Lawrence Letters, IX, 207.

7. Henry Adams Bullard to Amos Lawrence, June 4, 1848, *ibid.*, 219.

8. H. M. Judge to Amos Lawrence, May 2, 1848, *ibid.*, 191.

9. Hill, *op. cit.*, 78–79.

10. Glyndon Van Deusen, *Thurlow Weed* (Boston, 1947), 60–61. Also see Amos Lawrence to Mark Hopkins, June 12, 1848, Lawrence, *Diary*, 258–59.

11. Wilson, *op. cit.*, II, 137.

12. Robert C. Winthrop to Nathan Appleton, July 23, 1848, Winthrop Papers, Massachusetts Historical Society, XXXVI, 128.

13. Abbott Lawrence to John J. Crittenden, September 18, 1848, Crittenden Manuscripts.

14. Abbott Lawrence to Nathan Appleton, August 11, 1848, Hill, *op. cit.*, 80.

15. Mary Lawrence to Amos Lawrence, November 4, 1850, Amos Lawrence Letters, X, 645.

16. Wilson, *op. cit.*, II, 373–75.

17. Darling, *op. cit.*, 352–53.

18. Abbott Lawrence to John J. Crittenden, November [ ], 1848, Crittenden Manuscripts.

19. Nathan Appleton and Charles Sumner, Correspondence, July-September, 1848, Manuscripts, Rare Book Department, Boston Public Library, from the original letters in the possession of William S. Appleton, copied by F. B. Perkins, 1874.

20. J. F. Davis to Robert C. Winthrop, February 16, 1848, Winthrop Papers; Abbott Lawrence to Winthrop, February 4, 1848, *ibid.*; David Donald, *Charles Sumner and the Coming of the Civil War* (New York, 1961), 178–79.

21. W. P. Gentry to John J. Crittenden, November 20, 1848, Coleman, *op. cit.*, I, 326–28; Alexander H. Stephens to Crittenden, December 5, 1848, *ibid.*, I, 328–29.

22. Robert Toombs to John J. Crittenden, April 25, 1850, *ibid.*, I, 366; Jefferson Davis to Crittenden, January 30, 1849, *ibid.*, I, 399–400.

23. Amos Lawrence to Abbott Lawrence, February 28, March 3, 5, 1849, Lawrence, *Diary*, 267–68. Also see Robert C. Winthrop to Nathan Appleton, January 2, 1849, Winthrop Papers, XXXVI, 128; and Nathan Appleton to Millard T. Fillmore, February 6, 1849, Nathan Appleton Papers.

24. Amos Lawrence to a friend, July 18, 1849, Lawrence, *Diary*, 269.

25. Winthrop, *Memoir*, 91–92; Winthrop to Nathan Appleton, January 6, 1850, Winthrop Papers, XXXVI, 131. Also see Holman Hamilton, " 'The Cave of the Winds' and the Compromise of 1850," *Journal of Southern History*, XXIII (1957), 331–53.

26. *Congressional Globe*, 31st Congress, 1st Session, Appendix, 117–27, 567–73. Also see George Poage, *Henry Clay and the Whig Party* (Chapel Hill, 1936), 199–204; Glyndon Van Deusen, *The Life of Henry Clay* (Boston, 1937), 394–413.

27. Webster, *op. cit.*, X, 56–99.

28. Parrington, *op. cit.*, II, 314–15; Fuess, *Webster*, II, 218–27.

29. Amos Lawrence to Amos A. Lawrence, September 23, 1850, AAL Letters, VIII; Amos Lawrence to Mr. Woodburn, March 14, 1850, AAL Letterbook, I, 92. Also see Hughes, *op. cit.*, I, 142–43.

30. Boston *Daily Atlas*, March 11, 1850; David Van Tassel, "Gentlemen of Property and Standing—Compromise Sentiment in Boston, 1850," *New England Quarterly*, XXIII (1950), 307–19.

31. Diary of Philip Hone, February 9, 1850, cited in Foner, *op. cit.*, 23; Brown, *op. cit.*, II, 313.

32. Robert C. Winthrop to Edward Everett, March 17, 1850, Everett Papers, Massachusetts Historical Society; Robert C. Winthrop to George Morey, March 10, 1850, Winthrop Papers, XXXVI, 33. Also see Loring, *Diaries of William Appleton*, 143.

33. Boston *Daily Advertiser*, March 12, 1850.

34. *Ibid.*, March 11, 1850.

35. *Ibid.*, March 12, 1850. See Daniel Webster to Edward Everett, March 10, 1850; Everett to Webster, March 12, 1850, Everett Papers.

36. *Journal of Commerce*, March 7, 1850; Boston *Daily Advertiser*, March 9, 1850.

37. *Journal of Commerce*, March 8, 1850; Boston *Daily Advertiser*, March 12, 1850.

38. Brown, *op. cit.*, I, 162, 173–74; II, 310 ff.

39. Boston *Daily Advertiser*, April 3, 1850. For Webster's reply to the "Boston Letter," see *ibid.*, April 13, 1850.

40. Abbott Lawrence to General Dearborn, April 2, 1850, Hill, *op. cit.*, 79. Also see Abbott Lawrence to Edward Everett, March 18, 1850, Everett Papers.

41. Boston *Daily Advertiser*, April 6, 1850. Also see *ibid.*, April 11, 1850.

42. Abbott Lawrence to Amos Lawrence, August 16, 1850, AL Letters, X, 585; Winthrop, *Memoir*, 127.

43. Robert C. Winthrop to Nathan Appleton, July 26, 1850, Winthrop Papers, XXXVI, 135.

44. Winthrop, *Memoir*, 129.

45. Robert C. Winthrop to J. C. Warren, August 16, 1851, Warren Papers,

Massachusetts Historical Society, XXIX. Also see Abbott Lawrence to Amos Lawrence, August 16, 1850, AL Letters, X, 585.

46. Hill, *op. cit.*, 58. Also see Pierce, *op. cit.*, III, 217; C. S. Morehead to John J. Crittenden, March 30, 1850, Coleman, *op. cit.*, I, 361–64.

47. Boston *Daily Advertiser*, September 7, 1850.

48. Abbott Lawrence to Amos Lawrence, August 16, 1850, AL Letters, X, 585.

49. Robert C. Winthrop to Nathan Appleton, August 18, 1850, Winthrop Papers, XXXVI, 139; Winthrop to John C. Warren, August 16, 1851, Warren Papers.

50. R. N. Ogden to Amos Lawrence, December 29, 1850, AL Letters, X, 709.

51. Henry Adams Bullard to Amos Lawrence, January 25, 1851, AL Letters, X, 21.

52. James Ford Rhodes, *History of the United States from the Compromise of 1850* (7 Vols., New York, 1893–1906), I, 168–69, 181–83.

53. Whig Circular, November 8, 1850, signed by George Morey, Chairman of the Whig State Central Committee. Massachusetts Historical Society.

54. Boston *Post*, September 19, 1849.

55. See Henry Greenleaf Pearson, "Preliminaries of the Civil War," *Commonwealth History of Massachusetts*, IV, 477–78.

56. Amos Lawrence to Mark Hopkins, November 11, 1850, Lawrence, *Diary*, 287; Hopkins to Lawrence, November 27, 1850, AL Letters, X, 663. Also see Boston *Post*, January 7, 8, 1851; Boston *Daily Advertiser*, January 21, February 8, 19, 24, 1851.

57. Samuel A. Eliot to Amos A. Lawrence, January 23, 1851, AAL Letters, VIII, 200. Also see Robert C. Winthrop to Nathan Appleton, January 17, 1851, Winthrop Papers, XXXVI, 144.

58. John E. Tyler (Whig State Central Committee) to Amos A. Lawrence, February 11, 1851, AAL Letters, VIII, 210.

59. Amos A. Lawrence to John E. Tyler, February 12, 1851, AAL Letterbook, I, 266; Lawrence to Samuel Eliot, January 20, 1851, *ibid.*, I, 245.

60. Amos Lawrence to William Appleton, February 10, 1851, Lawrence to Ezra Lincoln, February 10, 1851, and Lawrence appeal for funds to defeat Sumner, March 14, 1851, AAL Letterbook, I, 261, 263, 296. Lawrence: Subscription "to defeat Sumner," March 14, 1851, and Lawrence: Subscription to Anti-Sumner Fund, April 24, 1851, AAL Letters, IX, 11, 25.

61. Robert C. Winthrop to George Morey, January 25, 1851, Winthrop Papers, XXXVI, 145; Lawrence to Dr. Green, November 16, 1850, AAL Letterbook, I, 211.

62. Boston *Daily Advertiser*, January 16, 17, February 8, March 11, 13, 1851. Also see Claude M. Fuess, *The Life of Caleb Cushing* (2 Vols., New York, 1923), II, 98–108.

63. Boston *Daily Advertiser*, April 25, 1851; Boston *Post*, April 25, 1851. Also see Elias Nason, *The Life and Times of Charles Sumner* (Boston, 1874), 139–40.

64. William S. Robinson, *"Warrington" Pen-Portraits* (Boston, 1877), 203–05.
65. Boston *Daily Advertiser*, September 7, 1850.
66. Edward Stanwood, *History of the Presidency* (2 Vols., Boston, 1916), I, 243–57.
67. Van Deusen, *Thurlow Weed*, 191–92.
68. Wilson, *op. cit.*, II, 361–62, 373–74.
69. Amos A. Lawrence to A. A. Richards, November 20, 1852, AAL Letter-book, II, 3.
70. Lawrence to Samuel Eliot, January 20, 1851, *ibid.*, I, 245.
71. Robinson, *op. cit.*, 203–05.
72. Winthrop, *Memoir*, 161; New York *Tribune*, November 13, 1852, January 14, 1853.
73. Lawrence, *Amos A. Lawrence*, 21–22; Lawrence, *Diary*, 335–36.
74. Amos A. Lawrence to Franklin Pierce, November 11, 1852, AAL Letter-book, I, 407; Lawrence to Mr. Conant, December 6, 1852, *ibid.*, II, 407. Lawrence, *Diary*, 335–36.
75. Amos A. Lawrence to William Appleton, December 28, 1852, AAL Letterbook, II, 23.
76. See W. O. Lynch, "Anti-Slavery Tendencies of the Democratic Party," *Mississippi Valley Historical Review*, II (1924), 319–31.
77. Winthrop, *Memoir*, 161.

6 ⚞ WAKE THE SLEEPING TIGER

1. Richardson, *op. cit.*, VI, 2730–36.
2. *Ibid.*, 2740–59.
3. R. N. Ogden to Amos Lawrence, December 29, 1850, AL Letters, X, 709.
4. Henry Adams Bullard to Amos Lawrence, January 24, 1851, *ibid.*, 21.
5. Nathan Appleton, *Letter to the Hon. William C. Rives of Virginia on Slavery and the Union* (Boston, 1860), 10.
6. Abbott Lawrence to Edward Everett, March 21, 1850, Everett Papers. Also see Hill, *op. cit.*, 94–97.
7. Reporting in *Harper's Magazine*, November, 1853, George William Curtis called it "Aladdin's Palace." Also see Boston *Daily Advertiser*, July 14, 1853.
8. *Journal of Commerce*, August 12, September 13, 1853.
9. *De Bow's Review*, October, 1853, 429. Also see Boston *Daily Atlas*, August 13, 1852.
10. *Ibid.*, July 2, 4, 1853.
11. William E. Dodd, *The Cotton Kingdom* (New Haven, 1920), 26; Allan Nevins, *The Ordeal of the Union* (2 Vols., New York, 1947), II, 245, 265–66.
12. *Hunt's Merchants' Magazine*, XXXII (1855), 583–85.
13. Boston *Daily Atlas*, September 21, 1853; Winthrop, *Memoir*, 149–50.

184 LORDS OF THE LOOM

14. Shlakman, *op. cit.*, 36–37.
15. Amos A. Lawrence to Rev. Dr. Scoresby, August 19, 1851, Lawrence, *Amos A. Lawrence*, 307.
16. Amos A. Lawrence to J. E. Tyler, February 12, 1851, AAL Letterbook, I, 266.
17. Nevins, *Ordeal of the Union*, II, 78.
18. Boston *Daily Advertiser*, February 17, 18, 20, 1851. Also see Harold Schwartz, "Fugitive Slave Days in Boston," *New England Quarterly*, XXVII (1954), 191–212.
19. William Means to Amos Lawrence, November 7, 1850, AAL Letters, X, 649; Amos A. Lawrence to Samuel Eliot, February 18, 1851, AAL Letterbook, I, 272.
20. Amos Lawrence to Amos A. Lawrence, September 25, 1850, AAL Letters, VIII, 127; Amos Lawrence to Mark Hopkins, November 11, 1850, Lawrence, *Diary*, 287.
21. Amos A. Lawrence to Giles Richards, June 1, 1854, AAL Letterbook, II, 338.
22. Robert C. Winthrop to John J. Crittenden, May 13, 1852, Coleman, *op. cit.*, II, 36.
23. Emerson, *op. cit.*, VIII, 363; Theodore Parker, *Additional Speeches, Addresses and Occasional Sermons* (2 Vols., Boston, 1855), I, 89.
24. Wendell Phillips, *op. cit.*, 65. Speech before the Massachusetts Anti-Slavery Society, Faneuil Hall, January 30, 1852.
25. *Life of Garrison*, III, 328.
26. Winthrop, *Memoir*, 147.
27. A. S. Packard to Amos Lawrence, October 28, 1850, AL Letters, X, 641.
28. Amos A. Lawrence to Dr. Green, November 16, 1850, AAL Letterbook, I, 211.
29. Amos A. Lawrence to Marshal Charles Devens, February 17, 1851, *ibid.*, 269.
30. Amos A. Lawrence to Samuel Eliot, February 18, 1851, *ibid.*, 272.
31. Amos A. Lawrence to William Lloyd Garrison, February 16, 1851, *ibid.*, 267.
32. Brown, *op. cit.*, II, 319.
33. Amos A. Lawrence to Giles Richards, June 1, 1854, AAL Letterbook, II, 338.
34. *33rd Congress, 1st Session,* Senate Report No. 15, p. 3.
35. Appleton, *Letter to Rives*, 10.
36. *Congressional Globe,* 33rd Congress, 1st Session, Appendix, 262 ff.
37. Boston *Daily Advertiser*, February 23, 1854; Boston *Times*, February 23, May 30, 1854.
38. Amos A. Lawrence to George S. Park, January 23, 1857, AAL Letterbook, IV, 1.
39. Winthrop, *Memoir*, 165–66.
40. Amos A. Lawrence to Hon. Samuel H. Walley, May 12, 1854, AAL

Letterbook, II, 325. Also see Lawrence to William Appleton, March 11, 1854, and Lawrence to Hon. J. W. Edmonds, March 16, 1854, *ibid.,* 272, 273.

41. Amos A. Lawrence to Mr. Andrews, May 26, 1854, *ibid.,* 335. Also see Edward Everett Diary, May 27, 1854, Massachusetts Historical Society.
42. Amos A. Lawrence to R. A. Crafts, New Orleans, March 7, 1854, AAL Letterbook, II, 270.
43. Amos A. Lawrence to Samuel H. Walley, May 12, 1854, *ibid.,* 325; Lawrence to J. W. Edmonds, March 16, 1854, *ibid.,* 273.
44. Charles Francis Adams, *Richard Henry Dana* (2 Vols., Boston, 1891), I, 269–70.
45. *Ibid.*
46. Amos A. Lawrence to Samuel Lawrence, June [ ], 1854, AAL Letterbook, II, 340. Also see Lawrence, *Amos A. Lawrence,* 75–76.
47. Boston *Times,* May 30, 1854.
48. Amos A. Lawrence to Mr. Andrews, May 26, 1854, AAL Letterbook, II, 335.
49. *Congressional Globe,* 33rd Congress, 1st Session, Appendix, 150 ff.
50. Amos A. Lawrence to Moses Grinnell, June 21, 1854, AAL Letterbook, I, 353.
51. Wilson, *op. cit.,* II, 464.
52. Eli Thayer, *A History of the Kansas Crusade* (New York, 1889), 25–30. See Robert E. Moody, "The First Year of the Emigrant Aid Company," *New England Quarterly,* IV (1931), 148–49; Samuel A. Johnson, "The Genesis of the New England Aid Company," *New England Quarterly,* III (1930), 90–100.
53. *Organization, Objects and Plan of Operations of the Emigrant Aid Company: Also a Description of Kansas for the Information of Emigrants* (Boston, 1854). Copy in the Eli Thayer Manuscripts, I, 5, John Hay Library, Brown University, Providence, Rhode Island.
54. Amos A. Lawrence to Moses Grinnell, June 21, 1854, AAL Letterbook, II, 352. Also see Lawrence to Rev. Edward Cook, Appleton, Wisconsin, June 20, 1854, *ibid.,* 350.
55. Thayer, *op. cit.,* 69–73; Charles Robinson, *The Kansas Conflict* (New York, 1889), 90–91.
56. Amos A. Lawrence to Rev. Edward Cook, June 20, 1854, AAL Letterbook, II, 350; Lawrence to Charles Robinson, August 9, 1854, *ibid.,* 398. Also see *ibid.,* 399, for a letter of recognition for Robinson to act as the "Agent of the Emigrant Aid Society," signed by Amos A. Lawrence as Treasurer.
57. Patrick Jackson to Amos A. Lawrence, June 10, 1854, AAL Letters, XI, 149; Eli Thayer to Lawrence, June 22, 1854, *ibid.*
58. Amos A. Lawrence to Eli Thayer, July 5, 6, 1854, AAL Letterbook, II, 365, 366; Thayer to Lawrence, July 15, 1854, AAL Letters, XI, 176.
59. Johnson, "Emigrant Aid Company," 105–07.

60. Lawrence, *Amos A. Lawrence*, 84; Amos A. Lawrence to Charles Robinson, September 30, 1854, AAL Letterbook, II; Lawrence to Rev. S. Y. Lum, Lawrence, Kansas, November 28, 1854, *ibid.*

61. Memorandum to be presented to Messrs. Williams and Thayer, co-trustees with myself of the Emigrant Aid Company. AAL Letterbook, II, 401.

62. Lawrence, *Amos A. Lawrence*, 80, 84.

63. Amos A. Lawrence to Thomas Hart Benton, January 2, 1855, AAL Letterbook, III, 1. This letter is erroneously dated "1854."

64. Memorandum to Messrs. Williams and Thayer, August 26, 1854, *ibid.*, II, 401.

65. Amos A. Lawrence to Eli Thayer, July 31, 1854; Lawrence to Hon. John Goodrich, August 2, 1854, *ibid.*, II, 388, 392.

66. Letter to be sent to every minister in New England, dated September, 1854, *ibid.*, II, 415.

67. Amos A. Lawrence to Governor Gardner, March 7, 1856, *ibid.*, IV, 26.

68. Amos A. Lawrence to President Franklin Pierce, April 17, 1855, *ibid.*, III, 89.

69. *National Intelligencer*, June 22, 1854.

70. Jay Monaghan, *The Civil War on the Western Border, 1854–1865* (Boston, 1955), 13–15.

71. Amos A. Lawrence to President Franklin Pierce, July 15, 1855, Lawrence, *Amos A. Lawrence*, p. 95.

72. Amos A. Lawrence to President Franklin Pierce, December 10, 1855, *ibid.*, 104.

73. Amos A. Lawrence to Senator David Atchison, March 31, 1855, AAL Letterbook, III, 78.

74. Charles Robinson to Eli Thayer, April 2, 1855; Robinson to Edward Everett Hale, April 9, 1855, cited in W. H. Isley, "The Sharps Rifle Episode in Kansas History," *American Historical Review*, XII (1907), 511, 522.

75. Thomas H. Webb to Charles Robinson, May 8, 1855, *ibid.*, 552–53.

76. Winston O. Smith, *The Sharps Rifle, Its History, Development and Operation* (New York, 1943), 11–12; Lawrence, *Amos A. Lawrence*, 97–98.

77. Amos A. Lawrence to Charles Robinson, July 20, 1855, AAL Letterbook, III, 203.

78. Amos A. Lawrence to Dr. Webb, July 20, 1855, *ibid.*, 204.

79. Amos A. Lawrence to President Pierce, July 15, 1855, Lawrence, *Amos A. Lawrence*, 95.

80. Charles Robinson to Salmon P. Chase, February 22, 1856, "Diary and Correspondence of Salmon P. Chase," *Annual Report of the American Historical Association, 1902*, II, 475, 476. See James C. Malin, "The Topeka Statehood Movement Reconsidered," *Territorial Kansas*, 33–69, for a detailed and scholarly appraisal of the complex factors which went to make up the demand for statehood.

81. Richardson, *op. cit.*, VI, 2860–83, esp. 2877.

82. *Congressional Globe*, 34th Congress, 1st Session, 639. See John J. Crittenden to Archibald Dixon, March 7, 1854; Abbott Lawrence to Crittenden, April 25, 1856, Coleman, *Crittenden*, II, 102–03, 119.

83. *Congressional Globe,* 34th Congress, 1st Session, Appendix, 529–44; Sumner, *Works*, IV, 137–249.

84. Amos A. Lawrence to Charles Sumner, October 10, 1856, Lawrence, *Amos A. Lawrence*, 141.

85. Amos A. Lawrence to Mrs. Charles Robinson, October 30, 1856, Robinson Papers, Folder IV, 4, Archives, University of Kansas, Lawrence, Kansas.

86. Amos A. Lawrence to Judge Hoar, May 10, 1859, AAL Letterbook, IV, 329.

87. Monaghan, *op. cit.*, 52–56; Alice Nichols, *Bleeding Kansas* (New York, 1954), 105–09.

88. New York *Tribune*, May 31, June 9, 10, 1856. Also see James C. Malin, *John Brown and the Legend of Fifty-Six* (Philadelphia, 1942), 589.

89. Amos A. Lawrence to Charles Robinson, December 17, 1857, January 29, 1858, Robinson Papers, Folder III, 12, 14.

90. Amos A. Lawrence to Charles Robinson, August 16, 1857, January 2, 1858, *ibid.*, 9, 13.

91. Lawrence to Robinson, January 29, 1858, *ibid.*, 14.

92. Lawrence to Robinson, December 17, 1857, February 3, 1858, *ibid.*, 12, 15. Also see Lawrence, Journal, November 5, 1856, Massachusetts Historical Society.

93. Amos A. Lawrence to Charles Robinson, March 31, 1857, Robinson Papers, Folder III, 3.

94. Lawrence to Robinson, August 16, 1857, *ibid.*, 9.

95. James C. Malin, *On the Nature of History* (Lawrence, Kansas, 1954), 201. Lawrence, writes Malin, "understood the issue of Federal Nationalism and advised the free-state men repeatedly against any course in Kansas that would compromise their position of loyalty to Federal Nationalism."

96. Richardson, *op. cit.*, VII, 2961–67.

97. Amos A. Lawrence to Charles Robinson, May 16, 1857, Robinson Papers, Folder III, 7.

98. *35th Congress, 1st Session,* House Reports, Vol. III, Report 377.

99. Amos A. Lawrence to John W. Geary, March 19, 1857, AAL Letterbook, IV, 32–33; Lawrence to Charles Robinson, January 29, 1858, Robinson Papers, Folder III, 14.

100. Lawrence to Robinson, January 2, 1858, *ibid.*, 13.

101. *35th Congress, 1st Session,* House Reports, Vol. V, Report 110, Testimony of Walker.

102. Lawrence to Robinson, February 3, 1858, Robinson Papers, Folder III, 15.

103. Richardson, *op. cit.*, VII, 2983.

104. *Ibid.*, 3002.

105. John J. Crittenden to Abraham Lincoln, July 29, 1858, Coleman, *op. cit.*, II, 162–64; George F. Milton, *Eve of Conflict: Stephen A. Douglas and the Needless War* (Boston, 1934), 271–93.

106. Amos A. Lawrence to John J. Crittenden, May 4, 1858, AAL Letterbook, IV, 179.

107. *Congressional Globe,* 35th Congress, 1st Session, Appendix, 194 ff.

108. Amos A. Lawrence to Charles Robinson, May 6, 1858, Robinson Papers, Folder III, 18.

109. See Frank Hodder, "The English Bill," *Annual Report of the American Historical Association, 1906,* I, 201.

110. Amos A. Lawrence to Charles Robinson, May 3, 4, 1858, Robinson Papers, Folder III, 17, 19.

111. Boston *Daily Advertiser,* February 4, 1858. Also see John C. Underwood to Eli Thayer, February, 1857, Thayer Manuscripts, I, 27, Brown University.

112. Undated Manuscript, Thayer Manuscripts, I, 57.

113. Speech of Gov. Charles Robinson of Kansas in favor of the election of Hon. Eli Thayer, delivered in Mechanics Hall, Worcester, Massachusetts, November 3, 1860, Thayer Manuscripts.

114. Lawrence, *Amos A. Lawrence,* 112–13.

115. Speech of Amos A. Lawrence in support of the election of Eli Thayer, November [ ], 1860, Manuscript, American Antiquarian Society, Worcester, Massachusetts.

7 ❦ COTTON WHIGS IN SEARCH OF A PARTY

1. R. P. Letcher to John J. Crittenden, December 26, 1857; George T. Curtis to Crittenden, July 10, 1856, Coleman, *op. cit.*, II, 141–42, 130–31.

2. New York *Tribune,* October 16, 1854.

3. *Commercial Advertiser,* June 28, September 19, 22, 23, 1855.

4. Springfield *Republican,* July 21–25, September 8, 1854; Boston *Traveler,* September 8, 1854.

5. Van Deusen, *Thurlow Weed,* 206–07.

6. Charles Sumner to Amasa Walker, April 26, 1854, cited in Donald, *op. cit.*, 266.

7. Winthrop, *Memoir,* 172–79.

8. *Ibid.*

9. *Ibid.*

10. *Ibid.*

11. T. D. Eliot to Charles Sumner, September 13, 1854, cited in Donald, *op. cit.*, 267.

12. *Ibid.*, 267–68; Robinson, *Pen-Portraits,* 63.

13. Boston *Pilot*, December 10, 1853; May 13, January 20, 1855.
14. Donald, *op. cit.*, 267–68; Robinson, *Pen-Portraits*, 63.
15. Rufus Choate to Hon. Charles Eames, June 29, 1855, Brown, *op. cit.*, I, 195–96.
16. Lawrence, *Amos A. Lawrence*, 140; George H. Haynes, "The Know-Nothing Legislature," *Annual Report of the American Historical Association, 1896* (Washington, 1897), I, 178.
17. Wilson, *op. cit.*, II, 49.
18. Amos A. Lawrence to George N. Briggs, October 6, 1859, AAL Letterbook, IV, 349. Also see W. D. Overdyke, *The Know-Nothing Party in the South* (Baton Rouge, 1950), 1–127.
19. Boston *Atlas*, November 14, 1854.
20. Foner, *op. cit.*, 114.
21. Donald, *op. cit.*, 271, 274. See *Commercial Advertiser*, October 18, 1855; Winthrop, *Memoir*, 167–68.
22. Avery Craven, *The Growth of Southern Nationalism, 1848–1861* (Baton Rouge, 1953), 238–45; Overdyke, *op. cit.*, 263–95.
23. Ray A. Billington, *The Protestant Crusade* (New York, 1938), 414–15.
24. Winthrop, *Memoir*, 185–86. Also see Wilson, *op. cit.*, II, 433; and Joel Parker, *The True Issue and the Duty of the Whigs* (Cambridge, 1856), a published version of an address before the citizens of Cambridge, October 1, 1856.
25. Rufus Choate to E. W. Farley and other gentlemen of the Maine Whig State Central Committee, August 9, 1856, Brown, *op. cit.*, I, 212–13; Foner, *op. cit.*, 120.
26. Winthrop, *Memoir*, 186–87.
27. Lawrence, *Amos A. Lawrence*, 142–43.
28. Winthrop, *Memoir*, 188–94.
29. Cited in Foner, *op. cit.*, 120.
30. Amos A. Lawrence to Charles Robinson, September 16, 1856, June 6, 1857, Robinson Papers, Folder III, 1, 8.
31. Amos A. Lawrence to Moses G. Cobb, July 8, 1857, AAL Letterbook, IV, 93–95.
32. *Ibid.*, 100–101.
33. *Ibid.*
34. George W. Van Vleck, *The Panic of 1857* (New York, 1943); Samuel Rezneck, "The Influence of Depression upon American Opinion, 1857–1859," *Journal of Economic History*, II (1942), 1–23.
35. Amos A. Lawrence to Eli Thayer, July 29, 1858, Thayer Manuscripts, I, 67.
36. Lawrence to Charles Robinson, November 25, 27, 1857, Robinson Papers,, Folder III, 10, 11.
37. Lawrence to Robinson, October 19, 1857, *ibid.*, 10. Also see John Murray Forbes to Edward Cunningham, September 28, 1857, Hughes, *op. cit.*, I, 167–68.

38. *Journal of Commerce,* December 1, 1858, August 18, 1859; *Commercial Advertiser,* April 1, 1859.
39. *Journal of Commerce,* April 2, August 28, September 25, October 2, 1858.
40. Charleston *Mercury,* October 14, 1857.
41. New York *Herald,* December 5, 12, 1859; January 30, 1860.
42. *Congressional Globe,* 35th Congress, 1st Session, Appendix, 70–71.
43. New York *Herald,* October, 1857. See Foner, *op. cit.,* 147–48, 162–63.
44. Boston *Post,* March 12, May 19, 1860.
45. Winthrop, *Memoir,* 201; *ibid.,* 202–03.
46. Foner, *op. cit.,* 141–42.
47. Amos A. Lawrence to Charles Hale, October, 1858, AAL Letterbook, IV, 259–60.
48. Lawrence to Charles Robinson, August 1, 1858, *ibid.,* IV, 223–24.
49. Lawrence to Eli Thayer, July 29, 1858, *ibid.;* IV, 222.
50. Lawrence to Charles Robinson, July 24, 1858, *ibid.,* IV, 220–21.
51. Lawrence to George Lunt and George S. Hillard, August 17, 1858, *ibid.,* 235–37.
52. *Ibid.*
53. Winthrop, *Memoir,* 207. Also see Boston *Daily Advertiser,* November 3, 5, 1858.
54. Amos A. Lawrence Journal, November 12, 13, 1858. Also see Boston *Daily Advertiser,* November 6, 1858.
55. AAL Letterbook, IV, 276–77. This letter was probably written in early December, 1858, but Lawrence neglected to include the name of his correspondent.
56. Thayer to Lawrence, November 16, 1858, AAL Letters, XVII, 114. Thayer's position proved so unacceptable to orthodox Republicans in the Bay State that they refused to renominate him in 1860 in his Worcester district. See Edith Ware, *Political Opinion in Massachusetts during the Civil War and Reconstruction* (New York, 1916), 36–37.
57. Edward Jay Morris to Lawrence; November 20, 1858, AAL Letters, XVII, 117.
58. AAL Letterbook, IV, 277.

8 ⅋ THE ELEVENTH HOUR

1. Amos A. Lawrence to Charles Robinson, January 7, 1859, Robinson Papers, Folder III, 20.
2. Lawrence to J. M. S. Williams, August 18, 1858, AAL Letterbook, IV, 239–40.
3. Lawrence to George N. Briggs, October 6, 1859, *ibid.,* 349.
4. *Ibid.*

5. Boston *Daily Advertiser*, October 12, 14, 1858. Also see Hudson Strode, *op. cit.*, 309–11. Elizabeth Cutting, *Jefferson Davis: Political Soldier* (New York, 1930), 124–25, provides a facsimile of Davis's speech.

6. Brian Waters, ed., *Mr. Vessey of England: Being the Incidents and Reminiscences of Travel in a Twelve Weeks' Tour Through the United States and Canada in the Year 1859* (New York, 1956), 164.

7. New York *Herald*, October 21, 1859.

8. Lawrence, *Amos A. Lawrence*, 130–31.

9. Octavius B. Frothingham, *Gerrit Smith* (New York, 1878), 254; Franklin B. Sanborn, *Recollections of Seventy Years* (2 Vols., Boston, 1909), I, 491–93.

10. Octavius B. Frothingham, *Theodore Parker, a Biography* (Boston, 1874), 462.

11. Frothingham, *op. cit.*, 243; Wilson, *op. cit.*, II, 605.

12. Edward Everett to Robert C. Winthrop, November 13, 1859, Everett Papers. Also see Boston *Advertiser*, February 24, June 19, 1860.

13. Amos A. Lawrence to W. W. Seaton, October 25, 1859, AAL Letterbook, IV, 352–53.

14. Amos A. Lawrence to Senator Jefferson Davis, December 22, 1859, *ibid.*, 368–69; Lawrence to Governor Henry Wise, October 26, 1859, *ibid.*, 355.

15. Foner, *op. cit.*, 171–72.

16. Ware, *Political Opinion*, 33.

17. Amos A. Lawrence to Levi Lincoln, March 21, 1860, AAL Letterbook, IV, 388–89; Boston *Daily Advertiser*, March 30, 1869; Ware, *Political Opinion*, 33–35.

18. *Ibid.*, 34.

19. Lawrence to John J. Crittenden, December 21, 1859, AAL Letterbook, IV, 365; Albert Morgan to Lawrence, December 13, 1859, AAL Letters, XIX, 21; Lawrence to H. and B. Douglas, December 22, 1859, AAL Letterbook, IV, 366–67.

20. Lawrence to Crittenden, December 22, 1859, *ibid.*, IV, 366–67. Also see Coleman, *op. cit.*, II, 183–84.

21. Lawrence to Crittenden, January 6, 1860, *ibid.*, 375–76; F. H. Walker to Lawrence, February 24, 1860, AAL Letters, XIX, 92. Also see Joseph Parks, *John Bell of Tennessee* (Baton Rouge, 1950), 366–67.

22. Brown, *op. cit.*, II, 303; Boston *Courier*, May 26, 1860.

23. Lawrence, *Amos A. Lawrence*, 163–64.

24. Amos A. Lawrence to Hon. Emerson Etheridge, April 2, 1860, AAL Letterbook, IV, 391–92.

25. Appleton, *Letter to Rives*, 4–9.

26. *Ibid.*, 12–13.

27. *Ibid.*, 14.

28. William C. Rives to Nathan Appleton, March [ ], 1860, Nathan Appleton Papers, Massachusetts Historical Society.

29. Amos A. Lawrence to John J. Crittenden, May 25, 26, 1860, AAL Letter-

book, IV, 400, 401; Boston *Daily Advertiser*, September 19, 1860. Also see Coleman, *op. cit.*, II, 206–07.

30. Edward Everett to Washington Hunt, May 29, 1860, cited in Boston *Daily Advertiser*, June 2, 1860.

31. Editorial, Boston *Post*, March 21, 30, April 2, 1860.

32. Cited in George S. Merriam, *The Life and Times of Samuel Bowles* (2 Vols., New York, 1885), I, 264.

33. Boston *Daily Advertiser*, March 30, 1860.

34. Robert C. Winthrop to Nathan Appleton, June 15, 1860, Nathan Appleton Papers.

35. Amos A. Lawrence to John J. Crittenden, May 25, 1860, AAL Letterbook, IV, 400.

36. Amos A. Lawrence to Emerson Etheridge, April 2, 1860, *ibid.*, IV, 391–92.

37. Foner, *op. cit.*, 172; New York *Tribune*, August 8, 15, 1860.

38. Ware, *Political Opinion*, 35–36.

39. Lawrence, *Amos A. Lawrence*, 156; Boston *Courier*, November 10, 17, 1860.

40. Robert C. Winthrop to Count Circourt, November 10, 1860, Winthrop Papers, XXXVI, 168.

41. Boston *Advertiser*, November 12, 15, 1860.

42. See Henry Adams, "The Secession Winter, 1860–61," *Proceedings of the Massachusetts Historical Society*, XLIII (1910), 660–87.

43. Boston *Daily Advertiser*, December 13, 1860.

44. *Ibid.*, January 23, 1861.

45. John J. Crittenden to Amos A. Lawrence, December 18, 1860, AAL Letters XX, 193.

46. Lawrence to Crittenden, December 29, 1860, Coleman, *op. cit.*, II, 240.

47. *National Intelligencer*, January 1, 1861. Speech of Nathan Appleton, December 15, 1860.

48. Sarah Norton and Mark De Wolfe Howe, *Letters of Charles Eliot Norton* (2 Vols., Boston, 1913), I, 213.

49. John Murray Forbes to Charles Sumner, December 22, 1860, Sumner Manuscripts, Harvard University.

50. L. B. Holbrook to Charles Sumner, December 22, 1860, *ibid.* Also see Boston *Courier*, December 16, 1860.

51. *Ibid.*, December 3, 1860.

52. Yorke, *op. cit.*, 44–45. Also see Stampp, *op. cit.*, 124–25.

53. *Springfield Republican*, December 5, 1859.

54. Phillips, *op. cit.*, 319–42.

55. *Life of Garrison*, IV, 1–10.

56. *Congressional Globe*, 36th Congress, 2nd Session, Appendix, 126–27; Boston *Courier*, February 6, 1861; Boston *Post*, February 6, 1861. Also see Charles Sumner to John Murray Forbes, January 13, 1861, Hughes, *op. cit.*, I, 186.

57. Loring, *Diaries of William Appleton*, 230–32.
58. Boston *Courier*, February 7, 1861; *Springfield Republican*, January 19, 24, 1861. Also see John J. Crittenden to Amos A. Lawrence, December 18, 1860, AAL Letters, XX, 193; Robert C. Winthrop to Crittenden, December 24, 1860, Winthrop Papers, XXXVI, 169.
59. *Springfield Republican*, January 28, 1861; Boston *Daily Advertiser*, February 23, 1861. Also see David M. Potter, *Lincoln and His Party in the Secession Crisis* (New Haven, 1942), 124–25.
60. Robert C. Winthrop to Edward Everett, January 21, 1861, Everett to Winthrop, January 22, 1861, Everett Papers. Also see Robert C. Winthrop, Diary Fragment, January, 1861, Winthrop Papers, XXXVI, 170–72.
61. New York *Times*, January 25, 1861; Lawrence, *Amos A. Lawrence*, 166–167; *National Intelligencer*, January 24, 26, 1861; *Journal of Commerce*, January 30, February 9, 1861; Foner, *op. cit.*, 250.
62. New York *Times*, January 25, 1861. See also Pierce, *op. cit.*, IV, 18.
63. Boston *Daily Journal*, February 6, 1861.
64. *Ibid.*
65. *Ibid.*, February 7, 1861.
66. *Ibid.*, February 6, 1861.
67. *Congressional Globe*, 36th Congress, 2nd Session, 862.
68. *Ibid.*, 862–63.
69. *Ibid.*, 863.
70. John Tyler to Edward Everett, January 29, 1861; Millard T. Fillmore to Everett, February 16, 1861, Everett Papers.
71. Robert C. Winthrop, Diary Fragment, Winthrop Papers, XXXVI, 170–172; Lawrence, *Amos A. Lawrence*, 167–68.
72. *Springfield Republican*, January 24, 1861.
73. Dwight Dumond, *The Secession Movement, 1860–1861* (New York, 1931), 239–46; Margaret Leech, *Reveille in Washington, 1860–65* (New York, 1941), 8–9.
74. Charles Francis Adams to John A. Andrew, January 28, 1861, Henry Greenleaf Pearson, *Life of John Andrew* (2 Vols., Boston, 1904), I, 155.
75. *Hunt's Merchants' Magazine*, XLIV (1861), 196–97; *Journal of Commerce*, March 1, 1861; New York *Tribune*, February 26, 28, 1861; Boston *Daily Advertiser*, March 20, 1861.
76. Yorke, *op. cit.*, 45.
77. For a firsthand account of the meeting between President-elect Lincoln and the members of the Peace Convention, see Lucius E. Chittenden, *Personal Reminiscences, 1840–1890* (New York, 1893), 391–93; and Lucius E. Chittenden, *Report of the Peace Convention in 1861* (New York, 1864), 465 ff.
78. Hughes, *op. cit.*, I, 200.
79. New York *Tribune*.
80. *Journal of Commerce*, March 4, 5, 7, 1861.

9 ఆ THE POINT OF NO RETURN

1. Roy Meredith, *Storm Over Sumter: The Opening Engagement of the Civil War* (New York, 1957); Bruce Catton, *The Coming Fury* (New York, 1967).
2. Loring, *Diaries of William Appleton*, 236.
3. Charles Hale to James S. Amory, April 24, 1861, Miscellaneous Manuscripts, Massachusetts Historical Society.
4. Loring, *Diaries of William Appleton*, 236–37.
5. William Appleton to Nathan Appleton, April 19, 1861, Nathan Appleton Papers. See also L. P. McDowell to Edward Everett, Columbia, South Carolina, April 20, 1861, Everett Papers.
6. Navin, *op. cit.*, 54–55. Also see Boston *Daily Advertiser*, April 17, 1861; Boston *Post*, June 18, 1861; Boston *Courier*, April 13, 16, 1861.
7. Robert C. Winthrop, Diary, April 19, 1861, Winthrop Papers, XXXVI, 173.
8. Amos A. Lawrence to William Appleton, April 5, 17, 20, 1861, AAL Letterbook, IV, 415, 420, 422. Also see Lawrence to Colonel Henry Lee, April 17, 1861, *ibid.*, 421.
9. Amos A. Lawrence to William Appleton, April 15, 1861; Lawrence to Senator Douglas, April 15, 1861, *ibid.*, 415, 416. Also see Lawrence, *Amos A. Lawrence*, 167–69, 173–77.
10. Lawrence, *Amos A. Lawrence*, 176.
11. Lawrence to Crittenden, April 15, 1861, AAL Letterbook, IV, 417–18.
12. Lawrence to Rev. R. J. Breckinridge, D.D., April 21, 1861, *ibid.*, 424–26.
13. *Ibid.* A note at the top of this letter in Lawrence's handwriting reads: "Letters similar in tenor sent to Hon. James Guthrie, Louisville, and to His Honor Mayor Brown, Baltimore."
14. Lawrence to Robert Ridgeway, April 16, 1861, *ibid.*, 419.
15. Lawrence to John Bell, April 26, 1861, *ibid.*, 428.
16. Navin, *op. cit.*, 54–55.
17. New York *Times*, March 2, 1861; New York *Tribune*, March 30, 1861.
18. *Hunt's Merchants' Magazine*, XLIV (1861), 665, 675–88. Also see E. Merton Coulter, *The Confederate States of America* (Baton Rouge, 1950), 240–43; Frank L. Owsley, *King Cotton Diplomacy* (Chicago, 1931), 31–33.
19. Yorke, *op. cit.*, 46; Amos A. Lawrence to Mrs. Arnold, May 27, 1861, AAL Letterbook, IV, 434.
20. Boston *Post*, May 8, 1862; Springfield *Republican*, May 12, 1862.
21. Charles Cowley, *History of Lowell* (Boston, 1868), 48–49; Yorke, *op. cit.*, 26; Thomas R. Smith, *The Cotton Textile Industry of Fall River, Massachusetts* (New York, 1944), 48–49; Clark, *op. cit.*, II, 29.

22. Navin, *op. cit.*, 54–55; Gibb, *op. cit.*, 195–96; George W. Browne, *The Amoskeag Manufacturing Company* (Manchester, N. H., 1915), 77–78.
23. Lawrence, *Amos A. Lawrence*, 181.
24. Amos A. Lawrence to Hon. John Z. Goodrich, August 2, 1854, AAL Letterbook, II, 392.

Bibliography

ꙮ MANUSCRIPTS

Nathan Appleton Manuscripts.
  Massachusetts Historical Society, Boston, Massachusetts.
Nathan Appleton and Charles Sumner, Correspondence, July-September, 1845.
  Rare Book Department, Boston Public Library, Boston, Massachusetts.
John J. Crittenden Manuscripts.
  Division of Manuscripts, United States Library of Congress, Washington, D.C.
Edward Everett Manuscripts.
  Massachusetts Historical Society, Boston, Massachusetts
William Lloyd Garrison Manuscripts.
  Rare Book Department, Boston Public Library, Boston, Massachusetts.
Amos Lawrence Letters.
  Massachusetts Historical Society, Boston, Massachusetts.
Amos Lawrence Papers.
  Massachusetts Historical Society, Boston, Massachusetts.
Amos A. Lawrence Letterbooks.
  Massachusetts Historical Society, Boston, Massachusetts.
Amos A. Lawrence Letters.
  Massachusetts Historical Society, Boston, Massachusetts.
Charles Robinson Manuscripts.
  Manuscript Archives, University of Kansas, Lawrence, Kansas.
Charles Sumner Manuscripts.
  Harvard College Library, Cambridge, Massachusetts.
Eli Thayer Manuscripts.
  John Hay Library, Brown University, Providence, Rhode Island.

John C. Warren Manuscripts.
    Massachusetts Historical Society, Boston, Massachusetts.
Robert C. Winthrop Manuscripts.
    Massachusetts Historical Society, Boston, Massachusetts.

❧ PRINTED PRIMARY SOURCES

Ames, H. V., ed., *State Documents on Federal Relations*. Philadelphia, 1906.

Annual Report of the American Historical Association, 1899, Vol. II. Correspondence of John C. Calhoun. Washington, 1899.

Appleton, Nathan, *Introduction of the Power Loom and the Origin of Lowell*. Lowell, 1858.

Appleton, Nathan, *Letter to the Honorable William C. Rives of Virginia on Slavery and the Union*. Boston, 1860.

Appleton, Nathan, *Memoir of Abbott Lawrence*. Boston, 1856.

Boutwell, George S., *Reminiscences of Sixty Years in Public Affairs*. 2 Vols.; New York, 1902.

Brown, Samuel G., *The Works of Rufus Choate with a Memoir of His Life*. 2 Vols.; Boston, 1862.

Chittenden, Lucius E., *Personal Reminiscences, 1840–1890*. New York, 1893.

(———), *Recollections of President Lincoln and His Administration*. New York, 1891.

(———), *Report of the Peace Convention in 1861*. New York, 1864.

Coleman, Chapman, *The Life of John J. Crittenden: With Selections from His Correspondence and Speeches*. 2 Vols.; Philadelphia, 1871.

Correspondence Between Nathan Appleton and John A. Lowell in Relation to the Early History of the City of Lowell. Boston, 1848.

Curtis, B. R., *A Memoir of Benjamin Robbins Curtis*. 2 Vols.; Boston, 1879.

Emerson, E. W., and Forbes, W. E., eds., *Journals of Ralph Waldo Emerson*. 10 Vols.; Boston, 1909–14.

Garrison, Wendell, and Garrison, Francis J., eds., *William Lloyd Garrison, 1805–1879: The Story of His Life told by his Children*. 4 Vols.; New York, 1885.

Hale, Edward E., Jr., *The Life and Letters of Edward Everett Hale*. 2 Vols.; Boston, 1917.

Higginson, Thomas W., *Cheerful Yesterdays*. Boston, 1898.

Hill, Hamilton A., *Memoir of Abbott Lawrence*. Boston, 1884.

Hoar, George F., *Autobiography of Seventy Years*. 2 Vols.; New York, 1903.

Hughes, Sarah, ed., *Letters and Reflections of John Murray Forbes*. 2 Vols.; Boston, 1900.

Kettell, Thomas P., *Southern Wealth and Northern Profits*. New York, 1860.

Lawrence, William, *The Life of Amos A. Lawrence: With Extracts from His Diary and Correspondence*. Boston, 1888.

Lawrence, William R., *Extracts from the Diary and Correspondence of the Late Amos Lawrence*. Boston, 1855.

Loring, Susan, ed., *Selections from the Diaries of William Appleton, 1786–1862*. Boston, 1922.

Lundy, Benjamin, *The War in Texas*. Philadelphia, 1836.

Morison, Samuel Eliot, *The Life and Letters of Harrison Gray Otis, Federalist, 1765–1848*. 2 Vols.; Boston, 1913.

Nevins, Allan, ed., *Polk: Diary of a President, 1845–1849*. New York, 1952.

Norton, Charles E., ed., *Letters of James Russell Lowell*. 2 Vols.; New York, 1894.

Organization, Objects and Plan of Operation of the Emigrant Aid Company: Also a Description of Kansas for the Information of Emigrants. Boston, 1854.

Parker, Theodore, *Additional Speeches, Addresses and Occasional Sermons*. 2 Vols.; Boston, 1855.

Phillips, Wendell, *Speeches, Lectures and Letters*. Boston, 1892.

Pierce, Edward L., ed., *Memoirs and Letters of Charles Sumner*. 4 Vols.; Boston, 1877.

Richardson, James D., comp., *Messages and Papers of the Presidents*. 11 Vols.; Washington, 1896.

Robbins, Chandler, "Memoir of Hon. William Appleton," *Proceedings of the Massachusetts Historical Society*, 1863, VI, 430–69.

Robinson, Charles, *The Kansas Conflict*. New York, 1889.

Robinson, William S., *"Warrington" Pen-Portraits*. Boston, 1877.

Sumner, Charles, *Complete Works*. 20 Vols.; Boston, 1900.

Thayer, Eli, *A History of the Kansas Crusade*. New York, 1889.

Ticknor, George, *Life, Letters and Journals of George Ticknor*. 2 Vols.; Boston, 1876.

Waters, Brian, ed., *Mr. Vessey of England: Being the Incidents and Reminiscences of Travel in a Twelve Weeks' Tour Through the United States and Canada in the Year 1859*. New York, 1956.

Webster, Fletcher, ed., *The Writings and Speeches of Daniel Webster*. 18 Vols.; National Edition, Boston, 1903.

White, George S., *Memoir of Samuel Slater*. Philadelphia, 1836.

Wilson, Henry, *History of the Rise and Fall of the Slave Power in America*. 3 Vols.; Boston, 1872–77.

Winthrop, Robert C., *Addresses and Speeches, 1852–67*. 2 Vols.; Boston, 1867.

Winthrop, Robert C., "Memoir of Hon. Nathan Appleton," *Proceedings of the Massachusetts Historical Society*, V (1861), 249–90.

❧ SECONDARY SOURCES

Adams, Henry, "The Secession Winter, 1860–61," *Proceedings of the Massachusetts Historical Society*, XLIII (1910), 660–87.

Adams, James T., *New England in the Republic*. Boston, 1926.

Albion, Robert G., *The Rise of the New York Port*. New York, 1939.

Atherton, Lewis E., "Mercantile Education in the Ante-Bellum South," *Mississippi Valley Historical Review*, XXXIX (1953), 623–40.

Austin, George L., *History of Massachusetts*. Boston, 1876.

Barnes, Gilbert H., *The Anti-Slavery Impulse: 1830–44*. New York, 1933.

Batchelder, Samuel, *Introduction and Progress of Cotton Manufacturing in the United States*. Boston, 1863.

Bean, William G., "An Aspect of Know-Nothingism—The Immigrant and Slavery," *South Atlantic Quarterly*, XXIII (1924), 319–34.

(————), "Party Transformation in Massachusetts, with Special Reference to Antecedents of the Republican Party, 1848–1860." Unpublished Doctoral Dissertation, Department of History, Harvard University, 1932.

Blackmer, F. W., *The Life of Charles Robinson*. Topeka, Kansas, 1902.

Boucher, C. S., *In Re That Aggressive Slavocracy*. Austin, Texas, 1921.

Bourne, E. G., "The United States and Mexico, 1847–48," *American Historical Review*, V (1900), 491–502.

Bowen, A., *A Picture of Boston*. Boston, 1829.

Bowen, James L., *Massachusetts and the War*. Springfield, Mass., 1890.

Brauer, Kinley J., *Cotton Versus Conscience: Massachusetts Whig Politics and Southern Expansion, 1843–1848*. Lexington, Kentucky, 1967.

Bretz, J. P., "Economic Background of the Liberty Party," *American Historical Review*, XXXIV (1929), 250–64.

Brewer, Daniel C., *The Conquest of New England by the Immigrant*. New York, 1926.

Browne, George W., *The Amoskeag Manufacturing Company*. Manchester, N.H., 1915.

Bruce, Kathleen, *Virginia Iron Manufacture in the Slave Era*. New York, 1931.

Burgess, John W., *The Middle Period, 1817–1858*. New York, 1897.

Carroll, E. Malcolm, *Origins of the Whig Party*. Durham, N.C., 1925.

Catterall, Ralph C., *The Second Bank of the United States*. Chicago, 1903.

Clark, Victor S., *History of Manufacturing in the United States*. 2 Vols.; New York, 1929.

Cohn, David, *The Life and Times of King Cotton*. New York, 1956.

Cole, Arthur C., *The Irrepressible Conflict, 1850–1865*. New York, 1934.

(————), "Lincoln's Election an Immediate Menace to Slavery in the United States?" *American Historical Review*, XXXVI (1931), 740–67.

Cole, Charles C., Jr., "Horace Bushnell and the Slavery Question," *New England Quarterly*, XXIII (1950), 19–30.

Copeland, Melvin T., *The Cotton Manufacturing System in the United States*. Cambridge, 1912.

Craven, Avery, *The Coming of the Civil War*. New York, 1942.

(————), *The Repressible Conflict*. Baton Rouge, 1939.

Current, Richard, *Daniel Webster and the Rise of National Conservatism*. Boston, 1955.

Curtis, George T., *The Life of Daniel Webster*. 2 Vols.; New York, 1870.

Cutting, Elizabeth, *Jefferson Davis: Political Soldier*. New York, 1930.

Dangerfield, George, *The Era of Good Feelings*. New York, 1952.

Darling, Arthur B., *Political Changes in Massachusetts, 1824–1848*. New Haven, 1925.

Davidson, Philip, "Industrialism in the Ante-Bellum South," *South Atlantic Quarterly*, XXVII (1928), 404–25.

De Voto, Bernard, *Year of Decision: 1846*. Boston, 1942.

Dewey, Davis R., *Financial History of the United States*. New York, 1934.

(———), *State Banking Before the Civil War*. Washington, 1910.

Dodd, Edwin M., *American Business Corporations until 1860: with Special Reference to Massachusetts*. Cambridge, 1954.

Dodd, William E., *The Cotton Kingdom*. New Haven, 1920.

Donald, David, *Charles Sumner and the Coming of the Civil War*. New York, 1961.

Duberman, Martin B., *Charles Francis Adams, 1807–1886*. Boston, 1961.

Dumond, Dwight, *Antislavery Origins of the Civil War in the United States*. Ann Arbor, 1939.

(———), *The Secession Movement, 1880–1861*. New York, 1931.

(———), *Southern Editorials on Secession*. New York, 1931.

Eaton, Clement, *History of the Old South*. New York, 1949.

(———), "Resistance of the South to Northern Radicalism," *New England Quarterly*, VIII (1935), 215–31.

Fite, Emerson D., *The Presidential Campaign of 1860*. New York, 1911.

(———), *Social and Industrial Conditions in the North during the Civil War*. New York, 1910.

Fladeland, Betty, *James Gillespie Birney, Slaveholder to Abolitionist*. Ithaca, 1955.

Foner, Philip S., *Business and Slavery: The New York Merchants and the Irrepressible Conflict*. Chapel Hill, 1941.

Foster, Herbert D., "Webster's Seventh of March Speech and the Secession Movement, 1850," *American Historical Review*, XXVII (1921), 245–70.

Fuess, Claude, *Daniel Webster*. 2 Vols.; Boston, 1930.

(———), *The Life of Caleb Cushing*. 2 Vols.; New York, 1923.

Fuller, John D. P., *The Movement for the Acquisition of all Mexico, 1846–1848*. Baltimore, 1936.

Gatell, Frank O., *John Gorham Palfrey and the New England Conscience*. Cambridge, 1963.

Genovese, Eugene, *The Political Economy of Slavery*. New York, 1965.

Gibb, George S., *The Saco-Lowell Shops: Textile Machinery Building in New England*. Cambridge, 1950.

Glover, Gilbert G., *Immediate Pre-Civil War Compromise Efforts*. Nashville, 1934.

Glover, John and Cornell, William, *The Development of American Industries.* New York, 1936.

Greenslet, Ferris, *The Lowells and Their Seven Worlds.* Boston, 1946.

Hacker, Louis M., *The Triumph of American Capitalism.* New York, 1940.

Hamilton, Holman, " 'The Cave of the Winds' and the Compromise of 1850," *Journal of Southern History*, XXIII (1957), 331–53.

Hammond, Bray, *Banks and Politics in America.* Princeton, N.J., 1957.

Harrington, Fred, "Nathaniel Prentiss Banks: A Study in Anti-Slavery Politics," *New England Quarterly*, IX (1936), 626–54.

Hart, Albert B., *Slavery and Abolition, 1831–1841.* New York, 1906.

Hart, Albert B., ed., *Commonwealth History of Massachusetts.* 5 Vols.; New York, 1927–30.

Hawk, Emory, *Economic History of the South.* New York, 1934.

Haynes, George H., "Causes of Know-Nothing Success in Massachusetts," *American Historical Review*, III (1897), 67–82.

Herbert, Hilary, *The Abolition Crusade and Its Consequences.* New York, 1912.

Hodder, Frank H., "The English Bill," *Annual Report of the American Historical Association, 1906*, I, 201–10.

(———), "The Railroad Background of the Kansas-Nebraska Act," *Mississippi Valley Historical Review*, XII (1925), 3–22.

Holdsworth, John, and Dewey, Davis, *The First and Second Banks of the United States.* Washington, 1910.

Hopkins, James H., *A History of Political Parties in the United States.* New York, 1900.

Isely, W. H., "The Sharps Rifle Episode in Kansas History," *American Historical Review*, XII (1907), 546–66.

Jennings, W. W., *The American Embargo, 1807–1809.* Iowa City, 1921.

Johnson, Allen, *Stephen A. Douglas.* New York, 1908.

Johnson, Samuel, "The Genesis of the New England Emigrant Aid Company," *New England Quarterly*, III (1930), 90–100.

Kirkland, Edward C., *A History of American Economic Life.* New York, 1949.

Knowlton, Evelyn H., *Pepperell's Progress.* Cambridge, 1948.

Korngold, Ralph, *Two Friends of Man: The Story of William Lloyd Garrison and Wendell Phillips and their Relationship with Abraham Lincoln.* Boston, 1950.

Lamb, Robert, "The Entrepreneurs and the Community," *Men in Business.* Cambridge, 1952.

Landers, Ernest M., "Manufacturing in South Carolina, 1815–1860," *Business History Review*, March, 1954.

Lawrence, Robert M., *Old Park Street and its Vicinity.* Boston, 1922.

Lloyd, Arthur Y., *The Slavery Controversy: 1831–1860.* Chapel Hill, 1939.

Luthin, Reinhard H., "Abraham Lincoln and the Massachusetts Whigs in 1848," *New England Quarterly*, XIV (1941), 619–32.

Madeleine, Sister M. Grace, *Monetary and Banking Theories of Jacksonian Democracy.* Philadelphia, 1943.

Malin, James C., *John Brown and the Legend of Fifty-Six.* Philadelphia, 1942.

(————), *The Nebraska Question, 1852–54.* Lawrence, Kansas, 1953.

(————), "Pro-Slavery Background of the Kansas Struggle," *Mississippi Valley Historical Review,* I (1923), 285.

Mann, Arthur, *Yankee Reformers in the Urban Age.* Cambridge, 1954.

McDowell, Tremaine, "Webster's Words on Abolitionists," *New England Quarterly,* VII (1934), 315.

McKee, Thomas H., ed., *The National Platforms of all Political Parties.* Washington, 1892.

McMaster, John B., *History of the People of the United States.* 8 Vols.; New York, 1883–1913.

Meserve, H. C., *Lowell: An Industrial Dream Come True.* Boston, 1923.

Milton, George F., *Eve of Conflict: Stephen A. Douglas and the Needless War.* Boston, 1934.

Mitchell, Broadus, *The Industrial Revolution in the South.* Baltimore, 1930.

(————), *William Gregg, Factory Master of the Old South.* Chapel Hill, 1928.

Monaghan, Jay, *The Civil War on the Western Border, 1854–1865.* Boston, 1955.

Moody, Robert E., "The First Year of the Emigrant Aid Company," *New England Quarterly,* IV (1931), 148.

Morgan, Robert J., *A Whig Embattled: The Presidency under John Tyler.* Lincoln, Nebraska, 1954.

Morison, Samuel Eliot, *Maritime History of Massachusetts, 1783–1860.* Boston, 1921.

Navin, Thomas R., *The Whitin Machine Works since 1831.* Cambridge, 1950.

Nevins, Allan, *The Emergence of Lincoln,* 2 Vols.; New York, 1950.

(————), *Ordeal of the Union.* 2 Vols.; New York, 1947.

Nichols, Roy F., *The Democratic Machine, 1850–1854.* New York, 1923.

(————), *The Disruption of American Democracy.* New York, 1948.

(————), *Franklin Pierce.* Philadelphia, 1931.

Nye, Russel B., *William Lloyd Garrison and the Humanitarian Reformers.* Boston, 1955.

Overdyke, W. Darrell, *The Know-Nothing Party in the South.* Baton Rouge, 1950.

Owsley, Frank L., *King Cotton Diplomacy.* Chicago, 1931.

Parks, Joseph H., *John Bell of Tennessee.* Baton Rouge, 1950.

Parrington, Vernon L., *Main Currents in American Thought.* 3 Vols.; New York, 1927.

Patton, James, "Notes on the Fifth Annual Meeting of the Southern Historical Society, From a Synopsis of a Speech by Thomas P. Martin, 'The Cotton Question at Home and Abroad, 1840–61,'" *Journal of Southern History* VI (1940), 86–87.

Peabody, Lucy W., *Henry Wayland Peabody, Merchant*. West Medford, Mass., 1909.

Perkins, Howard C., "The Defense of Slavery in the Northern Press on the Eve of the Civil War," *Journal of Southern History*, IX (1943), 501–31.

(———), ed., *Northern Editorials on Secession*. 2 Vols.; New York, 1942.

Pike, James S., *First Blows of the Civil War: The Ten Years of Preliminary Conflict in the United States, from 1850 to 1860*. New York, 1879.

Poage, George R., *Henry Clay and the Whig Party*. Chapel Hill, 1936.

Porter, Kenneth W., *The Jacksons and the Lees*. 2 Vols.; Cambridge, 1937.

Potter, David M., *Lincoln and His Party in the Secession Crisis*. New Haven, 1942.

Randall, James G., *The Civil War and Reconstruction*. Boston, 1937.

Rawley, James A., *Edwin D. Morgan, 1811–1883: Merchant in Politics*. New York, 1955.

Ray, P. Orman, *The Repeal of the Missouri Compromise*. Cleveland, 1909.

Rezneck, Samuel, "The Influence of Depression upon American Opinion, 1857–1859," *Journal of Economic History*, II (1942), 1–23.

Rhodes, James Ford, *History of the United States from the Compromise of 1850*. 7 Vols.; New York, 1893–1906.

Rives, George L., *The United States and Mexico, 1821–1848*. 2 Vols.; New York, 1913.

Russel, Robert R., *Economic Aspects of Southern Sectionalism, 1840–60*. Urbana, Illinois, 1924.

Sawyer, John E., "The Social Basis of the American System of Manufacturing," *Journal of Economic History*, XIV (1954), 361–79.

Schlesinger, Arthur M., Jr., *The Age of Jackson*. Boston, 1945.

Schouler, James, "The Whig Party in Massachusetts," *Massachusetts Historical Society Proceedings*, I (1917), 39–53.

Schwartz, Harold, "Fugitive Slave Days in Boston," *New England Quarterly*, XXVII (1954), 191–212.

Scrugham, Mary, *The Peaceable Americans of 1860–61*. New York, 1921.

Sears, Louis M., *Jefferson and the Embargo*. Durham, 1927.

Sellers, Charles G., "Who were the Southern Whigs?" *American Historical Review*, LIX (1954), 335–46.

Sellers, James L., "The Economic Incidence of the Civil War in the South," *Mississippi Valley Historical Review*, XIV (1927), 179–91.

Shlakman, Vera, "Economic History of a Factory Town: Chicopee," *Smith College Studies in History*, XX, 1936.

Simms, Henry H., *A Decade of Sectional Controversy*. Chapel Hill, 1942.

Smith, Justin, *The War with Mexico*. 2 Vols.; New York, 1919.

Smith, Theodore C., *Parties and Slavery, 1850–1859*. New York, 1906.

Smith, Walter, and Cole, Arthur, *Fluctuations in American Business, 1790–1860*. Cambridge, 1935.

Smith, Winston O., *The Sharps Rifle, Its History, Development and Operation*. New York, 1943.

Spring, L. W., *Kansas: The Prelude to the War for the Union*. Boston, 1885.

Stampp, Kenneth M., *And the War Came*. Baton Rouge, 1950.

(————), *The Peculiar Institution*. New York, 1956.

Stanwood, Edward, *American Tariff Controversies in the Nineteenth Century*. 2 Vols.; Boston, 1916, Vol. I.

(————), *History of the Presidency*. 2 Vols.; Boston, 1916, Vol. I.

Stephenson, Nathaniel H., *Texas and the Mexican War*. New Haven, 1921.

Stone, Alfred H., "The Cotton Factorage System of the Southern States," *American Historical Review*, XX (1915), 557–665.

Strode, Hudson, *Jefferson Davis: American Patriot*. New York, 1955.

Taussig, Frank W., *Protection to Young Industries*. Cambridge, 1883.

(————), *Tariff History of the United States*. New York, 1931.

Van Deusen, Glyndon, *Thurlow Weed, Wizard of the Lobby*. Boston, 1947.

Van Tassel, David, "Gentlemen of Property and Standing: Compromise Sentiment in Boston in 1850," *New England Quarterly*, XXIII (1950), 307–19.

Van Vleck, George W., *The Panic of 1857*. New York, 1943.

Villard, Oswald Garrison, *John Brown, 1800–1859*. Boston, 1910.

Walton, Perry, *The Story of Textiles*. Boston, 1912.

Ware, Caroline F., *The Early New England Cotton Manufacture*. Boston, 1931.

Ware, Edith E., *Political Opinion in Massachusetts during the Civil War and Reconstruction*. New York, 1916.

Weeden, William B., *Economic and Social History of New England, 1620–1789*. 2 Vols.; Boston, 1872–77.

Yorke, Dane, *The Men and Times of Pepperell*. Boston, 1945.

Young, Edward, *Special Report on the Customs-Tariff Legislation of the United States*. Washington, 1874.

Index

205

DATE DUE

SEP 2 9 75			
GAYLORD			PRINTED IN U.S.A.